Transitional Justice in Aparadigmatic Contexts

This book explores the practical and theoretical opportunities as well as the challenges raised by the expansion of transitional justice into new and 'aparadigmatic' cases.

The book defines transitional justice as the pursuit of accountability, recognition, and/or disruption and applies an actor-centric analysis focusing on justice actors' intentions of and responses to transitional justice. It offers a typology of different transitional justice contexts ranging from societies experiencing ongoing conflict to consolidated democracies and includes chapters from all types of aparadigmatic contexts. This covers transitional justice in states with contested political authority, shared political authority, and consolidated political authority. The transitional justice initiatives explored by the wide range of contributors are those of Afghanistan, Belgium, France, Greenland/Denmark, Libya, Syria, Turkey/Kurdistan, the United Kingdom/Iraq, the United States, and Yemen. Through these aparadigmatic case studies, the book develops a new framework that, appropriate to its expanding reach, allows us to understand the practice of transitional justice in a more context-sensitive, bottom-up, and actor-oriented way, which leaves room for the complexity and messiness of interventions on the ground.

The book will appeal to scholars and practitioners in the broad field of transitional justice, as represented in law, criminology, politics, conflict studies, and human rights.

Tine Destrooper is Associate Professor at the Human Rights Centre, Ghent University, Belgium.

Line Engbo Gissel is Associate Professor at Roskilde University, Denmark.

Kerstin Bree Carlson is Associate Professor at Roskilde University and The American University of Paris.

Part of the TRANSITIONAL JUSTICE SERIES

Series editor

Kieran McEvoy, *Queen's University Belfast, UK*

for information about the series and details of previous and forthcoming titles, see https://www.routledge.com/Transitional-Justice/book-series/TRANJ

a GlassHouse book

Transitional Justice in Aparadigmatic Contexts

Accountability, Recognition, and Disruption

Edited by Tine Destrooper, Line Engbo Gissel, and Kerstin Bree Carlson

Routledge
Taylor & Francis Group
a GlassHouse Book

First published 2023
by Routledge
4 Park Square, Milton Park, Abingdon, Oxon OX14 4RN

and by Routledge
605 Third Avenue, New York, NY 10158

Routledge is an imprint of the Taylor & Francis Group, an informa business

a GlassHouse book

British Library Cataloguing-in-Publication Data
A catalogue record for this book is available from the British Library

ISBN: 978-1-032-26617-6 (hbk)
ISBN: 978-1-032-26615-2 (pbk)
ISBN: 978-1-003-28910-4 (ebk)

DOI: 10.4324/9781003289104

Typeset in Bembo
by Deanta Global Publishing Services, Chennai, India

Contents

Tables and Figures

Tables

Figures

Acknowledgements

This book began as a panel for the International Political Science Association conference, which should have taken place in Lisbon in July 2020. After the conference was cancelled and travel rendered impossible by the COVID-19 pandemic, the panel was transformed into an online workshop, growing in numbers and ambition. Ultimately, the workshop included approximately a dozen participants and took place over three days in July and September 2020. Claiming quiet corners in their homes for hours at a time, participants discussed their selected cases of aparadigmatic transitional justice, and debated how their cases constructed or challenged the received wisdom of the field. This book is the fruit of these discussions, which seeded the theorisation developed in the Introduction and Concluding Remarks. Several of the cases discussed grew into the chapters included herein. All books owe many debts, and this one begins with those workshops, organised and chaired by Tine Destrooper, and energised by the workshop participants, some, but not all, of whom appear in the following pages.

Having determined that the topic was lively and significant, the editors – who met at a transitional justice pre-conference workshop at Eurocrim 2019, another debt – spent many hours in 2020 and 2021 building the book's edifice via the Introduction. As can be the case in fruitful collaborations, the resulting chapter is the product of that collective effort, debates carried out via track-changes and marginalia, and ideas developed via footnotes, diagrams, and live. Chapter contributors engaged with the emerging theory in successive Introduction drafts, a feedback loop that further clarified and honed the argument. We are profoundly grateful for the dedication and enthusiasm of our fellow editors and our fellow contributors in sculpting this book, a product of many months' group effort.

We are delighted that the book has found a home in Routledge's Transitional Justice Series, conversing directly with important books in the field. Routledge's anonymous reviewers provided valuable and constructive feedback, pushing us to sharpen our approach and its impact; the book is better for their comments.

No book is perfect, and we have some regrets. We lost some cases along the way, victims to challenges of timing or resources. There are several relevant and interesting examples of aparadigmatic transitional justice that are not included in the book, and indeed there are whole regions that the book does not visit at all. We can only hope that this book begins what we feel is an important and essential conversation about transitional justice outside the bounds of its paradigm. We especially hope that the book might add ideas or fodder to transitional justice practitioners and curious academics, and that they might be able to apply these ideas or examples in their own work and practice.

Individually, Tine Destrooper would like to thank her colleagues at the Human Rights Centre and Justice Visions at Ghent University for the inspiring conversations that enriched various parts of this book. Thanks to Kerstin and Line for the enthusing exchanges and to all the contributors of this volume for sharing their insights with us. Thanks also to Jef for so often sidestepping himself to make this and other projects possible and to Lilith for gently kindling a healthy amount of doubt, creativity, and sense of perspective. Line Engbo Gissel would like to thank Devapriyo for his immense support throughout this project. We juggled work and homeschooling, while trying to keep Maya and Milan sane, healthy, fed, clothed, and clean. I am grateful to Maya and Milan for insisting on the present and to Kerstin and Tine for academic sisterhood. For the Greenland chapter, I would like to thank Jens Heinrich, Mira Brandes, and Kim Falck-Petersen for their openness and interest in the research. Kerstin Bree Carlson thanks Lolo, Niamh and Claudio, who are always the first to feel stolen nights and weekends, and almost always very generous about it.

Author Biographies

Noha Aboueldahab (PhD) is Assistant Professor at Georgetown University, Qatar, and Senior Non-Resident Fellow at the Middle East Council on Global Affairs. She is the author of several research and policy publications about transitional justice in the Middle East, including *Transitional Justice and the Prosecution of Political Leaders in the Arab Region* (2017).

Nisan Alıcı (PhD) did her PhD project at the Transitional Justice Institute, Ulster University, focusing on the prospects for transitional justice in the ongoing Kurdish conflict from a victim-centred and grassroots-oriented perspective. She is the co-founder of the Demos Research Association, where she researches peace, gender, and transitional justice.

Veronica Bellintani (LLM) is Legal Researcher at the Syrian Legal Development Programme, where she provides capacity-building and technical assistance on issues pertaining to international law, transitional justice and the Syrian conflict. She holds an LLM in Human Rights & Transitional Justice from the University of Ulster, Belfast.

Kerstin Bree Carlson (JD, PhD) is Associate Professor at Roskilde University's Department of Social Sciences and Business and the American University of Paris. Kerstin researches the social impacts of law and is currently focusing on terror law.

Tine Destrooper (PhD) is Associate Professor at Ghent University's Human Rights Center and the Director of Justice Visions, an ERC-funded research project on victim participation in transitional justice. She is the former managing director of the Centre for Human Rights and Global Justice at New York University's Law School and of the Flemish Peace Institute.

Line Engbo Gissel (PhD) is Associate Professor at Roskilde University's Department of Social Sciences and Business, where she researches the relationship between law and politics: the judicialisation of politics and the politics of international law and transitional justice. She co-authored *Africa and the Backlash Against International Courts* (with Peter Brett, 2020). She is also the principal investigator of a project on the standardisation of transitional justice.

Par Engstrom (DPhil) is Associate Professor of Human Rights at the Institute of the Americas, University College London, and Visiting Professor at the Paris School of International Affairs (PSIA) at Sciences-Po. His research focuses on the politics of human rights and transitional justice with a geographical focus on Latin America.

Brigitte Herremans (MA) is Research Fellow in the Justice Visions project at Ghent University. She studies how arts can contribute to truth-seeking in Syria. Previously she worked as a Middle East policy officer for several NGOs and for the Centre of Fine Arts in Brussels.

Brianne McGonigle Leyh (PhD) is Associate Professor at Utrecht University's School of Law. Researching human rights law and global justice, she is a member of the Netherlands Institute of Human Rights and the Montaigne Centre for the Rule of Law and Administration of Justice.

Thomas Obel Hansen (PhD) is Senior Lecturer in the School of Law and a member of the Transitional Justice Institute at Ulster University. Thomas obtained his LLM and PhD in Law from Aarhus University Law School. He is currently (2023–2024) Maria Zambrano Distinguished Researcher with the Carlos III University in Madrid, Spain.

Cira Pallí-Asperó (PhD) is a postdoc at the Human Rights Centre of Ghent University. She is a historian whose research focuses on developing a theoretical and methodological framework for historical clarification commissions.

Huma Saeed (PhD) is Affiliated Senior Researcher at the Leuven Institute of Criminology (KU Leuven) and an independent research consultant with human rights and development organisations. Her research area is transitional justice and economic-state crime, with extensive fieldwork in Afghanistan. She is the author of *Transitional Justice and Socio-Economic Harm: Land Grapping in Afghanistan* (2022).

Stephen Winter (DPhil) is Associate Professor in Political Theory at the University of Auckland and works on transitional justice and related subjects. His book *Monetary Redress for Abuse in State Care* was published by Cambridge University Press in 2022.

Abbreviations and Acronyms

AHRDO	Afghanistan Human Rights and Democracy Organization
AIHRC	The Afghanistan Independent Human Rights Commission
AMT	*Association de malfaiteurs* (joint criminal responsibility)
BLM	Black Lives Matter
CIJA	The Commission for International Justice and Accountability
CSO	Civil society organisation
DRC	Democratic Republic of Congo
DMP	Diyarbakır Military Prison
ECCHR	European Centre for Constitutional and Human Rights
ECHR	European Convention of Human Rights
ECtHR	European Court of Human Rights
FARC	*Fuerzas Armadas Revolucionarias de Colombia* (Revolutionary Armed Forces of Colombia)
ICC	International Criminal Court
IHAT	Iraq Historic Allegations Team
IIIM	The International Impartial and Independent Mechanism to Assist in the Investigation and Prosecution of Those Responsible for the Most Serious Crimes under International Law
IMT	International Military Tribunal (at Nuremberg)
IS	Islamic State
JEP	*Jurisdicción Especial para la Paz* (Special Jurisdiction for Peace)
MNC	Multinational corporation
NGO	Non-governmental organisation
OHCHR	Office of the High Commissioner for Human Rights
PIL	Public Interest Lawyers
PKK	*Partiya Karkaren Kurdistan* (Kurdistan Workers Party)
PCACDR	Presidential Commission for the Analysis of the Communist Regime
TDC	Truth and Dignity Commission
UK	United Kingdom
UN	United Nations
UNAMA	UN Assistant Mission to Afghanistan
US	United States of America

Introduction

Transitional Justice in Aparadigmatic Contexts[1]

Tine Destrooper, Line Engbo Gissel, and Kerstin Bree Carlson

Introduction

Transitional justice is an established and well-theorised field of study and practice. Implemented in over 140 countries since 1970 and discussed in thousands of academic books and journal articles, it has become the dominant paradigm to address legacies of large-scale violence and disrupt the dynamics that contribute to authoritarianism and/or violent conflict (Shaw and Waldorf 2010). Where the past is defined by violence, transitional justice postulates that recognition of, and accountability for, past wrongs are necessary to break the cycle of violence and ensure a peaceful and just future (Quinn 2009). Over time, a paradigm has emerged which posits that societies need to deal with their past for their future to become stable. This claim is articulated by powerful global institutions, such as the UN Security Council, which states that '[t]o be able to rebuild lives without fear of recurrence and for society to move forward, suffering needs to be acknowledged, confidence in state institutions restored and justice done. Demands for justice can be denied, but they will not disappear' (the UN High Commissioner for Human Rights, quoted in UN Security Council 2020, 2).

This paradigm did not come from nowhere; it has a history. In the decade following the end of the Cold War, democratic regimes replaced authoritarian governance in sites across the globe, such as Argentina, Brazil, Chile, Hungary, Poland, reunified Germany, and South Africa. Incidents of mass violence were followed by 'wondrous, though painful and complex, transformations of the surrounding societies' and the emergence of '[l]ess oppressive, and even democratic regimes', while societies struggled over 'how much to acknowledge, whether to punish, and how to recover' (Minow 1998, 2). These transitions away from conflict or authoritarianism included a shift from illiberal to liberal governance, as well as various kinds of justice responses that provided some recognition and accountability (Elster 2004; Teitel 2000). In all of these

1 This research was partly funded through ERC-StG-804154 VictPart.

DOI: 10.4324/9781003289104-1

cases, the objects of redress – the atrocity, repression, or injustice – was in the recent past: conflict had just ended or authoritarian rulers had recently been brought down. These post-authoritarian and post-conflict settings became the 'paradigmatic' cases from which transitional justice was theorised and around which practitioners, scholars, and policy-makers built an inter-disciplinary field (Sharp 2018). Over the course of the 1990s and 2000s, processes of legalisation, internationalisation, and professionalisation consolidated this field, including its paradigmatic transitional state imaginary.

The paradigmatic cases that have fuelled most transitional justice theory involve a *transitional state*, where either power-sharing regimes or successor governments struggle to consolidate their new politics. These transitional states became conceptualised as a partner in the transition, no longer its adversary. The partner state sanctioned or carried out criminal trials, truth commissions, commissions of inquiry, reparations or vetting programmes, and institutional reform. It opened up archives, handed over incriminating information, and legally protected transitional justice institutions. As a result, the core transitional justice mechanisms – trials, truth commissions, reparations, and reform – are state-centric (Hamber and Lundy 2020, 748). One could even argue that the assumption and centrality of the transitional state represents an appropriation of transitional justice by the state. In South America, for example, transitional justice originated in the 1980s as popular responses to abuses committed by authoritarian regimes against their own citizens. The disruption demanded by this kind of bottom-up transitional justice distinguished itself both from state-centred transitional justice practices that are often less disruptive, and from other disruptive practices, like militarised opposition, because it resembled a movement (Rowen 2017). As the focus shifted from these disruptive movements and their demands towards the transitioning state, however, the substantive focus also shifted. The quest for accountability became central to the practice of transitional justice (Gissel 2017). Accountability, of course, relies on state institutions: the law, the public prosecutor, the courtroom, the judgeship, the prison, and the payroll.

This volume problematises transitional justice's long-standing, structural focus on the transitional state by identifying and theorising different understandings of accountability, recognition, and disruption that emerge from *aparadigmatic* cases. Aparadigmatic cases are those where transitional justice is pursued by varied actors in circumstances outside the paradigm of post-conflict or post-authoritarian states, i.e. in sites of ongoing conflict, fragile states, occupied territories, settler democracies, and consolidated democracies. These circumstances are aparadigmatic chiefly because they are not transitional in the classic sense. What these aparadigmatic cases have in common is that actors use transitional justice mechanisms in contexts that rarely envision the consolidation of a political transition but instead have more diverse, and sometimes ambiguous, objectives. In many of the aparadigmatic cases, transitional justice is conceptualised in ways that challenge straightforward conceptions of justice.

By one measure, the invocation of transitional justice in aparadigmatic contexts challenges the conceptual vigour of transitional justice by highlighting its amorphous ideological structure and unproven results (Israël and Mouralis 2014). By another, the fact that actors in aparadigmatic cases are invoking transitional justice discourse, concepts, and frameworks may signify a return to the foundations of transitional justice, which started as a disruptive mobilisation in opposition to the state.

The kind of disruption that animates practice both in early transitional justice and in contemporary aparadigmatic cases is specific to each society and is an empirical question. At the same time, the field lacks a rigorous theorisation of the disruptive potential of transitional justice. To develop this and map the evolving landscape of transitional justice, the book starts from the empirical question of why and how actors on the ground invoke or contest transitional justice. This volume gathers empirical chapters from a selection of aparadigmatic transitional justice cases to more fully theorise transitional justice's disruptive potential and analyse transitional justice in contexts without a transitional state. These insights add to and enrich mainstream transitional justice theory, discourse, and practice (Quinn 2014; Sharp 2014) and move some practices from the margins to the centre of the field.

Transitional Justice: Accountability, Recognition – and Disruption

Accountability and recognition are often considered the central aims of transitional justice (Quinn 2009). The mantra that there is 'no peace without justice' implies that accountability is necessary for stability and peace. Accountability processes may deter future violations and also provides recognition to victims. Legal and criminal accountability is provided through criminal trial processes, vetting or lustration programmes, and institutions such as truth commissions, commissions of inquiry, and historical commissions, which document a truth or the truth about the violent past.[2] While accountability does not necessarily imply only criminal or legal accountability, this is mainly how the field has conceptualised it. Yet, even within this state-centred conceptualisation of accountability, the notion has disruptive and transformative potential.

Truth-seeking efforts and reparations also contribute to the objective of recognition. Reports of truth-seeking bodies as well as material or symbolic reparations provide official recognition of the wrong that requires justice. They may be tied to accountability processes but can also exist independently of questions of guilt. In addition, various transitional justice initiatives, notably those rooted in traditional or restorative justice, seek to restore relations

2 Purges, on the contrary, represent a form of accountability for perpetrators, while violating rule-of-law safeguards.

between individuals and communities. In these initiatives too, some form of accountability and recognition are often deemed crucial for restorative justice to emerge. Accountability and recognition are, however, *potential* effects. Whether a particular transitional justice initiative actually results in more accountability or recognition is an empirical question.

Disruption is a third potential effect of transitional justice. Transitional justice processes enable a break with the past because they disrupt the practices and institutions of repression or violence. Institutional reform can be argued to seek to disrupt the practices and institutions that produce injustice. But other mechanisms, such as trials, truth-telling and vetting processes, may also disrupt. Empirically, however, and given the cooptation of many transitional justice initiatives by the state, transitional justice does not always disrupt or seek to disrupt. Instead, it is often 'managed' in ways that undermine disruption (Macdonald 2019) or 'instrumentalised' by actors wishing for, fearing or seeking to prevent its disruption (Arnould 2021). While recognition and accountability are well-established aims, disruption is rarely identified as a central objective of transitional justice; we therefore lack a rigorous theorisation of what disruption means for transitional justice.

'Disruption' can mean a disturbance that interrupts a process or practice and a radical change to an existing industry or institution. In paradigmatic transitional justice contexts, the object of interruption and radical change are the institutions and practices that produce harm and injustice, notably the *ad hoc* or institutionalised violence and discrimination produced by wars or authoritarian government institutions. In aparadigmatic cases, these institutions and practices could refer to colonial or post-colonial repression or, on the contrary, ongoing violence. Through transitional justice, it is hoped, practices and institutions of violence and discrimination will be replaced with non-violent, peaceful, and tolerant processes and behaviour.

Interruption and change are thus central to the concept of disruption, but so is power (Hayward 2020; Piven 2006). The status quo is reproduced by power and its disruption therefore requires (access to) power. This can be the power of institutions but also the power of the many, the disobedient, or the in-your-face survivors who refuse to go away. It can be used in opposition to the state or by a new political elite seeking to re-fashion the state in more modest ways. These various kinds of disruptive political actions 'can help shift the terms of political discourse' (Hayward 2020, 449).

In Argentina, *Madres y Abuelas de la Plaza de Mayo* provide an example of a disruptive political action that seeks to shift the political discourse. Beginning in 1977, these women demanded attention to the fate of those disappeared by the military government. They refused to stay silent or to go away (Bevernage 2012) and directed their practice against the transitional state. It resulted in the successor government investigating and prosecuting the military Juntas, which in turn changed the terms of political discourse and instituted a radical change in the military. To President Alfonsín (quoted in Sikkink 2011, 72), the main justification for the trials was 'prevention: to keep this from happening again'. This is a clear example of disruption taking place in response to the mobilisation of grassroots actors in a transitioning context. There are also more formal and institutionalised transitional justice initiatives that have explicitly sought to disrupt: South Africa's Truth and Reconciliation Commission, for example, which was imbued with legal and political authority, envisaged disruption using 'the full glare of publicity' to change the terms of political discourse (Tutu 1998, para. 3).

Against these paradigmatic cases, how does transitional justice in aparadigmatic contexts seek to provide accountability and recognition and disrupt the institutions and practices that produce injustice and harm, if at all? And given that transitional justice is so well-studied a field, what use is another volume? We argue that transitional justice scholarship is constructed around a limited typology of cases which have defined the paradigm of transitional justice, even if this paradigm has shifted across decades of practice. The concepts and methods of transitional justice practice, as well as the contexts in which it is applied, have all changed drastically in the past three decades. Yet most theorisation is still rooted in paradigmatic cases and, as such, fails to take into account all those experiences and insights emerging from the application of transitional justice in aparadigmatic cases. Aparadigmatic transitional justice practices are occurring in circumstances as varied as ongoing conflict and consolidated democracies. The promising avenues and questions opened up by these cases have so far not been addressed or theorised in a comprehensive way. Most analyses about the expansion of transitional justice to aparadigmatic contexts have either taken place within state-building, peace-building, and conflict studies (in case of transitional justice in ongoing conflict) or within comparative politics (in case of transitional justice in consolidated democracies). This has impeded a dialogue between scholars studying transitional justice in cases of ongoing conflict and those studying its use in consolidated democracies, as well as stifling the theoretical evolution of transitional justice as a field.

This volume brings these increasingly important transitional justice practice into the mainstream conversation, by mapping and exploring the changing terrain of transitional justice as it has expanded to contexts without a transitional state, either because they are cases of ongoing conflict or because they are consolidated democracies. The next section provides a brief account of the evolution of the field and then introduces a typology of transitional justice contexts centring on political authority and the nature of the state to show how paradigmatic and aparadigmatic cases stand in relation to each other.

The Evolution of Transitional Justice

Beginning in the 1980s, transitional justice focused mostly on how newly established democratic governments could use a unique and presumably confined 'transitional moment' to respond to the abuses committed by their repressive predecessors (McEvoy and McGregor 2008, 6). The implicit assumption was of a repressive and violent past, a (brief) transitional window of opportunity, and a (never-ending) peaceful and democratic future, at least in so far as transitional justice is used appropriately (Hansen 2017). Transitional justice was designed for, and evolved in relation to, a particular set of transitional states. These *paradigmatic contexts* were pacted transitions or those where successor governments took over from conflicted governments or dictatorships (e.g. Argentina, Peru, Rwanda, South Africa).

The comprehensiveness and versatility of the multitude of mechanisms that are now conceptualised as transitional justice, combined with the field's normative ambition of consolidating democracy and contributing to just societies, made the paradigm appealing in a much broader range of contexts than the paradigmatic cases for which it was developed. As the field expanded, it was also transformed, while still preserving some of its elements (Arnould 2021; Ni Aolain 2017). First, there was a *geographical* expansion from Latin America to Africa and, later, the Middle East, Australia, Canada, the United States, New Zealand, and Europe. This included a *contextual* expansion from post-dictatorship to post-conflict and further to ongoing conflict, settler democracies and, more recently, 'old democracies'.[3] Finally, there have been changes in the field's *applicability*, the sense of when transitional justice is a relevant paradigm, particularly in relation to the forms of harm for which it is appropriate. This is an expansion from situations of atrocity and physical violence to non-physical forms of suffering, such as colonial discrimination (e.g. in Greenland) and social justice (e.g. in the United States).[4] More recently, restitution of cultural property has been included in transitional justice discourse (O'Donnell 2011). The field became imbued with holistic normative ambitions rather than the narrower goals associated with facilitating liberal political transitions (Sharp 2014, 151).

Due to its expansion, transitional justice has been invoked and implemented in situations that belie the concept of 'transition', including in cases of ongoing conflict, consolidated democracies dealing with legacies of violence, or ambiguous contexts where there is neither obvious political transition nor an all-out war. The support for expansion can be observed in scholarly debate (e.g. Sarkin 2016), in calls by UN bodies to go beyond post-conflict settings (UN Advisory Group of Experts 2015, UN Framework Team 2012), and by activists and practitioners using transitional justice tools in aparadigmatic contexts. More conceptually, the processes of expansion changed the notion of justice from an exceptional justice to ordinary justice in exceptional contexts. In this process of 'normalisation', the 'transitional' prefix changed meaning, describing not the *nature* of justice but the *context* in which it occurs

3 See Destrooper in this volume.

4 See, respectively, Gissel and McGonigle Leyh in this volume; see also Joshi 2020.

(Gissel 2017). As the UN High Commissioner for Human Rights (2009, 2) argued, transitional justice was 'not a particular conception of justice, such as distributive or retributive justice', but rather 'a technical approach to exceptional challenges', such as dealing with massive human abuses committed in the course of armed conflict or by repressive regimes and in circumstances of scarce resources, urgently competing demands, and frequent institutional breakdown. In the past decade, transitional justice increasingly moved away from this 'politics of exception' so central to its foundational *raison d'etre* (Gissel 2017; Israël and Mouralis 2014). This coincided with the application of transitional justice in aparadigmatic cases, which was facilitated by the availability of an emerging standard.

Standardisation

Although accountability and recognition have been explicit objectives of transitional justice since the emergence of the field, scholars and practitioners have pursued these aims in increasingly standardised ways. The conceptualisation of transitional justice as revolving around four institutionalised mechanisms, or pillars, is the most obvious example of the standardisation process. Truth-telling, justice, reparations, and guarantees of non-recurrence constitute the 'model' relevant for application across local contexts (African Union 2019; European Union 2015; United Nations 2010). This standardised 'toolkit' prioritises a formal commitment to anti-impunity, defines harm in terms of violations of civil and political rights, and seeks to attribute (criminal) culpability for harm to individual perpetrators (see also Gissel 2022).

This standardised model, to which many central actors adhere, risks marginalising initiatives that do not easily fit the four-pillar model. Lustration and amnesties, for example, which are problematic from a rule of law perspective (McAuliffe 2010), came to be seen as undesirable. Memorialisation or community-based and artistic forms of engaging with a legacy of violence have also come to be seen as nice-to-haves rather than as necessary dimensions (Cohen 2020; Rush and Simic 2014).

Moreover, the model's mechanisms are state-centric. They require state backing and simultaneously reify the centrality of state institutions. Criminal justice needs to be state-sanctioned, while there is a vast literature on the role of criminal law and trials for consolidating state power (see, e.g. Shapiro 1981). Similarly, reparations programmes are difficult to implement without (national or local) public authority. Equally so, institutional reform constructs the state, while civil society can only shape the reform in an indirect manner and over the *longue durée*. Truth-telling is arguably the standardised justice mechanism that requires the least state involvement and gives the least state consolidation (but see Hamber and Wilson 2002). Yet, truth commissions, too, are often legally bounded, and their commissioners are officially appointed by parliaments or ministers. In summary, standardised transitional justice both depends on and strengthens politico-legal authority.

This standardisation process is remarkable, given the disruptive roots and ongoing disruptive potential of transitional justice.[5] It could be argued that the standardisation process is precisely an attempt to sanitise transitional justice and strip it of its excessive disruptive potential, as evidenced by other examples of state-generated standardisation (Scott 1999). Put differently, the field's legalisation and standardisation offer a way to bracket those disruptive promises that may threaten the powerful. Yet, standardised and non-standardised forms of transitional justice are in constant conversation with each other in ways that affect how we think about accountability, recognition and/or disruption.

For all its dominance, the standardised model has been heavily critiqued. For instance, its legalistic approach is criticised for being too narrow to work towards broader transitional justice objectives. Or North-based governments apply it in their foreign policy work but not domestically.[6] Lastly, it has blind spots, overlooking wrongs committed by multinational companies or involving structural injustice or colonial harm.

A Typology of Transitional Justice Contexts

Paradigmatic and aparadigmatic transitional justice contexts can be organised in a typology based on types of state and the status of political authority. The typology involves seven types of transitional justice context (A–G) in six different types of state, from ongoing conflict (type A) in a conflict state to consolidated democracy (type G) in an 'old' democracy. The types of contexts are organised on a spectrum of political authority that ranges from contested to consolidated. Authority is most contested and least consolidated in a context of ongoing conflict and it is least contested and most consolidated in an 'old' democracy. The typology highlights the fact that not all contexts where transitional justice has been implemented or rolled out are, in fact, transitional. There is neither a significant political transition in contexts of ongoing conflict or those marked by political violence or occupation (contexts A–C) nor in consolidated democracies (F and G).

The typology is not processual; it does not indicate the ideal or empirical path from ongoing conflict to consolidated democracy. Rather, it proposes a list of mutually exclusive contexts in which transitional justice takes place in practice. A state may have context A (ongoing conflict) and then D (pacted transition), but this does not necessarily mean it has also found itself in situation B or C (fragile state and occupation). As the typology is organised according

5 This is the topic of the definitional debate of first-generation transitional justice, the 'peace versus justice debate', and its accompanying queries regarding impunity and amnesty (Roht-Arriaza and Mariezcurrena 2006).

6 See Carlson in this volume.

to the status of political authority, political violence may be present in all of the contexts, but likely to different degrees: Where this authority is contested, there is likely to be more political violence, while less political violence is likely in areas of consolidated authority.

In typologies of modern state forms, categories are usually organised along constitutional (monarchy, republic) or regime (authoritarian, democratic, hybrid) type. More recently, scholars have proposed typologies based on state fragility (Ziaja et al. 2019). Risse and Stollenwerk (2018, 105) argue that most states are neither consolidated nor failed but are rather characterised by 'areas of limited statehood'. Although our seven types of context articulate different degrees of limited or consolidated statehood, the diversity of contexts requires more categories than afforded by the dichotomy of limited/consolidated statehood. For instance, both settler and former imperial democracies are consolidated democracies, but the potential for and modalities of accountability, recognition, and disruption are different in these two settings.

Table 0.1 illustrates the typology and the field's expansion from paradigmatic to aparadigmatic contexts. It shows that the expansion occurred in two directions from the paradigmatic transitions to different forms of non-transitions: first, to contexts of ongoing conflict, political violence, or occupation, all of which are characterised by contested political authority. This is a movement from the central columns towards the left of Table 0.1. Second, the field expanded to contexts, where political authority is consolidated. This movement was to settler and old democracies, respectively, which are located on the right of the table.

A conflicted state is a state of ongoing conflict, such as, presently, the Democratic Republic of Congo (DRC), Syria, and Yemen. Political authority is contested, as conflict parties build, challenge, and seek to preserve this authority. In this context, transitional justice initiatives can be used to disrupt political authority, hold perpetrators accountable while the conflict is still ongoing, or seek recognition for the suffering of victims. However, the government is not necessarily a partner in transitional justice; it may be involved in the conflict and is not interested in addressing any wrongs (Syria is an example), or it is instrumentalising transitional justice (like the DRC has done). A fragile state does not have ongoing conflict, but it does have political violence that transitional justice may seek to address. Occupied territories are controlled by a state, the United Nations (such as East Timor), or an 'international coalition' of states (until recently, Afghanistan and Iraq) or international organisations (Kosovo). There the political authority is imposed by the occupier and therefore likely contested by excluded political elites and the wider society. Transitional justice can play a role there by disrupting the existing status quo and seeking accountability and recognition for injustices and harm. The kind of accountability, recognition, and disruption envisaged here will necessarily differ substantially from that envisaged in paradigmatic cases. Pacted transitions and successor governments make up the category of paradigmatic contexts; as argued above, here

Table 0.1 Typology of paradigmatic and aparadigmatic transitional justice contexts

	Aparadigmatic			*Paradigmatic*		*Aparadigmatic*	
Context for Transitional Justice	**A. Ongoing conflict**	**B. Fragile state**	**C. Occupied territory**	**D. Pacted transition**	**E. Successor government**	**F. Consolidated democracy**	**G. Consolidated democracy**
State Form	Conflicted state	Fragile state	Occupied state	Transitional state	Transitional state	Settler democracy	Old democracy
Status of Political Authority	Very contested	Contested	Imposed, contested	Transitional	Transitional	Consolidated	Consolidated
Examples	DRC (2000s, 2010s) Uganda (2000s, 2010s) Syria (2010s, 2020s) Yemen (2020s)	Kenya (2000s) Burundi (2000s, 2010s) Myanmar (2020s)	Afghanistan* (2000s, 2010s) East Timor (1990s)	Chile (1990s) Poland (1990s) South Africa (1990s)	Argentina (1980s) Peru (1990s) Rwanda (1990s)	Australia (2010s) Canada (2010s) New Zealand (2010s) US (2010-2020s)	Belgium (2020s) Denmark (2020s) Spain (2010s)

Notes: Table compiled by the authors. *Afghanistan is categorised as an occupied state because the book was written when it was an occupied state. However, since August 2021, when NATO troops withdrew from the country, it has been a fragile state.

the state is more likely the partner in the justice process. Transitional justice has also taken place in two types of consolidated democracies: in settler democracies like Australia, Canada, New Zealand, and the United States, and, more recently, in old democracies like Belgium, France, and Denmark.

The Problem of the State

The different contexts vary on specific parameters that are of theoretical interest for this volume, including state form and the status of political authority. While a typology based on state form does not require state-centric analysis, it does require us to theorise the problem of the state and to think about how actors grapple with the nature of the state. Unpacking the issue of the state is crucial because the field of transitional justice assumes a particular form of state, the transitional state: a state that will engage in transitional justice processes, reform itself, support a truth process, and carry out trials, even if reluctantly. The field has generated a series of dichotomous concepts to accompany this assumption, such as before/after, backwards-looking/forwards-looking, authoritarianism/democracy, war/peace, impunity/accountability, perpetrator/victim, restorative/retributive, force/reason, politics/law, top-down/bottom-up, and (Global) North/South. In aparadigmatic contexts, transitional justice practitioners cannot assume a transitional state and this challenges the relevance of some of these binaries. Instead, as this volume demonstrates, aparadigmatic transitional justice contexts evidence civil-society-driven processes, the activism of third states, violence by third parties, and government refusal to partner in transitional justice.

There are good reasons why transitional justice became a state-centric field. On the one hand, the state is often central to the harms done, in the sense that the state either perpetrated them or failed to protect against them. On the other hand, transitional justice requires official state recognition of past harm. State acknowledgement of past harm affirms the idea that civilians ought to have been protected by their state, and thereby it performs sovereignty and enacts the fundamental structure of the contemporary state system.

There are nevertheless grounds for challenging the long-standing assumption that the state is the only logical focus in the quest for recognition and accountability. For many victims, state-based initiatives are not the only relevant approach to transitional justice. Alternative justice processes that include marginalised voices may be experienced as equally meaningful. For example, in post-war Guatemala, many indigenous women found alternative civil society processes (e.g. the *Tejidos que lleva el alma*) to be more meaningful than the work of the official *Comisión para Esclaracimiento Histórico*, the Commission for Historical Clarification. It was experienced as a more genuine form of recognition and acknowledgement of suffering than the official initiatives, which were perceived as remote (Destrooper and Parmentier 2018). Furthermore, national processes are primarily pursuing a national political agenda, which may be at odds with the pace or nature of individual or community-level processes to overcome trauma (Hamber and Wilson 2002). There are multiple contradictions, 'disjunctures', and 'convergences' between individual survivor responses and the transitional justice of national institutions (Hamber and Wilson 2002, 49).

The centrality of the state begs the question of how one can get justice from a state that is, or has been, involved in wrong-doing or which is not transitioning. This challenge is most visible in aparadigmatic contexts since there the violating regime is either still in place or long gone. Here the field's assumption of the constructive transitional state does not help the analysis. The expansion of transitional justice to aparadigmatic contexts has prompted actors to grapple with the problem of the state in new and different ways. They may develop new and different conceptions of justice as a result, introducing innovation into the field while consolidating other aspects. Moreover, innovation in one context may mean consolidation in another. Since the field has expanded to conflicted and failed states and contexts without regime change, it is urgent to learn from these aparadigmatic cases how stakeholders conceptualise recognition, accountability and disruption in the absence of a transition.

But how to empirically study accountability, recognition, and disruption in aparadigmatic contexts? How to identify the ways in which justice actors negotiate transitional justice in their non-transitional state? What does disruption look like when the state is anything but a constructive partner? We propose a focus on the dynamic relations between *intentions* and *responses* as a strategy to understand the practices, processes, or politics of aparadigmatic transitional justice.

Studying the Disruptive Potential: Intentions and Responses

Intentionality is central to the practice of transitional justice, as the intentions behind transitional justice processes constitute much of what meaningfully distinguishes them from other fields, such as peace-building, democratisation, and governance. Looking at intentionality helps to begin an empirical mapping exercise by asking what justice actors intend to achieve by turning to the transitional justice toolbox and discourse as well as how and which initiatives they apply, and in which ways, to further that intention. By examining intentionality, we may thus understand how transitional justice is understood or envisaged and what is at stake. These intentions may be either be articulated by activists, advocates, politicians, bureaucrats, diplomats, and so on, or they may be stated in formal documents such as reports, policies, and laws.

The analysis should, however, look beyond these stated intentions, and consider that 'real' intentions may be very different from stated ones. A criminal justice process, for example, may serve the official intention of holding specific perpetrators accountable, while enjoying elite support precisely because it leaves other individuals, policies, or institutions undisturbed (Carlson 2022). When it referred a conflict situation to the International Criminal Court in 2003, the Ugandan government stated that its intention was to ensure accountability. In practice though, it sought to incentivise rebel participation in peace negotiations, and/or mobilise international support for the military pursuit of its insurgent adversary (Branch 2011). Distinguishing 'real' from stated intentions is useful because the standardisation process made transitional justice a tool available for states to serve various ends, while inscribing themselves in the normatively appealing rhetoric of transitional justice.

A focus on intentions also allows us to acknowledge non-standardised transitional justice efforts, such as community-driven initiatives or artistic practice, as potential instances of transitional justice. This means moving our focus away from the state as the central object of analysis, and foregrounding instead the mobilisation for accountability, recognition, and disruption as it happens in practice. In the aparadigmatic cases in this volume, political will is often in short supply. Civil society practitioners, activists, survivors, or other stakeholders may be the ones pushing for some form of transitional justice in their quest for accountability, recognition, and/or disruption. Moreover, these actors do not always have access to state bodies. Their non-standardised transitional justice may be side-tracked, co-opted, or otherwise fail to ensure accountability, recognition, and/or disruption, but it is still a meaningful object of analysis. Indeed, the responses to this kind of mobilisation, too, shape what transitional justice is and becomes.

The second focus of the chapters in this volume is therefore on the responses to the stated and deduced intentions by actors such as activists, advocates, community members, leaders, officials, politicians, survivors, suspects, or even an opinion-surveyed population. Responses should be examined within their context and are likely to span a wide range, from wholesale uncritical adoption to a complete rejection. Julie Bernath and Sandra Rubli (2013) argue that rejection and resistance should be further explored in order to understand the importance and legitimacy of certain standardised and non-standardised approaches that might better align with victims' needs and resources. Indeed, the aparadigmatic cases in this volume describe a panorama of responses to transitional justice: resistance against an imposed foreign agenda; rejection by international actors of deeply contextualised proposals; government rejection of initiatives that would recognise past wrongs; principled and practical objections to certain objectives or mechanisms; critical or reluctant adoption of the model by ruling elites; or partial adoption by civil society actors who see it as a tool to further their own agendas.

Intentions and responses are interrelated; to analyse and understand their dynamic relationship we need to pay attention to context, positionality, and power. Rather than assuming the transitional state or, indeed, a genuine desire for accountability, recognition, and/or disruption, the chapters in this volume seek to understand the messiness and complexity of transitional justice on the ground, by providing a contextualised and actor-centred analysis rather than starting from the model of transitional justice.

By focusing on the relationship between intentions and responses, the basic framework may visibilise new actors and their agency. It may open the 'justice imagination' by offering new perspectives on what can be expected of transitional justice and how (Herremans and Destrooper 2021). For instance, a focus on trans-local transitional justice practice may destabilise North/South or bottom-up/top-down binaries.[7]

Our Cases

The chapters in this volume explore transitional justice in the five types of aparadigmatic contexts: ongoing conflict, fragile state, occupied territory, consolidated settler democracy, and consolidated old democracy (see Table 0.2 below). Together, they show that the contemporary practice of transitional justice takes many different forms, which are shaped and constrained by context. In spite of their position in Table 0.2, the cases can hardly be termed 'outliers'. Due to the expansion of the field, non-transitional states make up the majority of contexts where transitional justice is currently being implemented or imagined.

This typology does not seek to facilitate a controlled comparison, but instead problematises taken-for-granted assumptions of standardised transitional justice: its state centricity, the assumption of the transitional state, and the question of disruption. By exposing the limits of the model and its assumptions, the case studies interrogate and shed new light on the field of transitional justice.

Outline of the Volume

The structure of the volume follows our typology of transitional justice contexts presented in Table 0.2, beginning with ongoing conflict and fragile states, moving to occupied territory and then types of consolidated democracy, and ending with comparative considerations. The first two chapters therefore analyse Libya, Yemen, and Syria. Thereafter the volume turns to the fragile state of Turkey/Kurdistan, before moving to occupied Afghanistan. This is then followed by settler democracies and consolidated democracies, i.e. the United States, Greenland/Denmark, Belgium, Denmark, France, and the United Kingdom. Finally, the volume closes with a cross-cutting chapter on historical commissions and a theoretical discussion of stretching transitional justice from consolidated democracy to ongoing conflict. The concluding chapter reflects on the theoretical lessons that can be learnt from these empirical insights.

7 See Saeed and Aboueldahab in this volume.

Table 0.2 Case studies mapped onto the typology of paradigmatic and aparadigmatic contexts

	Aparadigmatic			*Paradigmatic*		*Aparadigmatic*	
Context for Transitional Justice	**A. Ongoing conflict**	**B. Fragile state**	**C. Occupied territory**	**D. Pacted transition**	**E. Successor government**	**F. Consolidated democracy**	**G. Consolidated democracy**
State Form	Conflicted state	Fragile state	Occupied state	Transitional state	Transitional state	Settler democracy	Old democracy
Status of Political Authority	Very contested	Contested	Imposed, contested	Transitional	Transitional	Consolidated	Consolidated
Case Studies and Analysis	**Libya and Yemen** (Aboueldahab) **Syria** (Herremans and Bellintani)	**Turkey/ Kurdistan** (Alıcı)	**Afghanistan** (Saeed)			**Greenland/ Denmark** (Gissel) **US** (McGonigle Leyh)	**Belgium** (Destrooper) **Denmark and France** (Carlson) **UK** (Hansen)
	Cross-cutting Analysis (Pallí-Asperó; Winter)						

Note: Table compiled by the authors.

The volume opens with a chapter by Noha Aboueldahab that links several cases of aparadigmatic transitional justice in situations of ongoing violence, notably Libya, Yemen and Syria. These are cases where the absence of state-endorsed transitional justice policies has prompted domestic and diaspora actors to shape truth and justice-seeking initiatives in ways that have disruptive potential. Their innovative conceptualisations of accountability and recognition cast a wider net of accountability that includes international actors, including Western-based multinational corporations. The chapter suggests that in contexts where the state continues to exercise repressive rule, unexpected opportunities for accountability, recognition, and disruption may emerge.

The chapter by Brigitte Herremans and Veronica Bellintani likewise explores how certain local and international actors are testing and advancing elements of the transitional justice toolkit while abuses are ongoing. They argue that Syrian justice actors have turned to the transitional justice toolkit to counter the reigning defeatism about the impossibility of pursuing justice while the conflict is ongoing, building on a diverse international justice network. The chapter empirically describes the evolution of the initial transitional justice efforts, examining the intentions of justice actors who embraced transitional justice tools as a way to defy the accountability gap, achieve recognition and disrupt violent state practices. The chapter shows how justice actors are animated by this potential for accountability, recognition and disruption, thus explaining why justice actors are using transitional justice even in cases where the state is not transitional.

The non-transitional state is also the background to Nisan Alıcı's chapter on Kurdish transitional justice activists in Turkey. Turkey has never adopted an official, overarching transitional justice agenda to deal with the past atrocities in its Kurdish areas, and the Kurdish question poses a particular threat to the contested political authority of the Turkish state. Nonetheless, Alıcı follows two engagements seeking to disrupt the hegemonic state narrative in pursuit of recognition and eventual accountability; the Diyarbakır Commission, which was led by civil society actors, and managed to push the Parliament to open up an investigatory sub-commission, and Erdoğan's apology for the Dersim massacre, which led to controversies around the underpinning motivation, but disrupted the public silence over the issue.

Huma Saeed's chapter on transitional justice in Afghanistan addresses the question of how domestic and diaspora attempts at transitional justice are shaped by the lack of political will from international and local (institutional) actors to address legacies of mass atrocities. Saeed examines how Afghanistan's complex societal and political structure was affected by direct and indirect foreign interventions, in ways that relegated formal transitional justice initiatives to the background. Through an analysis of various policy reforms, including a contested amnesty law, she demonstrates how an unjust and unaccountable status quo was consolidated. The chapter underlines the need for innovations to the standardised transitional justice paradigm by arguing in favour of a transnational

transitional justice that integrates diaspora and refugee communities both as agents of change and as beneficiaries of transitional justice programmes in their host countries. In doing so, the chapter expands the scope of how we commonly think about accountability and recognition within a transitional justice context, and paves the way for the disruption of rights-violating policies and regimes.

The framing possibilities that transitional justice's categories can offer to social justice challenges in democratic states outside of conflict or transition is the topic of Brianne McGonigle Leyh's chapter. She considers how the four pillars of paradigmatic transitional justice could direct more effective social justice initiatives. Her chapter visits several lesser-known social justice initiatives that pursue the accountability, recognition and disruption upon which transitional justice is premised. Her chapter argues that the significant challenges that impede the facilitation of social transformation include a decentralised and disjointed legal system, underlining the importance of a coherent and comprehensive response at the federal level to complement and fully realise the innovative and disruptive potential of local-level initiatives.

The government rejection of transitional justice is central to Line Engbo Gissel's chapter analysing the politics of potential accountability, recognition, and disruption in Greenland and Denmark. In 2013 the Danish government rejected participation in the Greenland Reconciliation Commission, which therefore became a unilateral project seeking recognition and – to some extent – disruption. In the absence of Danish involvement, the Commission's work turned towards intra-Greenlandic relations, outlining the contours of a disruptive potential that may shape the island's future independence. The case illuminates the state-centric nature of both standardised truth-telling and transitional justice in post-colonial Denmark.

In his chapter on justice for crimes by the UK military, Thomas Obel Hansen provides a detailed analysis of justice measures in the United Kingdom and internationally relating to crimes committed by British military forces in campaigns abroad. He explores the added value of model transitional justice in contexts like these. His case goes beyond the typical way in which consolidated democracies have been implementing – parts of – the model transitional justice agenda, i.e. in relation to historical abuses. Instead, he asks what transitional justice's intentionality of accountability, recognition and disruption can mean in the context of violations committed by the United Kingdom's armed forces in recent military campaigns. By considering several government efforts that de facto obstruct rather than promote accountability, he underlines the need for standardised and innovative practices to be in conversation to allow for some form of accountability to materialise.

The limits of permissible disruption frame the two examples in Tine Destrooper's chapter on the adoption of certain model transitional justice mechanisms in Belgian case. Destrooper contrasts the scepticism and rejection she observed regarding the applicability of transitional justice approaches to

Flanders' educational programme aimed at dealing with societal polarisation and conflict transformation with the 2020 Special Parliamentary Commission on Belgium's colonial past. Explicit transitional justice architecture was rejected for one, while it was nominally, arguably instrumentally, adopted for the other. Destrooper's chapter demonstrates how engaging with transitional justice's core intentions of accountability for and recognition of past harm, requires the state to engage in a rethinking of, and potential challenge to, the legitimacy of the existing state institutions and of the existing narratives about those institutions.

Government actors rejecting transitional justice discourses also feature in Kerstin Bree Carlson's chapter on Danish and French legal responses to domestic terror actors and foreign fighters. Carlson explores the potential benefits of applying transitional justice as a tool to counter emerging illiberal terror laws in European states, arguing that transitional justice has the capacity to circumvent the security/rights impasse in which liberal democracies find themselves regarding domestic terror actors. Carlson explores how objections to illiberal terror law highlight intentionality and response in seeking to disrupt state terror law practices.

These contested narratives are also at the heart of the historical clarification commissions (HCCs) used in consolidated democracies to address a legacy of the past. Cira Pallí-Asperó relies on a functional definition of what these commissions do, i.e. using the historical method as a fact-finding to shed light on social and political events of the past that were linked to the origin, causes or developments of conflict. She explores the extent to which HCCs fit the model of transitional justice. Functionally they may show overlaps, but do they share the intentionality of accountability, recognition, and disruption? While their history of being used as political, diplomatic, or clarification tools, suggests otherwise, Pallí-Asperó sheds light on their potential as accountability mechanisms for crimes and other violations of human rights committed in the distant past, which makes them relevant in light of the intentionality of transitional justice, even if they have not always been framed as such.

Stephen Winter's chapter challenges some of the arguments presented above in asking whether it is relevant to refer to transitional justice-like practices as transitional justice in cases where there is no regime or political change. He relies on a legitimating theory of transitional justice to argue that transitional justice is both performative and political in that it can help states, with various forms of political authority, to discharge duties of justice to create a more reasonable political order. Transitional justice is necessarily a driver of transition, bringing state practice into accord with developing legitimating discourses, in cases of illegitimacy created by authorised wrong-doing. His legitimating account argues that political institutions necessarily aim to exercise political authority, but that transitional legitimation is necessary both

when political authorities have negated their purpose by committing systemic injuries and/or when their weakness or absence requires the constitution of new institutions. As such, the chapter explicitly engages with this Introduction's discussion of state forms and how they relate to the disruptive potential of transitional justice.

The concluding chapter by Par Engstrom and Tine Destrooper pulls together the insights emerging from the empirical chapters about how to do transitional justice in different contexts, and what 'doing transitional justice' in different contexts tells us about transitional justice as a field. It shows that what we see as innovative today sometimes entails an expansion of the transitional justice repertoire and sometimes entails a stripping back of layers and going back to practices in ways that make transitional justice more context sensitive. It reflects on the cross-cutting themes, such as issues related to bottom-up/top-down perspectives; accountability politics/law; the scope and objectives of transitional justice. The chapter shows that transitional justice norms and politics remain locally embedded in many places around the world, including in some very inhospitable contexts.

References

African Union (2019) 'Transitional Justice Policy'. 12 February. Available at: https://au.int/en/documents/20190425/transitional-justice-policy.

Arnould, V. (2021) 'Developments in the Field of Transitional Justice'. Leuven Transitional Justice Blog, 23 June. Available at: https://blog.associatie.kuleuven.be/ltjb/tag/colonialism/.

Bevernage, B. (2012) '"Unpopular Past": The Argentine Madres de Plaza de Mayo and Their Rebellion against History'. In: S. Berger, C. Lorez and B. Melman, eds. *Popularizing National Pasts: 1800 to the Present* (pp. 331–351). Abingdon: Routledge.

Branch, A. (2011) *Displacing Human Rights: War and Intervention in Northern Uganda.* Oxford: Oxford University Press.

Carlson, K.B. (2022) *The Justice Laboratory: International Law in Africa.* London, UK and Washington, DC: Chatham House/Brookings.

Cohen, C. (2020) 'Reimagining Transitional Justice'. *International Journal of Transitional Justice* 14(1), 1–13.

Destrooper, T. and S. Parmentier (2018) 'Gender-Aware and Place-Based Transitional Justice in Guatemala: Altering the Opportunity Structures for Post-Conflict Women's Mobilization'. *Social and Legal Studies* 27(3), 323–344.

Elster, J. (2004) *Closing the Books: Transitional Justice in Historical Perspective.* Cambridge: Cambridge University Press.

European Union (2015) 'The EU's Policy Framework on Support for Transitional Justice'. 16 November 2015. Available at: www.eeas.europa.eu.

Gissel, L.E. (2017) 'Contemporary Transitional Justice: Normalising a Politics of Exception'. *Global Society* 31(3), 353–369.

—— (2022) 'The Standardisation of Transitional Justice'. *European Journal of International Relations* 28(4), 859–884.

Hamber, B. and P. Lundy (2020) 'Lessons from Transitional Justice? Toward a New Framing of a Victim-Centered Approach in the Case of Historical Institutional Abuse'. *Victims and Offenders* 15(6), 744–770

—— and R.A. Wilson (2002) 'Symbolic Closure through Memory, Reparation and Revenge in Post-conflict Societies'. *Journal of Human Rights* 1(1), 35–53.

Hansen, T.O. (2017) 'The Time and Place of Transitional Justice'. In: C. Lawther, L. Moffett and D. Jacobs, eds. *Research Handbook on Transitional Justice* (pp. 34–51). Cheltenham: Edward Elgar.

Hayward, C.R. (2020) 'Disruption: What Is It Good For?' *The Journal of Politics* 82(2), 448–459.

Herremans, B. and T. Destrooper (2021) 'Stirring the Justice Imagination: Countering the Invisibilization and Erasure of Syrian Victims' Justice Narratives'. *International Journal of Transitional Justice* 15(3), 576–595.

Israël, L. and G. Mouralis (2014) *Dealing with Wars and Dictatorships: Legal Concepts and Categories in Action*. The Hague: T.M.C. Asser Press.

Jones, B., J. Bernath and S. Rubli (2013) *Reflections on a Research Agenda for Exploring Resistance to Transitional Justice*. Working Paper 3/2013. Bern: Swiss Peace Foundation.

Macdonald, A. (2019) '"Somehow This Whole Process Became So Artificial": Exploring the Transitional Justice Implementation Gap in Uganda'. *International Journal of Transitional Justice* 13(2), 225–248.

McAuliffe, P. (2010) 'Transitional Justice and the Rule of Law: The Perfect Couple or Awkward Bedfellows?' *Hague Journal on the Rule of Law* 2, 127–154.

McEvoy, K. and L. McGregor (2008) *Transitional Justice from Below: Grassroots Activism and the Struggle for Change*. Oxford and Portland: Hart.

Minow, M. (1998) *Between Vengeance and Forgiveness*. Boston, MA: Beacon Press.

Ni Aolain, F. (2017) 'After Things Fall Apart: Challenges for Transitional Justice Futures'. *Human Rights and International Legal Discourse* 11(1), 23–40.

O'Donnell, T. (2011) 'The Restitution of Holocaust Looted Art and Transitional Justice: The Perfect Storm or the Raft of the Medusa?' *European Journal of International Law* 22(1), 49–80.

Piven, F.F. (2006) *Challenging Authority: How Ordinary People Change America*. New York: Rowman & Littlefield.

Quinn, J. (2009) 'Introduction'. In: J. Quinn, ed. *Reconciliation(s): Transitional Justice in Postconflict Societies*. Quebec: McGill-Queens University Press.

—— (2014) 'Whither the "Transition" of Transitional Justice?'. *Interdisciplinary Journal of Human Rights Law* 8(1), 63–79.

Rowen, J. (2017) *Searching for Truth in the Transitional Justice Movement*. Cambridge: Cambridge University Press.

Roht-Arriaza, N. and J. Mariezcurrena, eds. (2006) *Transitional Justice in the Twenty-First Century. Beyond Truth Versus Justice*. Cambridge: Cambridge University Press.

Rush, P.D. and O. Simic, eds. (2014) *The Arts of Transitional Justice. Culture, Activism, and Memory after Atrocity*. New York: Springer.

Sarkin, J. (2016) 'Refocusing Transitional Justice to Focus Not Only on the Past, But Also to Concentrate on Ongoing Conflicts and Enduring Human Rights Crises'. *Journal of International Humanitarian Legal Studies* 7, 294–329.

Scott, J.C. (1999) *Seeing Like a State: How Certain Schemes to Improve the Human Condition Have Failed*. New Haven: Yale University Press.

Shapiro, M. (1981) *Courts: A Comparative and Political Analysis*. London and Chicago: The University of Chicago Press.

Sharp, D. (2014) 'Emancipating Transitional Justice from the Bonds of the Paradigmatic Transition'. *International Journal of Transitional Justice* 9(1), 150–169.

—— (2018) *Re-Thinking Transitional Justice for the 21st Century: Beyond the End of History*. Cambridge: Cambridge University Press.

Shaw, R. and L. Waldorf, eds. (2010) *Localizing Transitional Justice*. Stanford: Stanford University Press.

Sikkink, K. (2011) *The Justice Cascade: How Human Rights Prosecutions are Changing World Politics*. New York and London: W.W. Norton & Company.

Teitel, R. (2000) *Transitional Justice*. Oxford: Oxford University Press.

Tutu, D. (1998) 'Chairperson's Foreword'. In: Truth and Reconciliation Commission, *Truth and Reconciliation Commission of South Africa Report* (vol. 1, pp. 1–23). Pretoria: Government of South Africa.

UN Advisory Group of Experts (2015) *Identical Letters dated 29 June 2015 from the Chair of the Advisory Group of Experts on the Review of the Peacebuilding Architecture Addressed to the President of the General Assembly and the President of the Security Council*. A/69/968-S/2015/490, 30 June. New York: General Assembly, Security Council.

UN Framework Team (2012) 'The United Nations Interagency Framework Team for Preventive Action'. Available at: https://www.un.org/en/land-natural-resources-conflict/pdfs/FRAMEWORK_TEAM_FLYER-2July12.pdf.

UN High Commissioner for Human Rights (2009) *United Nations Approach to Transitional Justice, Address by Navanethem Pillay*. 15 October. New York: United Nations.

UN Security Council (2020) *[Summary Minutes from the] 8723rd Meeting*. S/PV.8723, 13 February. New York: United Nations.

United Nations (2010) *Guidance Note of the Secretary General: United Nations Approach to Transitional Justice*. New York: United Nations.

Ziaja, S., J. Grävingholt and M. Kreibaum (2019) 'Constellations of Fragility: An Empirical Typology of States'. *Studies in Comparative International Development* 54, 299–321.

Chapter 1

Diasporic and Domestic

Leveraging Criminal Accountability for Transitional Justice in the Middle East[1]

Noha Aboueldahab

Introduction

In several countries in the Middle East and North Africa, actors have been striving to stake their claim over transitional justice processes within contexts that are marked by renewed authoritarianism and ongoing violent conflict. More than ten years after the Arab Spring, where protesters took to the streets across the region and demanded justice for and freedom from decades of repressive rule, the state remains a primary perpetrator of mass human rights abuses and of an entrenched system of repression.[2] This leaves non-state actors, particularly activist lawyers and civil society leaders at home and in the diaspora, with the difficult task of pursuing transitional justice without and against their home state (Gready and Robins 2017). As such, the empirical analysis presented in this chapter relates to the book's theorisation about transitional justice in contexts where the perpetrator state presents significant challenges to the pursuit of transitional justice.

However, this state of affairs has created opportunities for an expanded transitional justice process that is not limited to the crimes of domestic perpetrators. Transnational networks and alliances of domestic and diasporic transitional justice actors have set in motion a movement that casts a wider net of accountability, targeting the role of other states and of multinational corporations (MNCs) in the perpetration of crimes within a given context. By virtue of their physical mobility and the advocacy access that comes with it, activist lawyers in the diaspora are a particularly underexplored transitional justice actor that disrupts contexts of ongoing conflict and renewed authoritarianism (Adamson

1 The author would like to thank Haider Ahmar for his research assistance for this chapter, and the editors for their insightful feedback on earlier drafts.

2 The role of the state as primary perpetrator varies across states within the region; in Yemen, for instance, the Houthi rebels, though operating in state-like ways, are not recognised as a state but have been implicated in war crimes and other grave human rights violations. The Yemeni 'state' and its international allies have also been involved in grave crimes, as will be explained in this chapter. In addition, militias and other non-state actors are also involved in the perpetration of crimes.

DOI: 10.4324/9781003289104-2

2016; Aboueldahab 2018; Baser and Swain 2010; Beaugrand and Geisser 2016; Koinova 2018; Van Hear and Cohen 2017).

This chapter is concerned with the 'new' Arab diasporas that actively pursue transitional justice in aparadigmatic contexts where the state continues to be the perpetrator. Lawyers, human rights professionals, civil society actors, journalists, artists, former politicians, and others have either left or have been forced to flee their home states for security reasons, especially in the immediate aftermath of the 2010/2011 Arab uprisings. This chapter argues that in transitional contexts where the state continues to exercise repressive rule, unexpected opportunities for a wider reckoning with the past emerge, especially when engaged by a mixture of domestic *and* diasporic transitional justice advocates that aim to disrupt ongoing violence. Such actors pursue criminal accountability and recognition in the immediate term as a strategy aiming to effect political change in the longer term. They leverage criminal accountability processes to draw more attention to a broader and deeper history of injustices.

The opportunities that such contexts present include a broader reckoning that takes into account the adverse role of both domestic and external actors in the perpetration of crimes. They also emerge from non-state-led justice processes that seek to protect the documentation of histories of injustice. The examples discussed in this chapter briefly refer to Libya and Yemen. Valuable lessons can also be drawn from Syria, where the absence of state-endorsed transitional justice policies has created opportunities for Syrian victims to shape their truth and justice-seeking initiatives (Aboueldahab 2018; see also Herremans and Bellintani in this volume). This has enabled them to imagine that the deeper and more complex history of injustice, including socio-economic violations, can be addressed. This has the potential to disrupt both state governance structures as well as the paradigmatic transitional justice model that this volume examines.

Drawing on this volume's theorisation of disruption and recognition in transitional justice, this chapter will proceed as follows. First, it argues that the disruptive potential of transitional justice in contexts where the perpetrator state is entrenched has been driven by domestic and diaspora transitional justice actors through legal advocacy. It has also served as a means to recognise victims through documentation and criminal investigations. Second, it argues that leveraging criminal accountability in the short term, especially through universal jurisdiction, does not diminish the value, nor prevent the future pursuit, of reparative and other forms of justice. This is particularly important in aparadigmatic contexts where conflict rages and repression is rampant. Finally, the chapter uses brief examples from Yemen, Libya, and Syria to demonstrate that leveraging criminal accountability by domestic and diasporic transitional justice actors may constitute an effective strategy to target the more complex web of complicity that involves foreign governments and MNCs. These efforts, in turn, make transitional justice a potentially powerful framework for a reckoning with a complex history of atrocities that are not confined to domestic spaces.

Legal Advocacy to Disrupt the State and Recognise Victims

Transitional justice has often required a certain level of state endorsement and involvement. This is particularly true for a range of transitional justice mechanisms, including institutional reform, reparations, national truth commissions, and criminal accountability. However, state fragmentation and conflict, such as in Libya and Yemen, present a significant obstacle to a state-endorsed transitional justice process. This is why justice advocates, particularly those based at international organisations, tend to advocate for a *post-conflict* transitional justice process, rather than one that begins before an armed conflict has ended (Mendes 2021). As the Syrian case clearly demonstrates, a paradigmatic transition to democratic rule need not be in place in order to pursue truth and justice-seeking processes. In such cases, transitional justice may even be a way to keep conflicts on the agenda of the international community, despite the waning political will to resolve them (Aboueldahab 2018).

As the civic space continues to shrink within several countries in the Middle East, new Arab diasporas have grown as has their capacity to coordinate with other diasporic communities that advocate for justice and accountability. Such transnational networks involving domestic and diasporic actors powerfully demonstrate how criminal accountability can be leveraged to pursue a transitional justice that reckons with a broader set of violations and a broader history of injustice. Moreover, the impact of legal advocacy is neither confined to the courts nor does it generate limited judicial truths (Accatino and Collins 2016). It also generates a form of political resistance, i.e. disruption, to ongoing authoritarian rule and conflict, as well as a form of protection for the stories and histories of victims, i.e. recognition. These diasporic transnational networks also play an important role in widening the accountability focus by targeting the role of external actors, including governments and corporations. Their efforts are striking, not least because they pursue them within contexts of ongoing violent conflict and in the absence of domestic state endorsement.

Since the mass Arab uprisings that swept the region in 2011, the number of cases targeting the role of foreign perpetrators has increased. Transitional justice has served as a useful framework through which this deeper reckoning with the past is made possible. As transitional justice often places emphasis on the importance of addressing the past, the role of Western governments and corporations will inevitably fall into the orbit of justice-seeking actors in post-colonial authoritarian states. Tunisia's Truth and Dignity Commission (TDC) offers an excellent example of how such transitional justice processes, even when domestically implemented, can hold external complicit actors accountable – or at least draw more attention to their complicity.

The TDC was established in 2013 with a mandate to investigate crimes committed from the final year of French colonial rule in 1955 to the post-independence governments of Habib Bourguiba and Zine El Abidine Ben Ali ending in 2013. This expanded mandate thus allowed Tunisia's domestic transitional justice process to target the French colonial state, the detrimental impact of Western multilateral institutions of the World Bank and the International Monetary Fund, as well as crimes committed by Tunisian state officials. Tunisians who had fled and resettled in the diaspora participated in the TDC hearings by providing testimony, some of which was aired live for millions of Tunisians to watch (Aboueldahab 2020a; Gall 2017).[3] A crucial difference, however, is that Tunisia did not suffer from ongoing armed conflict during its transitional justice process, which allowed the TDC to conduct its work with relative security.[4]

In transitional contexts marked by renewed authoritarianism and ongoing violent conflict, non-state actors, such as activist lawyers and diasporic civil society leaders, tend to take the reins of transitional justice processes without and against the state. The Syrian case demonstrates that, contrary to what many scholars of critical transitional justice would argue, the focus on criminal accountability is not 'narrow' and does not necessarily impose a hierarchy of justice that overlooks reparative and transformative justice (Accatino and Collins 2016; see also Saeed's chapter on Afghanistan in this volume).

Instead, the focus on criminal accountability is a practical tactic that generates greater international attention to the plight of victims, while also putting high-level perpetrators in the spotlight as cases and international arrest warrants mount against them. Criminal accountability, especially when pursued through universal jurisdiction avenues, presents a viable option in the short term compared to reparative and transformative justice, which are more complex, require state endorsement, and take more time. Setting aside critiques of the inherently limited justice that prosecutions and arrest warrants serve, they nevertheless constitute a highly symbolic effort that draws attention from both domestic and international levels, garnering much-needed support from international NGOs for actors working within contexts where the state remains a primary perpetrator.

Importantly, they serve as tangible and *possible* steps that set justice-seeking efforts in motion, thereby breathing momentum into other longer-term, yet equally important, truth and justice-seeking mechanisms, such as land and property restitution. Leveraging criminal accountability in this way also leads transitional justice actors to focus part of their work on ensuring accountability for allies of authoritarian transitional contexts, such as foreign governments

3 Approximately 4 million Tunisians tuned in to watch and/or listen to the hearings live.

4 That said, the Truth and Dignity Commission faced significant pushback from the Tunisian government.

and MNCs. Collaborations between international, diasporic, and home-state justice advocates lay the groundwork for such efforts. Criminal accountability, then, could be a step towards changing a broader political trajectory that includes a political transition away from authoritarianism and towards a future where the affected society has dealt with – rather than forgotten – its past and the role of those who helped perpetrate its injustices. The LaFarge case in Syria provides a powerful example of how this could work in Libya and Yemen.

The LaFarge case demonstrates the potential for holding MNCs accountable for their complicity in war crimes, while also underscoring the value of the work of diasporic and international alliances. LaFarge is a French multinational cement company, whose subsidiary, LaFarge Cement Syria, operated in Syria throughout the war. This case opened following the filing of a criminal complaint in November 2016 by 11 former Syrian employees together with the European Centre for Constitutional and Human Rights (ECCHR) and its French partner organisation, Sherpa. In 2018, French judges indicted individuals from LaFarge on charges of complicity in crimes against humanity, financing of a terrorist enterprise, and endangering people's lives. In 2022, the Paris Court of Appeals confirmed the charges of complicity in crimes against humanity against LaFarge, the organisation. The same year, LaFarge pleaded guilty before a US court to financing Islamic State (IS), and was ordered to pay a fine of USD 778 million (Cohen and Freifeld 2022).

LaFarge was accused of forcing its employees to continue to work in unsafe conditions between 2012 and 2014, thereby endangering their employees' lives to keep the factory open and running in north-eastern Syria. LaFarge was also accused of being an accomplice to crimes against humanity because it financed IS in a number of ways. It is believed that LaFarge purchased oil and other commodities from IS, paid fees to IS to obtain passes for mobility, and may have also sold cement to IS. This was regarded as empowering IS to commit massive atrocities in Syria. The investigation into LaFarge so far has revealed that it may have paid up to 13 million Euros to various armed groups in order to keep its factory running in Syria. Eight LaFarge executives, including two CEOs, were charged. It is the first time that France held a criminal inquiry into the actions of a French company in a foreign country.

Criminal accountability efforts in other parts of the Middle East have similarly targeted the role of corporations in perpetrating human rights violations and in propping up repressive governments. For example, the International Federation for Human Rights (FIDH) filed complaints against French company Amesys for its role in supplying electronic surveillance systems to the Libyan and Egyptian governments, who used them to target political dissidents. Victims of these systems provided testimony for these cases. French bank BNP Paribas is under investigation by the war crimes unit of the Tribunal of Paris for its alleged complicity in torture, genocide, and crimes against humanity in Sudan between 2002–2008. The complaint was filed on behalf of nine Sudanese plaintiffs (International Federation for Human Rights 2020). BNP

Paribas is also facing a lawsuit in the US, where it is accused of facilitating human rights violations in Sudan. A judge involved in the case stated that

> the victims had made a sufficient showing that BNP was aware of the atrocities being carried out by Sudan's government and continued providing it with access to the global financial system anyway, taking steps to conceal it in the process. In helping the regime sell oil on global markets, the bank had a role in helping Sudan fund a military that was engaged in a campaign of human rights abuses.
>
> (Berthelsen 2021)

In yet another case involving a corporation, SNC-Lavalin, a Canadian construction company, in 2019 pleaded guilty to money laundering and bribery to win contracts in Libya. To secure the contracts, millions of dollars were paid to the son of Libyan dictator Muammar Gaddafi, thereby depriving Libyans of resources that were instead swallowed by the black hole of corruption for which the Gaddafi era was infamous (Hinkson 2019). The role of Western governments in facilitating arms transfers from weapons companies to conflicts in Libya and Yemen has also increasingly come under scrutiny by key non-state actors who have long taken matters into their hands when their states could not or would not investigate it. These actors are primarily activist lawyers, diasporic and domestic transitional justice practitioners, and civil society organisations (CSOs).

Leveraging 'Narrow' Prosecutorial Justice For 'Broader' Transitional Justice

Criminal accountability, particularly through universal jurisdiction channels, has thus emerged as an impactful outlet for transitional justice in aparadigmatic contexts. These cases illustrate the power of transnational alliances between home-state victims and international CSOs, propelled by diasporic members who are both victims and lawyers. The spaces in which the state can be disrupted and where victims can be recognised have thus expanded in unexpected ways: through third-state judicial institutions and through a strategy that leverages criminal accountability for multiple purposes, including disruption and recognition.

The absence of strong and effective domestic judicial institutions, ongoing conflict, and few viable options to involve the International Criminal Court (ICC) are factors that have contributed to the tendency of transitional justice actors to go the universal jurisdiction route. Importantly, however, transitional justice actors who pursue criminal accountability in this way are more than well aware that it is but one form of justice needed to reckon with the past. Forms of reparative justice, crucial in contexts where socio-economic inequality and grievances are widespread, are a more distant possibility given the necessity of state endorsement and legislation in order to facilitate and implement them. While criminal accountability relies on state institutions (see the Introduction to this volume), it does not rely on the domestic perpetrator state in the same way as other forms of transitional justice. This is a key reason that domestic and diasporic actors actively pursue transnational criminal accountability mechanisms in the short term: they are accessible, somewhat effective, keep the transitional justice wheels turning, and do not prevent the pursuit of reparative or transformative justice in the future.

Given the internationalised nature of the conflicts in Libya and Yemen, legal advocacy for *transitional* and *transnational* justice is particularly important. Western arms exporters have especially come under fire as a result of such advocacy because of their complicity in the perpetration of crimes in Libya and Yemen. The following sections discuss the implications of the work of transitional justice advocates in the cases of Yemen and Libya, with a focus on the role of diasporic efforts.

Yemen

Although the conflict in Yemen is classified as non-international, it is overwhelmingly internationalised (RULAC n.d.). This has created a context in which Yemeni domestic and diasporic transitional justice actors are able to pursue attempts to disrupt the role of external actors in the perpetration of crimes committed in Yemen. Before I elaborate on this, it is worth summarising how the conflict in Yemen is internationalised.

In September 2014, the rebel group known as the Houthis took over the Yemeni capital, Sanaa, in an attempt to oust President Abed Rabbo Mansour Hadi. Earlier that year, the country had completed its National Dialogue Conference, a months-long process to decide on the country's future after the ouster of Yemen's long-time president, Ali Abdallah Saleh, during the mass anti-government uprising in 2011. At the request of President Hadi, a Saudi-led military coalition of ten states intervened in March 2015.[5] At the time of writing, this war is about to enter its eighth year. The United Nations has described Yemen as one of the world's worst humanitarian disasters (International Crisis Group 2020).[6] Both the Houthis, who are said to receive support from Iran, and the Saudi-led coalition are responsible for grave human rights violations in

5 The Saudi-led coalition, also referred to as the Arab coalition, initially included ten states: Jordan, Morocco, Qatar, Sudan, Kuwait, Bahrain, Egypt, the United Arab Emirates, and others. Several of these states are no longer a part of this coalition and for a long time, it has essentially been led by Saudi Arabia and the United Arab Emirates. Since 2019, however, the United Arab Emirates has scaled back its military presence in Yemen.

6 According to the International Crisis Group, 112,000 people have been killed, and 24 million Yemenis require humanitarian assistance. Starvation, malnutrition, cholera, and other diseases including now COVID-19, have contributed to the devastating human cost of the war.

the Yemen conflict. The Saudi-led coalition would not be able to carry out its operations without political and military support from Western countries, particularly the US. Both the United States and the United Kingdom have been the largest providers of weapons for the coalition, making billions of dollars in profit through such arms deals. France, Germany, Australia, and Canada have also sold weapons to this side. Some paused these sales due to human rights concerns, while others did not.

UN reports that outline these violations have increasingly called out countries such as Canada, Iran, the US, France, and the United Kingdom for continuing to sell arms to the conflict parties, despite these ongoing violations of international law and the mass suffering inflicted on innocent Yemenis (Group of Eminent Experts 2020; UN Office of the High Commissioner for Human Rights 2019). As a result of mounting evidence of war crimes and complicity in perpetrating them, and because of the work of civil society, in particular, certain politicians in the United States have called for an end to American involvement in this war. US senators have made attempts to block the sale of American weapons to Saudi Arabia and the United Arab Emirates, fearing that the United States would be held accountable for aiding and abetting war crimes in Yemen through its role as an arms exporter and military trainer. In May 2020, the Trump administration fired Steve Linick, a state department inspector general, who was about to complete an investigation into the lawfulness of American arms sales to Saudi Arabia and the United Arab Emirates in 2019 (Wong and Sanger 2020). Ultimately, more attention is given to the complicity of Western actors in what could amount to war crimes in Yemen.

The work of Yemeni civil society actors and their international allies has been instrumental in garnering this attention. For example, Mwatana (2020), a Yemeni human rights NGO, has played a significant role in advocating for accountability for crimes committed in Yemen. Operating both inside and outside Yemen, Mwatana employees have researched, documented, published, and advocated at international fora for justice for Yemeni victims. Together with the Berlin-based ECCHR, Mwatana and Italian organisations filed a joint criminal complaint with the Italian Prosecutor's Office in April 2018, and another complaint with the ICC in December 2019 (ECCHR 2020). Both complaints address the complicity of Italian arms exporters in the perpetration of grave crimes in Yemen.

International efforts to halt arms sales while also holding arms exporters and their governments accountable demonstrate how diasporic and home-state actors in Yemen have been successful, to an extent, in applying pressure on third states to end their support for the war in Yemen (LaForgia and Wong 2020). Often, the role of external actors in exacerbating conflicts in the region – including in Libya, Yemen, and Syria – is insufficiently addressed because the transitional justice focus is largely on domestic perpetrators. This creates an incomplete picture of historical injustices, which weakens prospects for a more effective transitional justice trajectory.

However, while criminal accountability is restrictive in the sense that it aims to establish a judicial truth about a particular incident or policy, it is also highly symbolic and can lead to the establishment of more contextual truths. The process of building evidence, especially for cases pursued through universal jurisdiction mechanisms, becomes both a truth-seeking and justice-seeking process that is not limited to prosecutorial accountability. Unlike those who remain in their home state where authoritarian rule or violent conflict persists, victims in the diaspora, especially where such universal jurisdiction cases are pursued, might feel more comfortable sharing their testimonies and stories because of the reduced risk to their safety.

Nevertheless, the trajectory of transitional justice for Yemen will require a stronger effort to garner attention and resources to allow diasporic transitional justice advocates to have a greater impact. Europe, where the universal jurisdiction cases targeting Syrians have taken place, saw a significant influx of Syrian refugees and asylum seekers following the outbreak of the war in 2011. As mentioned earlier, among them were victims who were also human rights lawyers and who saw an opportunity to pursue universal jurisdiction cases by partnering with networks of international legal advocacy organisations.

The new Yemeni diaspora that emerged after 2014 was, however, faced with obstacles that have mitigated opportunities to pursue universal jurisdiction cases similar to the Syrian ones. These challenges include general difficulties in being granted refugee or asylum seeker status in countries where universal jurisdiction mechanisms are strong. In addition, the 'Trump travel ban', whereby individuals from mostly Muslim-majority states were banned from entering the US, prevented a sizeable Yemeni population to resettle there. Moreover, apathy among the international community regarding the conflict in Yemen meant that the plight of Yemeni victims has often been overlooked or dismissed. This context, however, is not static. Yemeni civil society actors both within and outside Yemen are increasingly strengthening their advocacy networks and may be bolstered by the end of the Trump era and beginning of a Biden administration that, at the time of writing, has made statements in favour of ending the armed conflict in Yemen (Al Jazeera 2021).

In contexts where there is ongoing armed conflict or authoritarian rule, diasporic justice advocates play a crucial role in supporting their fellow citizens at home by documenting violations and advocating for accountability for ongoing atrocities. In doing so, they contribute to the evolving practice of employing the language and the tools of transitional justice before a transition to peace has taken place. Their relative security and access to international policymakers and CSOs position them in ways that generate greater momentum for transitional justice initiatives that, as explained earlier, are not confined to domestic perpetrators. Alliances and partnerships with host-state NGOs are increasingly focusing their criminal accountability gaze on the complicity of foreign governments and MNCs in crimes committed in the home state. Like Yemen and Syria, Libya presents a valuable contribution to this underexplored area of transitional justice praxis, where diasporic actors play an important role.

Libya

Similarly to Yemen, Libya's domestic turmoil has long been impacted by international actors' heavy involvement. Foreign diplomatic and military interventions, foreign mercenaries, and other actions driven by external actors, particularly in the Gulf and in Europe, have all resulted in heightened transitional justice consciousness and activity among Libyan diasporic figures. I first provide a brief explanation of the key developments of the conflict and accountability efforts.

The Libyan anti-government uprising of February 2011 was soon followed by a NATO military intervention that culminated in the death of Muammar Gaddafi, who had ruled Libya for over four decades. Prior to his death in October 2011, the ICC had issued arrest warrants targeting him, his son Saif Al-Islam Gaddafi, and the former intelligence chief Abdallah Al Senussi. The ICC has since issued additional arrest warrants for individuals suspected of committing war crimes in Libya; at the time of writing, none have been transferred to The Hague, while some have died.[7] Domestic prosecutions targeting more than 35 members of Gaddafi's regime were marred by an ineffective judiciary and security challenges (International Commission of Jurists 2019). In 2018, a consultative process that surveyed 7,000 Libyans across the country and garnered the attention of 1.8 million Libyans focused on their expectations for national reconciliation. The final report of this consultative process was meant to be a foundational document for Libya's National Conference Process planned for 2019. However, Libyan General Khalifa Haftar's offensive against Tripoli in April 2019 ground these plans to a halt (Aboueldahab 2019a).

The protracted violence in Libya has meant that transitional justice advocates have had to ramp up their efforts in the diaspora. The Libya Platform Coalition, formed in 2016, is one example of a cluster of 15 NGOs that coordinate efforts in Libya and abroad to advocate for the integration of justice and accountability policies into the country's tumultuous transition. The Libya Platform includes the Cairo Institute for Human Rights Studies, an NGO originally based in Egypt, but which had to move its headquarters to Tunisia due to repressive laws that stifled civil society activism. Such South–South mobilisation amplifies the visibility and access of these transitional justice actors in multiple geographical locations, although there is still room for improvement

7 In October 2013, the ICC decided that Senussi was no longer admissible following an appeal which argued that Senussi was already being tried in Libya (ICC 2014).

in how international policymakers engage with them (Aboueldahab 2020b; Aboueldahab 2021).

The Libya Platform serves several objectives, including '[b]reaking the isolation between civil society organisations working in the field of human rights and defenders inside and outside Libya with a better distribution of roles among them' (Cairo Institute for Human Rights Studies 2019). Another Libyan NGO, the Tunis-based Defender Center for Human Rights, provides a platform through which 'Libyan human rights defenders, activists and media workers inside and outside Libya' can document human rights violations. The Center also provides capacity-building initiatives that focus on digital security, networking and advocacy campaigns, and the documentation of human rights violations. A key feature of its advocacy strategy is its engagement with the UN Human Rights Council in Geneva, among several other major international human rights institutions. The role of the diaspora, then, is integral to the Libyan human rights and transitional justice movement.

Many of these CSOs consist of individuals who have been working in the areas of human rights, justice, and accountability for decades. As a result, they have amassed an institutional memory that enables them to trace continuities and discontinuities in the history of injustices in Libya. In light of the ongoing conflict and the multiple parties involved, the focus of accountability efforts in Libya has been on the documentation of ongoing crimes, while calling for criminal accountability for crimes perpetrated since 2011.[8]

Consequently, efforts to coordinate and form transnational coalitions aiming to mobilise and advocate for transitional justice lay the foundations for greater impact at the international, regional and domestic levels. Lawyers for Justice in Libya, a Libyan human rights NGO with headquarters in London and staff in Libya, uses its focus on criminal accountability as a pressure point to trigger a broader and deeper transitional justice process in Libya. Indeed, the organisation's accountability programme states that 'legal intervention [is] a starting point for change and not simply an end in itself. Using judicial mechanisms to ensure accountability leads to the establishment of useful precedent and jurisprudence' (Lawyers for Justice in Libya n.d.). Without a reliable or stable Libyan state to work with, this and other Libyan transitional justice advocates focus their efforts on transnational civil society partnerships as well as engagement with international institutions, including the ICC. Their disruptive potential, then, has emerged mainly on international planes.

8 For a discussion on the implications for this temporal focus in Libya and other states in the Middle East, see Aboueldahab (2019b).

Conclusion

This chapter has drawn on the volume's theorisation of transitional justice's disruptive potential as well as its objective of recognition by underscoring the opportunities for a reckoning with the past that emerge in the absence of state endorsement. It has argued that the disruptive potential of transitional justice in contexts where the perpetrator state is entrenched has been driven by domestic and diasporic transitional justice actors through legal advocacy. Recognition of victims has taken many forms, including through documentation of the past and through criminal investigations. This chapter has also outlined how the tactic of leveraging criminal accountability in the short term, especially through universal jurisdiction, does not diminish the value of, nor prevent the future pursuit of, reparative and other forms of justice. This is particularly important in aparadigmatic contexts of conflict and repression. Finally, using examples from Yemen, Libya, and Syria, the chapter argued that leveraging criminal accountability by domestic and diasporic transitional justice actors constitutes an effective strategy to target the more complex web of complicity that involves foreign governments and multinational corporations. These efforts, in turn, make transitional justice a potentially powerful framework for addressing a complex history of atrocities that are not confined to domestic spaces.

While ongoing conflict and authoritarian rule have shrunk the civic space in several countries in the Middle East and North Africa, there are powerful transnational transitional justice networks linking domestic and diasporic actors. Resistance to the oppressive post-colonial state, as well as to its international allies, is becoming increasingly central to transitional justice practices in the Middle East. The diaspora plays an important role in shaping this resistance by leveraging short-term criminal accountability for long-term objectives aiming for political change. The parameters for the timing and purpose of transitional justice have expanded. It has been pursued in contexts involving ongoing violent conflict and renewed authoritarian rule. It provides a framework to address multiple legacies of oppression and to address the role of international actors in that history of injustices. Without such a reckoning, transitional justice practices would risk drawing up a severely limited picture of historical injustices that focused on domestic perpetrators while overlooking the complicit role that their external allies played.

Competing visions of transitional justice in the Middle East involve a political and legal playing field in which the state, civil society, and other non-state actors battle to maintain control of justice processes and historical justice narratives. Those who manage to take charge of these processes will determine which part of the past is addressed. Leveraging criminal accountability by both diasporic and domestic actors presents unexpected opportunities to embark on a broader, deeper social justice process in states plagued by authoritarian rule and conflict. The role of the diaspora in implementing this strategy is an important innovation in transitional justice, one that is particularly useful when the state functions as a perpetual antagonist.

References

Aboueldahab, N. (2018) 'Writing Atrocities: Syrian Civil Society and Transitional Justice'. *Brookings Doha Center Analysis* Paper 21, May. Available at: https://www.brookings.edu/research/writing-atrocities-syrian-civil-society-and-transitional-justice/

—— (2019a) 'Views: Peace and Justice in Libya's Transition'. *ROWAQ Arabi*, 24(1), 39–49.

—— (2019b) 'Time, Transition, and Justice in Arab States'. In: Z. Azzam and I.K. Harb (eds), *The Arab World Beyond Conflict* (pp. 77–86). Washington, DC: Arab Center Washington DC.

—— (2020a) 'The United States Needs a Truth Commission. It Should be Televised," Foreign Policy, 24 July. Available at: https://foreignpolicy.com/2020/07/24/united-states-racism-truth-commission-televise-south-africa-tunisia/

—— (2020b) 'Views: A Renewed Call for Indigenous-Led Conflict Resolution in the Arab States'. *ROWAQ Arabi* 25(1), 85–92.

—— (2021) 'How Western Policymakers Can Engage the New Arab Diasporas'. Brookings Institution, 16 July. Available at: https://www.brookings.edu/blog/order-from-chaos/2021/07/16/how-western-policymakers-can-engage-the-new-arab-diasporas/

Accatino, D. and C. Collins (2016) 'Truth, Evidence, Truth: The Deployment of Testimony, Archives and Technical Data in Domestic Human Rights Trials'. *Journal of Human Rights Practice* 8(1), 81–100.

Adamson, F.B. (2016) 'The Growing Importance of Diaspora Politics'. *Current History* 115(784), 291–297.

Al Jazeera (2021) 'Biden Ends Support for Saudi's Yemen War in Foreign Policy Shift'. *Al Jazeera*, 5 February.

Baser, B. and A. Swain (2010) 'Stateless Diaspora Groups and their Repertoires of Nationalist Activism in Host Countries'. *Journal of International Relations* 8(1), 37–60.

Beaugrand, C. and V. Geisser (2016) 'Social Mobilization and Political Participation in the Diaspora During the 'Arab Spring''. *Journal of Immigrant & Refugee Studies* 14(3), 239–243.

Berthelsen, C. (2021) 'BNP Paribas to Face Human Rights Claims Over Sudan Work'. Bloomberg, 16 February.

Cairo Institute for Human Rights Studies (2019) 'Libya Platform: The Situation of Human Rights in Libya: Extrajudicial Killing and Enforced Disappearance'. 21 August. Available at: https://cihrs.org/the-situation-of-human-rights-in-libya/?lang=en

Cohen, L. and K. Freifeld (2022) 'Lafarge Pleads Guilty to U.S. Charge of Supporting Islamic State, to Pay $778 million', *Reuters*, 20 October. Available at: https://www.reuters.com/legal/french-cement-maker-lafarge-plead-guilty-us-charges-supporting-islamic-state-2022-10-18/.

ECCHR (2020) 'Italian Arms Exports to Yemen: State and Corporate Responsibility'. 27 October. Available at: https://www.ecchr.eu/en/event/italian-arms-exports-to-yemen-state-and-corporate-responsibility/

Gall, C. (2017) 'Tunisia's Truth-Telling Renews a Revolution's Promise, Painfully'. New York Times, 22 April.

Gready, P. and S. Robins (2017) 'Rethinking Civil Society and Transitional Justice: Lessons from Social Movements and "New" Civil Society'. *The International Journal of Human Rights* 21(7), 956–975.

Group of Eminent Experts (2020) 'Yemen: A Pandemic of Impunity in a Tortured Land'. 28 September. Available at: https://www.ohchr.org/Documents/HRBodies/HRCouncil/GEE-Yemen/2020-09-09-report.pdf

Hinkson, K. (2019) 'SNC-Lavalin Pleads Guilty to Fraud for Past Work in Libya, Will Pay $280M Fine'. *CBC News*, 18 December.

International Commission of Jurists (2019) 'Accountability for Serious Crimes under International Law in Libya: An Assessment of the Criminal Justice System'. March. Available at: https://www.icj.org/wp-content/uploads/2019/07/Libya-Accountability-serious-crimes-Publications-Reports-Thematic-reports-2019-ENG.pdf

International Criminal Court (2014) 'Al-Senussi Case: Appeals Chamber Confirms Case is Inadmissible before ICC'. Press release, 24 July. Available at: www.icccpi.int/en_menus/icc/press%20and%20media/press%20releases/Pages/pr1034.aspx

International Crisis Group (2020) 'Rethinking Peace in Yemen'. 2 July. Available at: https://www.crisisgroup.org/middle-east-north-africa/gulf-and-arabian-peninsula/yemen/216-rethinking-peace-yemen

International Federation for Human Rights (2020) 'Judicial Investigation Opened into BNP Paribas' Role in Atrocities in Sudan'. 11 October. Available at: https://www.fidh.org/en/issues/international-justice/judicial-investigation-opened-into-bnp-paribas-role-in-atrocities-in#:~:text=In%20the%20criminal%20complaint%20against,laundering%20and%20handling%20the%20proceeds

Koinova, M. (2018) 'Diaspora Mobilisation for Conflict and Post-conflict Reconstruction: Contextual and Comparative Dimensions'. *Journal of Ethnic and Migration Studies* 44(8), 1251–1269.

LaForgia, M. and E. Wong (2020) 'War Crime Risk Grows for U.S. Over Saudi Strikes in Yemen'. New York Times, 14 September.

Lawyers for Justice in Libya (n.d.) 'Accountability and Transitional Justice'. Available at: https://www.libyanjustice.org/en/programmes/accountability

Mendes, M.A. (2021) 'A Passage to Justice. Selected Yemeni Civil Society Views for Transitional Justice and Long-Term Accountability in Yemen'. Open Society Foundation, February. Available at: https://www.opensocietyfoundations.org/publications/a-passage-to-justice

Mwatana for Human Rights (2021) 'UN Human Rights Council: Prioritize Yemen Accountability and Redress'. 29 September. Accessible at: https://mwatana.org/en/prioritize-yemen-accountability-and-redress/

RULAC (n.d.) 'Non-international Armed Conflicts in Yemen'. Available at: https://www.rulac.org/browse/conflicts/non-international-armed-conflicts-in-yemen#collapse2accord

UN Office of the High Commissioner for Human Rights (2019) *Yemen: Collective Failure, Collective Responsibility – UN Expert Report*. 3 September. Geneva: United Nations.

Van Hear, N. and R. Cohen (2017) 'Diasporas and Conflict: Distance, Contiguity and Spheres of Engagement'. *Oxford Development Studies* 45(2), 171–184.

Wong, E. and D.E. Sanger (2020) 'State Department Investigator Fired by Trump Had Examined Weapons Sales to Saudis and Emiratis'. The New York Times, 18 May.

Chapter 2

Overcoming the Justice Impasse in Syria[1]

Brigitte Herremans and Veronica Bellintani

Introduction

After the start of the 2011 Syrian uprising, Syrian and international stakeholders advanced the transitional justice paradigm to support the hoped-for transition. The regime's obliteration of the protest movement and the transformation of the uprising into a civil war, along with the international disagreement over the conflict's resolution, have undermined efforts to pursue accountability and justice. Despite the fading transitional moment, Syrian and international stakeholders, whom we refer to as justice actors, continue to use transitional justice concepts and mechanisms to mobilise for justice, including but not limited to court cases. In so doing, Syrian justice actors are seeking both to address the accountability gap and to further resistance by foregrounding their demands for freedom and justice that unleashed the uprising. We argue that the transitional justice paradigm has allowed Syrian and international justice actors to counter the pervasive defeatism about the pursuit of justice for Syrians. This has taken place through justice actors' blending of standardised and non-standardised approaches to transitional justice. Moreover, the ingenious use of the transitional justice toolkit in this aparadigmatic context has important implications for other justice efforts in situations of ongoing conflict. It demonstrates that even when the international justice architecture is impaired, justice actors can still develop concrete initiatives to overcome the accountability gap and make a tangible difference for victims. In this chapter, we demonstrate how transitional justice's potential for accountability, recognition, and disruption has inspired a broad group of justice actors to overcome the justice impasse in Syria.

The crystallisation of the no-transition scenario has forced both Syrian and international justice actors to reconsider the initial transitional justice programme. Consequently, they have moved away from a comprehensive approach to a more limited practice, focusing strongly on criminal accountability with the prioritisation of documentation efforts and court cases under the principle of universal jurisdiction. However, the zeal for criminal

1 This research was partly funded through ERC-StG-804154 VictPart.

DOI: 10.4324/9781003289104-3

accountability initiatives does not reflect a conviction by Syrian and international justice actors that trials ensure the strongest form of justice. By and large, they acknowledge that criminal accountability can only provide a modicum of justice. Importantly, however, it can open a crack in the wall of impunity. In order to address pressing justice needs, such as clarity about the fate of the forcibly disappeared and the missing, NGOs and victim groups are increasingly turning to other transitional justice initiatives, such as truth-seeking.

In the first section, we describe the evolution of the initial transitional justice programme, looking into the intentions of justice actors who embraced transitional justice mechanisms as a way to defy the accountability gap. In the following section, we analyse how the materialisation of a non-transitioning scenario has forced Syrian and international actors to change strategies, bringing to life a transnational justice network. Finally, we examine how, despite the evolution towards a non-transition and growing apprehensions about the feasibility of the transitional justice paradigm, innovative justice efforts saw the light in the field of criminal accountability, documentation, and victims' activism. For this chapter, we draw on secondary sources and empirical material, collected throughout professional activities with CSOs and victim groups and semi-structured interviews with 14 representatives of Syrian and international NGOs and CSOs. The topic list for these interviews was centred around the introduction and the relevance of the transitional justice paradigm in the Syrian context, the role of international and local justice actors, and developments with regard to the application of the transitional justice toolkit, formal justice avenues and victim groups' initiatives.

Transitional Justice: From a Way out of The Deadlock to a Metaphor for Comprehensive Justice

In this section, we examine how, early on in the uprising, Syrian civil society embraced the concepts and mechanisms of the transitional justice paradigm as a way to uphold the revolutionary demands for freedom and justice, and to initiate the quest for accountability, for past human rights violations perpetrated by the Assad regime as well. Syrian justice actors proactively developed ways to pursue some form of justice in this fluid context, focusing strongly on documentation (Aboueldahab 2018). The introduction of transitional justice concepts and tools, along with best practices implemented in other countries, allowed Syrian justice actors to probe avenues that have been unexplored in the Syrian context, such as criminal accountability and truth-seeking, to defy the justice impasse at the international level, and to pursue a victim-centred, locally relevant approach.

The protests that erupted in 2011 initiated the hope for a transition away from a long history of regime-sponsored human rights violations (Ziadeh 2020). Despite the hostile climate for civil society activism and restricted space for self-expression in the public realm, dissent and resistance are by no means new phenomena in Syria. Throughout the 2000s, human rights activists, artists, and dissidents increasingly chipped at the wall of fear, thus laying the basis for civil society mobilisation and the creation of dozens of CSOs after 2011 (Salamandra and Stenberg 2015, 3). Some individuals even precociously played with the concept of truth-seeking to determine the fate of those disappeared during the 1982 atrocities, when the regime killed thousands of people during a military assault in Hama (Darwish 2020). This experiment in truth-seeking was by no means imagined as a prelude to a broader transitional justice programme as it was inconceivable to lead to any kind of recognition or accountability at that time. It was seen as a way to prevent the erasure of victims' experiences and to enable memorialisation and potentially even some form of disruption (Darwish 2020; Sawah 2020). The 1982 atrocities and the regime's efforts to erase these crimes provided a strong motivation to document crimes after the 2011 uprising (Nassar 2021).

At that time, Syrian human rights activists and CSOs initially adopted a holistic approach to transitional justice, premised on the aspiration of a transition, despite the regime's prompt escalation of violence. International actors were paramount in this early justice mobilisation. Notably, Western states and institutions sought to play a role in the transition and attempted to lay the groundwork of an – overtly – ambitious transitional justice programme. In this context, Syrian justice actors translated transitional justice concepts and mechanisms to the local context, despite their general lack of experience with the paradigm and despite the regime's persecution of justice actors, forcing them into exile. A milestone in this early mobilisation was the report 'Supporting a Democratic Transition in Syria' by a diverse group of Syrian justice actors aiming to design a strategy for a transition away from dictatorship (The Day After Project 2012). The international passivity after the regime's first use of chemical weapons in 2013 entrenched the non-transitioning scenario and gradually demoted the transitional justice programme in the Syrian context (Sawah 2020). While most Syrian justice actors continued to explore the potential of transitional justice for accountability, recognition, and disruption, a more classic understanding of transitional justice moored to state-sanctioned mechanisms gained ground.

In this early justice mobilisation, justice actors insufficiently acknowledged the consequences of the military escalation and the difficulty of establishing a fully-fledged transitional justice programme in the absence of a transition. As we discuss in the next section, international institutions and states contributed to this as they promoted plans that often proved disconnected from the local reality (Nassar 2020). The transformation of the uprising to a civil war and the dissolution of the hope for change, prompted Syrian civil society to explore avenues to advance justice while violations were ongoing. This resulted in a second early mobilisation milestone: the establishment of a transitional justice coordination group uniting 15 to 17 NGOs. This coordination group served as a laboratory to develop relevant transitional justice initiatives in an increasingly messy situation (Sawah 2020). While the evaporation of the transition led to this group's gradual demise, Syrian justice actors remained determined to tailor initiatives to the Syrian context in order to assert control over justice efforts (Nassar 2020).

Despite the unavoidable elimination of initial transitional justice plans, justice actors have not formally renounced the application of the paradigm in the Syrian context. This has led to an interesting situation in which theorisation about the desired, standardised model was not abandoned while in practice justice actors increasingly experimented with transitional justice in a non-standardised way. The absence of effective multilateral initiatives to prevent atrocity crimes and overcome the accountability gap has emboldened Syrian CSOs to experiment with transitional justice initiatives (Al Abdallah 2020; al-Bunni 2021). Their implementation in this no-transition scenario is also marred by the multiplication of perpetrators, and the absence of a unified vision within the Syrian justice community (Kawabat and Travesi 2018).

As we discuss in the next section, many early believers became disillusioned with the utility of transitional justice claims in the short term, eliciting lively debates about the effectiveness of the paradigm in the current context. Several respondents indicated that they do not consider justice efforts focusing predominantly on criminal accountability as transitional justice. In the long run, they estimate that a transition is required to provide a comprehensive framework to address justice and accountability (Alhaj Saleh 2021; al-Hallaq 2021; Darwish 2020; Ghazi 2021; Nassar 2021). A classical transitional justice programme would allow for the prosecution of the main perpetrators to provide redress for victims and mitigate the risks of revenge or amnesty (al-Bunni 2021; Sawah 2020). We contend that given the obstacles to the application of this model version of transitional justice, the paradigm turned into a metaphor for a comprehensive justice programme within Syria.

A Moving Justice Landscape

In this section, we critically reflect on how international, multilateral, and Syrian stakeholders adopted, modified, or contested transitional justice claims and initiatives. We argue that a diverse collection of Syrian justice actors, including lawyers, NGOs, and victim groups, was the driving force for a move away from justice efforts solely related to existing judicial mechanisms, testing more grounded ways to centralise victims' experiences and justice needs. The implosion of the early mobilisation forced Syrian and international actors to relinquish the holistic approach to overcome the accountability gap. As a result, different forms of cross-sectional cooperation arose between international institutions, governments, and civil society actors that either joined efforts in a variety of spaces or developed their own, distinct justice initiatives.

The transformation of the conflict into a civil war involving multiple perpetrators was a critical game-changer for international justice mobilisation. When the Assad regime perpetrated its first large chemical weapons attack in 2013, an international agreement mediated by Russia initiated a shift away from conflict resolution and accountability for mass atrocities to feasibility politics.[2] The situation on the ground became increasingly complicated: Russia and Iran enabled the regime through their military interventions to reacquire control over the majority of the areas held by the opposition, while the Gulf States and Turkey supported armed opposition groups that gradually became radicalised. Furthermore, the emergence of Islamic State (IS) in 2014 decreased attention in the Global North for the government's crimes as the narrative in many policy and media circles evolved from a regime having lost legitimacy to a government fighting violent jihadist groups (Stokke and Wiebelhaus-Brahm 2019; Üngör 2019). On the multilateral level, the UN Security Council reserved its strongest accountability language for IS and violent jihadist groups (Van Schaack 2020a, 60). The predominant focus on jihadi violence has paralysed the 'justice imagination', i.e. the faculty to generate new ideas about how to curb injustices and to stretch the boundaries of what is conceivable in terms of justice and accountability beyond present mechanisms and potentially beyond the judicial realm (Herremans and Destrooper 2021). The regime's strategy of narrative warfare, discrediting oppositional narratives, augmented the climate of uncertainty about the evidence of atrocity crimes.

Therefore, international support was key in laying the groundwork for the mobilisation of transitional justice, as governments in the Global North hoped to play a role in this transition. In an era when the regime appeared to falter, several states implemented projects on the ground (Van Schaack 2020b, 249). As in other countries in the Middle East and North Africa, the transitional justice industry often presented concepts and templates that could not be easily adapted to the local context (Nassar 2020). The United States were, for instance, intent on developing a full transitional justice programme, with the State Department establishing projects on the rule of law and draft laws before there was any clarity about the outcome of the uprising (Nassar 2014, 70).

The unravelling of the initial transitional justice programme obliged Western governments, which had not sufficiently anticipated a scenario in which the Syrian government and Russia would initiate an annihilation campaign, to abandon their holistic perspective (Haugbølle 2019; Ismail 2018, 55). The United States, for example, halted its transitional justice programme on the

2 On 21 August 2013, the Assad regime fired rockets containing sarin on the Damascus suburb al-Ghouta. Although the use of chemical weapons crossed President Obama's 'red line', following negotiations with Russia the United States agreed to suspend its attack on the condition that the Syrian government destroyed its arsenal of chemical agents under the supervision of the Organization for the Prohibition of Chemical Weapons. However, the Assad regime has continued its use of chemical weapons. Since the start of the conflict, there has been at least 336 chemical weapons attacks, of which 98% can be attributed to the regime while IS is responsible for the rest (Schneider and Lütkefend 2019).

ground and developed a preference for prosecution (Sawah 2020). To that end, it supported the establishment of organisations such as the Commission for International Justice and Accountability to bolster documentation efforts in the framework of (future) accountability processes. Yet, as we discuss in the next section, Syrian justice actors refuse a narrow criminal accountability focus, insisting that criminal prosecutions cannot be equated with justice. In light of the justice impasse, they recognised the feasibility of a justice-centred approach to documentation. However, there is a risk that the prioritisation of documentation creates unrealistic expectations among victim communities, raising false hopes with regard to the potential impact of documentation on criminal prosecutions.

While the UN Security Council has constituted a major source of frustration and an obstacle to further accountability, documentation was prioritised at the multilateral level with the establishment of important judicial and truth-finding UN entities. In August 2011, the Human Rights Council established the Independent International Commission of Inquiry on Syria. Since the beginning of its work, it has produced over 20 mandated reports as well as papers on specific issues such as sexual and gender-based violence and detention in Syria. To circumvent the Russian and Chinese veto in the Security Council, the General Assembly established a new justice mechanism for Syria in 2016, the International Impartial and Independent Mechanism to Assist in the Investigation and Prosecution of Those Responsible for the Most Serious Crimes under International Law Committed in Syria since March 2011 (the so-called 'IIIM'). While the UN Security Council's role became increasingly marginal, it managed to set up a Fact-Finding Mission in 2014 to investigate allegations of the use of chemical weapons. The Mission's findings provided the basis of a Joint Investigative Mechanism by the Organisation for the Prohibition of Chemical Weapons and the United Nations to identify the perpetrators of the chemical weapons attacks.

The justice-centred approach to documentation generated responses among UN bodies, states, and non-governmental sectors and gave rise to a new justice architecture (Nassar and Rangelov 2020;Van Schaack 2020b, 7). New international entrepreneurial mechanisms emerged, with private justice entrepreneurs collecting evidence and cooperating with states to launch criminal prosecutions. One of the most influential actors is the Commission for International Justice and Accountability, which gathers and preserves evidence from Syria and supports domestic and international justice institutions, such as national prosecutors and the IIIM (Burgis-Kasthala 2019). In collaboration with Syrian justice actors, NGOs, such as the European Centre for Constitutional and Human Rights (ECCHR) and the Open Society Justice Initiative, are leading the strategic litigation efforts before European courts focusing on forcible disappearance, torture, sexual and gender-based violence, and chemical weapons use.

The international justice impasse has led individual states to seek remedies outside the multilateral framework, with some states also pursuing new justice avenues. In September 2020, the Netherlands announced its decision to 'hold Syria responsible under international law for gross human rights violations and torture in particular', indicating that it is prepared to formally submit a case before the International Court of Justice for Syria's violation of the UN Convention Against Torture if diplomatic routes fail and arbitration attempts are unsuccessful (Guernica 37 2020; Nahlavi and Sekkarie 2020). Canada followed suit in March 2021, announcing that it also requested formal negotiations under the Convention Against Torture. As we describe below, another important development is the strategic use of universal jurisdiction in European countries to prosecute international crimes.

Beyond any doubt, the main driver behind the pursuit of new justice avenues is the Syrian justice community. Its determination to identify new opportunities has entailed a diversification of Syrian civil society with NGOs and CSOs that continue to work in Syria, and NGOs and victim-led initiatives that mostly operate in the diaspora. Several Syrian NGOs continue to work inside Syria, both in opposition-controlled areas and in regime-controlled areas, despite the security conditions that prevent a broader involvement at the domestic level. These initiatives strongly focus on women, youth, and community empowerment to continue documentation efforts to pursue awareness raising about criminal accountability and other ways to address victims' needs, such as truth-seeking (Nassar 2021). Other specific initiatives have involved lawyers living in Syria in training on justice-related issues. These projects also aim at tackling the growing distance between the diaspora and the lived reality of Syrians within the country. Even if a lot of these efforts are focused on the future, enabling domestic mobilisation remains a key aspiration as many Syrian civil society actors esteem that change will have to come from inside the country (Al Abdeh 2020).

However, the majority of Syrian civil society activists were forced into exile, from where they continue to promote concrete justice efforts. This diasporic activism created new opportunity structures in the field of documentation and truth-seeking as a wide variety of actors mobilised in different global locations (Orjuela 2018; Tenove 2019). Civil society groups that also remained active in Syria, such as The Day After Project, the Syrian Justice and Accountability Centre, Women Now For Development, Dawlaty, and Release Me, became major laboratories for experimenting with practitioner-driven transitional justice initiatives. By 2016, these practices had concretely resulted in a focus on strategic litigation and the conception of victim groups initiatives (Nassar 2020). As we discuss in the next section, this innovation was also rendered possible through transnational cooperation between international and Syrian NGOs.

While the scholarship and broader analysis of transitional justice efforts in Syria have focused largely on the work of institutionalised NGOs, victim/survivor-led groups have opened new spaces and approaches rooted in victims' perspectives, allowing them to occupy a central position in justice efforts. This activism thrived mainly as a result of partnerships with Syrian NGOs, which either provided support to groups during or after their founding process, or as groups that had been conceived as NGO programmes became independent. Overall, these victim groups refuse the passive notion of 'victims', highlighting that their pivotal role in justice efforts derives from their ownership of experiences of victimhood (Alhaj Saleh 2021; al-Hallaq 2021; Mahmoud 2021; Serriya 2021). Their creation was rooted in the conviction that the role of survivors and their families cannot be reduced to directly supporting survivors or being witnesses, depriving them of agency and decision-making (Helmi 2021). Participation in victim groups has enabled survivors and families to mobilise for their needs and demands before UN bodies and other international avenues. Moreover, several groups started working independently on justice initiatives which we discuss below, thus effectively adopting the transitional justice toolkit to prioritise their most urgent justice needs, such as knowing the fate of the missing and the disappeared.

Transitional Justice Contested: Between Resistance and Innovation

Despite transitional justice being the sole paradigm to advance justice, it provokes resistance, not only among the regime and the warring parties, but also among justice actors such as Syrian NGOs and victim groups. As we discussed earlier, the entrenchment of a non-transition and the multiplication of perpetrators, entailed doubts about the aptness of transitional justice, especially among victim groups who increasingly challenge the relevance of ongoing—criminal—justice efforts for victims and question the power dynamics within the Syrian and international justice community. Transitional justice interventions in the Syrian context have created a Syrian civil society elite that has advanced an understanding of what justice efforts should look like, also inspired by the prioritisation of retributive justice initiatives by the international transitional justice industry that have initially dominated the justice efforts. Moreover, donor patronage relations and the disavowal of the capacities of nascent victim groups entailed power inequalities within the burgeoning civil society scene, resulting in rivalries between NGOs and victim groups (Stokke and Wiebelhaus-Brahm 2019). The changing local and international context confronted Syrian and international justice actors with the need to review the suitability of the transitional justice toolkit (Al Abdallah 2020; Darwish 2020; Ghazi 2021).

The transformation of the conflict also entailed questions about the possible success of transitional justice initiatives among citizens as the assumptions on what they could and should achieve became more removed from their experiences, especially in the growing refugee community (Ghazi 2021; Macdonald 2013; Nassar 2021). Whereas the human rights movement embraced transitional justice at the start of the uprising, for most Syrians it was a new concept that needed to prove its merits. This originally prompted civil society to focus on awareness raising, as many citizens associated transitional justice with forgiveness and reconciliation and feared it might increase impunity (Sawah 2020). Furthermore, generous donor funding and the development of an NGO elite strengthened apprehensions among many citizens that transitional justice initiatives are a fantasy, even evoking disdain (Darwish 2020; Nassar 2021). Moreover, the transformation of the conflict has created different justice needs among diaspora communities. Over 12 million Syrians have been displaced, among whom 6 million are internally displaced and 6 million are refugees, creating distinct justice needs that are mostly linked to immediate and concrete forms of justice, such as addressing and remedying violations of housing, land, and property rights (Al Abdallah 2020). While some victims, notably within communities present in Europe, advocate for criminal accountability, this endeavour has only symbolic or even no meaning for other victims who are primarily concerned with socio-economic needs (Ghazi 2021). Moreover, victims' conceptualisations of justice can be very different from what transitional justice practice promotes (Al Abdeh 2020). As surveys conducted by Syrian NGOs indicate, a lot of Syrian citizens adhere to the notion of divine justice and have very different perspectives on punishment (Charney and Quirk 2014; The Day After Project 2020).

It might seem that the transformation of the conflict, the evolving justice needs and the growing grassroots resistance abolished the momentum for transitional justice in the Syrian context. Nonetheless, we argue that the paradigm has enabled Syrian – and international- justice actors – to develop concrete and creative initiatives in the domain of criminal accountability, documentation, and victims' activism. Even if these initiatives do not offer innovations to the transitional justice framework as such, they are innovative as they open the justice imagination, advancing possibilities beyond existing mechanisms and even beyond the judicial realm. First, criminal prosecutions in foreign national courts under the principle of universal jurisdiction became the main justice avenue in the absence of an effective adjudicative multilateral mechanism. While the focus on criminal accountability is not innovative in itself, strategic litigation in the Syrian context is breaking new ground as it illustrates the ongoing resistance of Syrian victims/survivors and justice actors against both the injustices and the reigning international defeatism. Second, Syrian justice actors have advanced innovative and forward-looking documentation initiatives for purposes beyond criminal prosecutions. Third, a coalition of victim groups managed to present a unified vision to reconnect justice efforts increasingly to the grassroots level by proposing concrete initiatives, moreover with regard to the fate of forcibly disappeared and missing people.

Syrian civil society actors, mostly located in the diaspora, acted on the need to reassess the potential of the transitional justice framework. With the aim of opening an initial formal justice avenue, several Syrian justice actors promoted the application of universal jurisdiction by European domestic courts to prosecute internationally recognised crimes committed in Syria (Kaleck and Kroker

2018). In several European national jurisdictions, judicial authorities initiated or concluded court cases on war crimes or crimes against humanity committed in Syria, mostly the result of Syrian justice actors' investment in strategic litigation in cooperation with lawyers, victims, and their families, teaming up with European NGOs (Elliot 2017; Kroker 2021).[3] The first trial against Syrian torture worldwide that started in the Higher Regional Court in Koblenz, in which two former officials of President Bashar al-Assad's security apparatus were charged with crimes against humanity, is the result of such intense cooperation between the ECCHR, the Syrian Centre for Media and Freedom of Expression, the Syrian Centre for Legal Studies and Research, and the Caesar Files Group (ECCHR 2020). The al-Khatib trial, named after the Damascus detention centre where the accused worked, became the first judicial avenue in which victims of the regime could testify in court. Alongside, civil society managed to draw attention to the widespread practice of torture by government officials. The central place of witness testimony in the proceedings has given victims and survivors a forum in which to raise hitherto underexplored issues, such as sexual and gender-based violence.

The cases under universal jurisdiction illustrate the importance of diaspora-initiated justice activism for awareness raising about the erasure and invisibilisation of crimes. The al-Khatib trial has outcomes that reach far beyond the logic of criminal proceedings. It has stimulated debate within diverse Syrian communities on the potential and limitations of concrete justice initiatives and on difficult questions of justice, such as about who is considered a perpetrator and who is not. The trial has also served as a catalyst to foreground sexual and gender-based violence and the need to prosecute it as a crime against humanity. Moreover, it sparked a debate on transformative justice-related perspectives on gender-based violence, for example, on the predominant focus on violence that women endure, while Syrian men and children have also been subjected widely to sexual violence (Al Abdeh 2020; Kroker 2021). However, the al-Khatib trial also provoked dismay, mainly among victim groups that argue that victims benefit little from this type of criminal accountability given the lack of genuine participation of victims. They deem that it is largely symbolic and cannot replace a future tribunal in Syria (Alhaj Saleh 2021). Additionally, the inability of European courts to fully address the experiences of victims in Syria, highlighted by the refusal to include enforced disappearance in the charges against defendants in the al-Khatib trial, also triggered criticism (Schmitz-Buhl 2021).

3 Since 2016, the ECCHR, for example, has been filing torture cases together with more than 50 Syrians (torture survivors, relatives, activists, and lawyers) in Austria, Germany, Norway, and Sweden. The two countries that have initiated the largest number of investigations under universal jurisdiction are Germany and Sweden.

A second important innovation is the multiple uses of documentation by Syrian civil society (Tenove 2019). While documentation in the transitional justice paradigm is conceived as a precursor to other mechanisms, documentation efforts in the Syrian context also open possibilities for truth-seeking, reparations, and memorialisation and could almost be seen as a stand-alone mechanism because of its centrality and its transformative potential (Aboueldahab 2018; Kabawat and Travesi 2018; Nassar 2021). Therefore, Syrian justice actors criticise the disposition within institutional circles to view documentation predominantly from a criminal justice perspective. Victim groups, for example, document their experiences as former detainees and victims to resist the erasure and invisibilisation of their experiences of harm, as they understand the dramatic effects of the regime's and Russia's narrative warfare, the discrediting of evidence of atrocity crimes and of oppositional narratives (Üngör 2019). Through documentation, they forbid forgetting and also preserve and highlight their agency (Alhaj Saleh 2021; Serriya 2021).

In this respect, documentation is part and parcel of Syrian justice actors' non-violent resistance. This way of looking at documentation is a rebuttal of the adage that 'history repeats itself', as justice actors are determined not to let the regime suppress the memory of atrocity crimes as happened in 1982. Syrian justice actors increasingly address legacies of rights violations and multiple victimisations through truth-seeking and memorialisation initiatives, notwithstanding the limitations such as the impossibility of establishing an official truth commission and the complexity of truth-seeking in an ongoing conflict (al-Bunni 2021; Darwish 2020; Nassar 2021). Artistic practices play an important role in these efforts to offer more complex understandings of truth.[4] This is not a new phenomenon, as socially-engaged artists have traditionally challenged and stretched the boundaries of permissible public discourse (Bank 2020, 101; cooke 2016, 31). The artistic response to the current conflict has focused strongly on experiences of harm, with many artists bearing witness and 'presencing' the plight of victims, resisting the erasure of their stories and offering counternarratives to hegemonic discourses about the Syrian conflict.

Many justice actors sense that the merit of documentation also lies in its future possibilities. To date, the entire spectrum related to reparations, compensation, restitution, rehabilitation, and guarantees of non-recurrence has largely been left out of transitional justice claims in Syria. However, some Syrian CSOs started documentation work to collect property documents to record and challenge housing, land, and property rights violations, with a view

4 Families for Freedom and The Syria Campaign, a human rights advocacy group, initiated activities such as a European tour with the *Freedom Bus* to ask for freedom for the detained and forcibly disappeared in Syria. Together with the Caesar Families Association, these groups organised sit-ins outside the Koblenz court with pictures of their beloved ones. Visual artist Khaled Barakeh set up the installation *Mute*, involving Families for Freedom and The Syria Campaign, to remember those who asked for freedom and dignity in 2011.

to laying the foundation for a future restitution and compensation mechanisms (Enab Baladi 2020).[5] Despite the impossibility of establishing an official reparations programme, the question of how reparations may address victims' needs and overall Syrian society, is not left unaddressed. Yet, invoking the restorative justice paradigm in the Syrian context is a sensitive undertaking as many Syrian justice actors and victims deem it incompatible with criminal accountability (al-Omari 2020).[6] Furthermore, there is a fear that invoking restorative justice claims could be interpreted as an openness towards reconciliation or a sign of victims' willingness to waive rights in return for material compensation. We believe that this fear stems from a lack of acquaintance with the restorative justice paradigm, fuelling an inadequate understanding of what remedy and reparations could entail in practice.

The third, and possibly most surprising innovation in ongoing justice efforts is led by victim groups that initiated ingenious efforts to address the priorities of the primary beneficiaries of justice, such as survivors of torture, families of the disappeared, and the detained. Activities taking mostly place in informal spaces, such as workshops, protests, or sit-ins, foreground issues and voices that risk being erased or invisibilised in formal spaces. In the absence of judicial avenues other than universal jurisdiction cases, only a fraction of the international crimes, such as torture and arbitrary detention, are raised in formal processes, which had as an unintended consequence the erasure of other issues (Herremans and Destrooper 2021). This has prompted victim groups to claim a larger space in justice efforts to highlight crimes that have hitherto not received sufficient exposure, such as sexual and gender-based violence. Furthermore, this activism has reinvigorated the justice landscape at a moment when justice efforts were largely equated with criminal accountability.

In this respect, the Truth and Justice Charter of the Association of Detainees and Missing of Sednaya Prison, Caesar Families Association, the Coalition of Families of Persons Kidnapped by IS-Massar, Families for Freedom, and the Ta'afi Initiative (2021) presents a milestone. This joint Charter is primarily promoting collective mobilisation and cooperation among victims and their families, besides appealing to NGOs, states, and international institutions to strengthen their commitment to victim participation. The Charter is built upon the idea of providing small, cumulative steps in the short, medium, and long term to eventually achieve truth and justice for victims and their families. It provides a victim-centred reading of what transitional justice efforts should look like in the Syrian context, pursuing a timeline based on the urgency of

5 The Day After Project and Free Syrian Lawyers have been leading the work in collecting and safeguarding property-related documents.

6 A reference to the concept of restorative/reparative justice in a UN Security Council briefing by the Special Envoy for Syria, Geir Pedersen, on 16 December 2020 was met with criticism by some Syrian civil society representatives. While it related to a translation error, their outrage reveals a malaise about restorative justice.

certain measures for victims and their families. Key short-term justice demands are the release of the detainees, information about the fate of the disappeared, an immediate halt to torture, inhuman treatment and sexual crimes, and the return of the remains of those killed under conditions of enforced disappearance and detention.

As more than 100,000 persons have been forcibly disappeared or kidnapped by several parties to the conflict (Syrian Network for Human Rights 2020), clarity about their fate is a central justice priority. Hence, the Charter's associations initiated a campaign for a mechanism to find Syria's disappeared and detained in order to fulfil Syrian families' right to the truth (Sarkin 2021). Even though victim groups have continuously called for attention to the fate of the disappeared and the missing, the issue did not figure strongly on the international agenda until March 2021, when both the UN Commission of Inquiry and the High Commissioner for Human Rights supported their call for the establishment of a mechanism. The victim groups' action for change has highlighted the importance of justice initiatives centred upon the lived reality of victims and their families. Moreover, it reinvigorated the international community's efforts, spurring other stakeholders and UN actors to adopt a victim-centred approach in processes or initiatives conducted in the Syrian context.

Conclusion

Despite the transformation of the conflict, the absence of prospects for a transition, and the gradual shift of international attention to perpetrators other than the Assad regime, Syrian and international justice actors have spearheaded ingenious transitional justice initiatives. Yet, the evolution to a non-transitioning scenario has fundamentally altered the understanding of the transitional justice paradigm in the Syrian context, nurturing apprehensions among practitioners and victims regarding the paradigm's relevance. Justice actors nevertheless continue to draw upon it to overcome the justice impasse. Dwindling international mobilisation for justice hampered their efforts as the belief in advancing justice subsided and governments in the Global North prioritised the fight against IS. Thereby they unwillingly exacerbated the fragmentation among Syrian and international justice actors who designed different, and sometimes competing, justice pathways.

Nonetheless, Syrian NGOs and victim groups have used the transitional justice toolkit as a conduit for resistance, brokering accomplishments in the field of documentation, criminal accountability, and victim group activism. Victim groups, in particular, have demonstrated a prodigious capacity to reflect on and advance their own participation in justice processes. Intuitively and forcibly, they adopted an eco-systemic approach that eschews neat categories and views victims' trajectories as ongoing processes which have an inherent meaning and value (Evrard et al. 2021). The non-transition compelled them to stall a comprehensive transitional justice programme in favour of concrete actions.

Syrian and international justice actors' achievements also highlight the murkiness of non-paradigmatic transitional justice contexts. Rather than waiting for a transition to happen, justice actors tailor the transitional justice toolkit to substantial needs, insisting on the need to prioritise other elements besides criminal accountability, such as truth-seeking, reparations, and guarantees of non-recurrence. They prove that even in dark times, when advancing justice for victims of international crimes seems futile, the transitional justice paradigm can provide a way to push the boundaries of a realistic justice and make a tangible difference for victims.

References

Aboueldahab, N. (2018) 'Writing Atrocities: Syrian Civil Society and Transitional Justice'. *Brookings Doha Center Analysis Paper 21*, May. Available at: https://www.brookings.edu/research/writing-atrocities-syrian-civil-society-and-transitional-justice/

Al Abdallah, M. (2020) Interview. Director, Syrian Justice and Accountability Centre, 8 December.

Al Abdeh, M. (2020) Interview. Director, Women Now for Development, 6 December.

Al-Bunni, A. (2021) Interview. Director, Syrian Centre for Legal Studies and Research, 8 January.

Alhaj Saleh, K. (2021) Interview, Member, Coalition of the Families Kidnapped by IS-Massar, 20 April.

al-Hallaq, M. (2021) Interview, Member, Caesar Families Association, 29 April.

al-Omari, M. (2020) 'Al-adalah al-tasalahiya fi siyaq al-'adalah al-intiqaliya' [Restorative Justice in the Contect of Transitional Justice]. Enab Baladi, 27 December. Available at: https://www.enabbaladi.net/archives/443424.

Association of Detainees and Missing of Sednaya Prison, Caesar Families Association, the Coalition of Families of Persons Kidnapped by ISIS-Massar, Families for Freedom, and Ta'afi Initiative (2021) 'Truth and Justice Charter'. February. Available at: https://www.impunitywatch.org/_files/ugd/f3f989_ea2bcacb68664b52a2b9dc090b3c775e.pdf.

Bank, C. (2020) *The Contemporary Art Scene in Syria: Social Critique and an Artistic Movement*. London: Routledge.

Burgis-Kasthala, M. (2019) 'Entrepreneurial Justice: Syria, the Commission for International Justice and Accountability and the Renewal of International Criminal Justice'. *European Journal of International Law* 30(4), 1165–1185.

Charney, C. and C. Quirk (2014) 'He Who Did Wrong Should be Accountable: Syrian Perspectives on Transitional Justice'. Washington, DC: Syrian Justice and Accountability Center. Available at: https://syriaaccountability.org/content/files/2022/04/SJAC_Syrian_Perceptions_2014_EN.pdf

cooke, m (2016) *Dancing in Damascus: Creativity, Resilience, and the Syrian Revolution*. New York: Routledge.

Darwish, M. (2020) Interview. Director, Syrian Centre for Media and the Freedom of Expression, 11 December.

ECCHR (2020) 'First Criminal Trial Worldwide on Torture in Syria before a German Court'. Available at: https://www.ecchr.eu/en/case/first-criminal-trial-worldwide-on-torture-in-syria-before-a-german-court/.

Elliot, I. (2017) 'Meaningful Step towards Accountability? A View from the Field on the United Nations International, Impartial and Independent Mechanism for Syria'. *Journal of International Criminal Justice* 15(2), 239–256.

Enab Baladi (2020) 'Syrian Human Rights NGO Calls on Real Estate Owners to Document their Properties to Avoid Palestine's West Bank Scenario'. 11 December. Available at: https://english.enabbaladi.net/archives/2020/06/syrian-human-rights-ngo-calls-on-real-estate-owners-to-document-their-properties-to-avoid-palestines-west-bank-scenario.

Evrard, E., G.M. Bonifazi, and T. Destrooper (2021) 'The Meaning of Participation in Transitional Justice: A Conceptual Proposal for Empirical Analysis'. *International Journal of Transitional Justice* 15(2), 428–447.

Ghazi, N. (2021) Interview. Director, No Photo Zone, 23 April.

Guernica 37 (2020) 'Guernica 37 Assists the Government of the Netherlands in Holding Syria Accountable'. 18 September. Available at: https://www.guernica37.com/post/press-statement-guernica-37-assists-the-government-of-the-netherlands-in-holding-syria-accountable.

Haugbølle, S. (2019) 'Holding out for the Day After Tomorrow: Futurity, Memory and Transitional Justice Evidence in Syria'. In: I. Bramsen, P. Poder and O. Wæver, eds. *Resolving International Conflict: Dynamics of Escalation, Continuation and Transformation* (pp. 229–244). Abingdon: Routledge.

Helmi, A. (2021) Interview. Founder, Ta'afi Initiative, 29 April.

Herremans, B. and T. Destrooper (2021) 'Stirring the Justice Imagination: Countering the Invisibilization and Erasure of Syrian Victims' Justice Narratives'. *International Journal of Transitional Justice* 15(3), 576–595.

Ismail, S. (2018) *The Rule of Violence: Subjectivity, Memory and Government in Syria*. Cambridge: Cambridge University Press.

Kaleck, W. and P. Kroker (2018) 'Syrian Torture Investigations in Germany and Beyond Breathing New Life into Universal Jurisdiction in Europe?' *Journal of International Criminal Justice* 16(1), 165–191.

Kawabat, N. and F. Travesi (2018) 'Justice for Syrian Victims Beyond Trials: The Need for New, Innovative Uses for Documentation of Human Rights Violations in Syria'. New York: International Center for Transitional Justice.

Kroker, P. (2021) Interview. International criminal lawyer, ECCHR, 29 April.

Macdonald, A. (2013) 'Local Understandings and Experiences of Transitional Justice: A Review of the Evidence'. Justice and Security Research Programme, London School of Economics and Political Science. Available at: http://eprints.lse.ac.uk/56354.

Mahmoud, F. (2021) Interview. Member, Families for Freedom, 27 April.

Nahlavi, Y. and S. Sekkarie (2020) 'We'll See You in Court: How the Netherlands May Finally Bring Syria to The Hague'. Opinio Juris, 2 October. Available at: http://opiniojuris.org/2020/10/02/well-see-you-in-court-how-the-netherlands-may-finally-bring-syria-to-the-hague.

Nassar, H. (2014) 'Transitional Justice in the Wake of the Arab Uprisings: Between Complexity and Standardisation'. In: J.F. Fisher and R. Stewart, eds. *Transitional Justice and the Arab Spring* (pp. 54–74). Routledge: Abingdon.

—— (2020) Interview, Director, Policy and Research at Impunity Watch, 25 November.

Nassar, S. (2021) Interview, researcher and human rights defender, 2 April.

Nassar, S. and I. Rangelov (2020) 'Documentation of Human Rights Violations and Transitional Justice in Syria: Gaps and Ways to Address Them'. Conflict Research

Programme, London School of Economics and Political Science. Available at: http://eprints.lse.ac.uk/106206.

Orjuela, C. (2018) 'Mobilising Diasporas for Justice. Opportunity Structures and the Presencing of a Violent Past'. *Journal of Ethnic and Migration Studies*, 44(8), 1357–1373.

Sarkin, J. (2021) 'The Case for an International Mechanism to Address the Detainees and Disappeared Crisis in Syria'. Available at: https://taafi-sy.org/wp-content/uploads/2021/05/Humans-Not-Numbers-EN-FINAL-20MAY2021.pdf.

Sawah, W. (2020) Interview. Independent transitional justice expert, former director, the Day After Project, 30 November.

Salamandra, C. and L. Stenberg (2015) 'Introduction'. In: C. Salamandra and L. Stenberg, eds. *Syria from Reform to Revolt. Volume 2: Culture, Society, and Religion* (pp. 12–27). New York: Syracuse University Press.

Schmitz-Buhl, L. (2021) 'Missing Perspectives'. Völkerrechtsblog, 30 August. Available at: https://voelkerrechtsblog.org/missing-perspectives/.

Schneider, T. and T. Lütkefend (2019) 'Nowhere to Hide: The Logic of Chemical Weapons Use in Syria'. February. Berlin: Global Public Policy Institute. Available at: https://www.gppi.net/2019/02/17/the-logic-of-chemical-weapons-use-in-syria.

Serriya, D. (2021) Interview. Director, Association of Detainees and the Missing in Sednaya Prison, 26 April.

Stokke, E. and E. Wiebelhaus-Brahm (2019) 'Syrian Diaspora Mobilization: Vertical Coordination, Patronage Relations, and the Challenges of Fragmentation in the Pursuit of Transitional Justice'. *Ethnic and Racial Studies* 42(11), 1930–1949.

Syrian Network for Human Rights (2020) 'Record of Enforced Disappearances'. https://sn4hr.org/blog/2021/08/04/record-of-enforced-disappearances1.

Tenove, C. (2019) 'Networking Justice: Digitally-enabled Engagement in Transitional Justice by the Syrian Diaspora'. *Ethnic and Racial Studies* 42(11), 1950–1969.

The Day After Project (2012) 'Supporting a Democratic Transition in Syria: Vision, Principles, Objectives, Challenges, and Recommendations'. August. Available at: https://www.swp-berlin.org/en/publication/the-day-after-democratic-transition-in-syria.

—— (2020) 'Conditions of Victims and Their Attitudes Towards Accountability and Reparations'. Available at: https://tda-sy.org/2020/05/05/conditions-of-victims-and-their-attitudes-towards-accountability-and-reparations.

Üngör, U. (2019) 'Narrative War is Coming'. *Al-Jumhuriya*, 7 June. Available at: https://www.aljumhuriya.net/en/content/narrative-war-coming.

Van Schaack, B. (2020a) 'The International Community's Efforts in Syria'. In: H. Moodrick-Even Khen, N. Boms, and S. Ashraph, eds. *The Syrian War: Between Justice and Political Reality* (pp. 243–267). Cambridge: Cambridge University Press.

—— (2020b) *Imagining Justice for Syrians. Lieber Studies Volume 4*. Oxford: Oxford University Press.

Ziadeh, R., ed. (2020) *Accountability in Syria: Achieving Transitional Justice in a Postconflict Society*. London: Lexington Books.

Chapter 3

Imagining Transitional Justice in Turkey's Ongoing Kurdish Conflict[1]

Nisan Alıcı

Introduction

Turkey has never adopted an official, overarching transitional justice agenda to deal with past atrocities in its Kurdish areas. However, grassroots organisations in partnership with several international actors have used the transitional justice discourse to pressure the government in their pursuit of truth, justice, and accountability. By the early 2000s, the state put limited efforts for prosecutions and reparations in place, while activist groups led unofficial transitional justice initiatives to deal with the past. These efforts, however, did not disrupt the nature of governing, and they gradually faded away following the collapse of the peace process in 2015.

The current socio-political context of Turkey does not allow much room for activists to engage actively with a transitional justice framework. This is because the contested political authority of the Turkish state is particularly threatened by the Kurdish question, making disruption particularly costly to the state. For this reason, the chapter foregrounds the perspective of grassroots justice activists – rather than that of the rights-violating state – and highlights the disruptive potential of their actions; this potential has so far been undertheorised in the literature.

There are several experiences of grassroots actors seeking to foster changes by mobilising transitional justice rhetoric. In this chapter, I draw on two of these examples to analyse how transitional justice's truth and accountability goals could be pursued and partly achieved. The first example is the Diyarbakır Commission, led by civil society actors, which managed to push the parliament to open up an investigatory sub-commission. The second is the Dersim Apology of then Prime Minister Recep Tayyip Erdoğan, which led to controversies around the underpinning motivation, but disrupted the public silence over the issue. Both processes were significant in breaking the cycle of silence and denial and lifting the veil on gross human rights violations in Turkey's

1 This research was funded by the Peace Research Grant Program of the International Peace Research Association Foundation.

DOI: 10.4324/9781003289104-4

recent past. Although they failed to deliver legal accountability, they are crucial to show how transitional justice discourse can be mobilised, at least partly, through the pressure of civil society actors.

Drawing on the past experiences and current perspectives of grassroots actors, the chapter explores the possibilities of using a transitional justice framework in the absence of any state support for transitional justice. It demonstrates a need for a differentiated approach to analyse the prospects, challenges, and opportunities that might arise when transitional justice is applied in conflicted societies. I highlight the need for scholarly analysis of such projects because the role played by these initiatives can strengthen our understanding of the practice of transitional justice.

This chapter is part of a broader, victim-centred research project focusing on transitional justice in Turkey's ongoing Kurdish conflict (Alıcı 2022). The theoretical arguments in this chapter are supported by 11 in-person and 13 online interviews with practitioners, lawyers, and activists based in Istanbul and Diyarbakır. The interviews focused on their understanding of transitional justice, how they think it could help deal with the Kurdish conflict, their interpretation of past transitional justice initiatives, and how they make sense of transitional justice while dealing with an ongoing conflict.

The following section provides brief contextual information on the Kurdish conflict and human rights violations. I then set out how grassroots actors make sense of transitional justice and transition in the given situation. In the empirical section, I analyse the two past transitional justice practices: the Truth and Justice Commission for the Diyarbakır Prison and the Apology for Dersim Massacre. I analyse the intentionalities and responses of different actors during different phases of those practices. These two examples highlight the value of a new and nuanced framework to understand the complexities of transitional justice interventions on the ground. I then conclude that transitional justice can be a meaningful paradigm for non-state actors in contested states who can use its intentionality to pursue accountability, recognition, and disruption.

The Broader Context

Kurdish Conflict

The Kurdish conflict is rooted in the history and the formation of the Turkish Republic in 1923. The armed conflict started in 1984 when the *Partiya Karkaren Kurdistan*, the Kurdistan Workers Party (PKK), launched its first major attack against the Turkish military forces. Modern Turkey was founded as a nation-state based on creating a homogenous Turkish nation and a particular cultural identity which the citizens should adopt (Jongerden 2018). Until recently, Turkish governments refused to recognise the Kurdish population as a distinct people with a distinct identity with collective rights. This resulted in widespread assimilation policies towards the Kurds and systematic human rights violations in the Kurdish region (Gunes 2013). Among some groups, this led to the idea that violence was the only means through which to achieve Kurdish liberation (Gunes 2013).

Within the context of the armed conflict, it is estimated that 35,567 people died between 1984–2013: 7,918 of these were public servants and the rest were civilians and guerrilla fighters (Türkiye Büyük Millet Meclisi 2013). The Kurdish-populated regions were ruled under a state of emergency between 1987 and 2002. The conflict reached its peak in the 1990s when there was an 'extended implementation of extreme violence against civilians' by the state armed forces and several paramilitary organisations (Işık 2020). Systemic human rights violations committed by the state during that period include thousands of extrajudicial killings and enforced disappearances (Göral et al. 2013), the evacuation of more than 4,000 villages and towns, the forced displacement of approximately 2,5 million people (Ayata and Yükseker 2005), arbitrary detention, and torture.

Jongerden (2018, 723) argues that the conflict is the manifestation of the 'systematic denial and degradation of Kurds'. However, the Turkish state has tried to deal with the Kurdish conflict using a security discourse and heavy military interventions (Yıldız 2012). Mainstream Turkish political parties considered the Kurdish issue as an existential threat to national security and refused to settle this complex ethno-political question politically (Bozarslan 2008; Gunes 2013). Until the early 2000s, the official stance on the Kurdish issue was based on the denial of any state involvement in human rights violations against Kurdish citizens (Çelik B. 2020). This denial of state responsibility accompanied the government's reluctance to implement transitional justice measures aimed at accountability and recognition. This would have required acknowledging the role of the state in systemic human rights violations and an inevitable disruption of the critical pillars upon which contemporary Turkey is built.

The 1990s were also central to the political mobilisation and empowerment of the Kurdish people. Alongside PKK's armed campaign, many Kurds resisted political violence through peaceful means, such as mass rallies, school boycotts, and shutdowns of shops (Çelik 2015). Those who were most affected by the conflict became active political actors who, to date, have mobilised around demands for justice and accountability for conflict-related crimes. Kurdish political parties started to gain widespread support in Turkey. At the same time, the Kurdish diaspora started to organise campaigns in Europe to expose state violence. In cooperation with their foreign colleagues, Kurdish lawyers filed lawsuits before the European Court of Human Rights (ECtHR), which became an essential tool for holding the Turkish state accountable to a wider audience (Uçarlar 2015). Kurdish lawyers used the ECtHR as a tool for legal mobilisation and social transformation (Kurban 2020). The hearings before the ECtHR provided the applicants with the opportunity to be heard publicly in a legal forum for the first time (Çalı 2010, 312). Hundreds of judgements issued by the ECtHR played a significant role in documenting state-sponsored human rights violations (Kurban 2014) and challenging the official policies of denial and silence (Çalı 2010; Budak 2015; Uçarlar 2015; Jongerden 2018).

During the conflict, the warring parties attempted several peace talks. Most recently, a failed peace process took place between the PKK and the state between 2012–2015. After its collapse, the conflict took a turn towards its deadliest period. The clashes in Kurdish cities and towns killed approximately 1,200 residents and displaced around 350,000 people (International Crisis Group 2017). The consolidation of the authoritarian regime accompanied the escalation of violence in the Kurdish region. Most mayors of the Kurdish municipalities were replaced by government-appointed trustees, leading Kurdish political figures and human rights activists were imprisoned, and numerous civil society organisations (CSOs) were shut down by decrees (Alici et al. 2020). This period marked the beginning of a political atmosphere where many of those who used to work actively for peace and transitional justice were either imprisoned or had to leave the country. Those who remained continued their activities under state surveillance (Yabanci 2019).

Seeking Justice During Conflict

Turkey has long been characterised by social amnesia (Bakiner 2013) and the denial of state-sponsored human rights violations against Kurdish people. Recognition of these violations is assumed to challenge the very foundation of modern Turkey (Cengiz 2011). These dynamics of forgetting, however, started to change due to popular demands for truth and remembrance, especially in the period 2005–2015 (Budak 2015; Kaya 2015). Demands for transitional justice gained popularity among victims, survivors, lawyers, and activists who used the transitional justice discourse to pressure the government in the search for truth, justice, and accountability. The demands gained visibility with the support of the European Union and the ECtHR (Budak 2015, 231). As part of the peace process in 2012–2015, the interest in and demands for transitional justice reached their highest level and sparked several discussions on different approaches to transitional justice. Dealing with the past was seen as a fundamental component of conflict transformation and peace-building; justice and accountability thereby became even more needed.

Exploring grassroots actors' understanding of transition and transitional justice provides insights into how and why they have been engaging with transitional justice at different times. Budak (2015) suggests that transitional justice provides a valuable framework to come to terms with the legacies of the past in Turkey and that it could play a vital role in resolving Turkey's Kurdish conflict. This view seems to be widely shared by grassroots actors who have engaged in justice-seeking efforts. Some of them consider the transitional justice framework to offer a basis to think about how to handle a substantial social problem and how it might bring about sustainable resolutions. It is also perceived not to be limited to post-conflict transitions but rather something that grassroots actors can also benefit from during conflict.

A nuanced and broad understanding of transition is key to grassroots transitional justice efforts in Turkey. Grassroots actors perceive transition as a long-term, non-linear process. Because a transition does not happen at a particular moment, transitional justice seems relevant and useful before, during, and after a peace accord that could bring the Kurdish conflict to an end. Grassroots justice activists moreover imagine transitions as a dynamic terrain for a political struggle initiated bottom-up. According to this bottom-up understanding, a transition cannot be driven from above or started by the political elite. Moreover, transitional justice is part of a broader struggle for transition (personal interview, July 2019). This understanding foregrounds agency while also giving grassroots actors the responsibility for initiating transitional justice processes.

From a bottom-up and agency-oriented approach, civil society actors and human rights advocates are the ones most likely to initiate transitional justice in cases of ongoing conflict. This would mean that justice efforts are not the province of political elites but belong to a broader consortium of justice actors. For instance, an interviewee, who has been working closely with the forcibly displaced Kurdish population, expressed the need for creating a network and trying to push the state:

> We should form a network in this transitional process and involve all the segments of society. There should be two people from the state or the civil society with close ties to the state. It would indeed create a change. Otherwise, waiting for peace means choosing an easy way out.
>
> (Personal interview, July 2019)

Another interviewee, who has extensive experience working with the families of the disappeared, acknowledged the challenges of implementing various transitional justice mechanisms during the conflict. She found it crucial to identify what is feasible in the given conditions. According to her, although not every transitional justice mechanism is suitable for the current situation, some could be highly beneficial and relatively easier to implement. She believes in the need to acknowledge the challenges faced in the current situation and identify prospective aspects or measures of transitional justice:

> Is there ground for a truth commission now? No. However, neither does it pose an obstacle to revealing the bigger picture or even laying the groundwork for establishing such a mechanism. What could be the disadvantages of thinking about it when the conflict is ongoing? Obviously, I know what my challenges are. But as a human rights advocate, if I assumed the responsibility of reminding the state of its responsibilities and adopted this

> approach as a lawyer, what could prevent me from learning how to benefit from transitional justice best?
>
> (Personal interview, July 2019)

A recurrent theme in the interviews was reflection on what could be done given the limited space for civil society. One interviewee addressed the importance of accumulating small experiences and considered archival work and memorialisation efforts significant in the context of the impossibility of establishing mechanisms like truth commissions:

> Every stone we put is meaningful, and every small step counts. Official mechanisms that could only be started with the state's involvement are not employable right now. However, it does make much sense to do something with the organised activist groups, local administrations, or local initiatives.
>
> (Personal interview, August 2019)

Another participant identified the main contributions of using transitional justice in the early stages as building civil society networks and collecting data (personal interview, August 2019). This is a common thread in most interviews. Everything that could be done now would count as 'infrastructure work' to enable civil society actors to actively and meaningfully get involved once an official process starts. Another interviewee states:

> For instance, memorialisation is a crucial mechanism offered to me by the transitional justice framework, and there is no obstacle to do that right now. I do what I can do; I collect what I can collect under today's circumstances. I cannot make the government apologise, but I can inform people about what an official apology means. For example, I cannot create a new historical narrative, but I can discuss what it should look like.
>
> (Personal interview, July 2019)

When I asked the interviewees about what they are doing at present that could be examined under the transitional justice banner, the most mentioned practices were archival work, documentation, database forming, reporting, and research. Aboueldahab (2018) states that in ongoing conflicts such as in Syria, the documentation of violations serves as a function of transitional justice and becomes an act of resistance by keeping the justice demands alive. She argues that agency is at the centre of documentation by involving various actors in recording and revealing the truth about violations. In Turkey, as well, documentation plays a crucial role in recording human rights violations. During curfews in Kurdish areas in 2015–2016, the authorities prevented national and international human rights organisations from entering the curfew regions to document mass abuses against civilians (Human Rights Watch 2016). Several CSOs, who managed to document the abuses, were later shut down by a decree. An interviewee highlights the importance of continuing the documentation work:

> In the future [when there is an official peace process], these violations will be more visible and become part of the resolution of the Kurdish conflict and access to justice. This is why we do archival work, documentation, data collection, and research. This will be our contribution to transitional justice.
>
> (personal interview, July 2019)

Both the interviews and the analysis of previous initiatives show that truth-seeking has been a crucial cross-cutting activity for different actors. The denial of past atrocities has been so prevalent in Turkish institutions (Ayata and Hakyemez 2013) that justice advocates see truth recovery as a critical aspect of any justice process. A state-sanctioned truth-seeking process, according to these activists, would imply an official willingness to acknowledge what happened in the past and end impunity. Moreover, it would signal that society was ready to acknowledge its responsibility for the silence and denial.

The prevailing denial and impunity stem from, and result in, a lack of sufficient data about the causes of abuse. Documentation and truth recovery, therefore, are essential for two reasons. The first is to collect data to be used in a judicial process holding the perpetrators accountable. The other is to achieve public recognition of the harm done to victims and survivors. Both purposes are present in civil society's efforts, as I will explore in the next section examining different initiatives.

The interest in truth recovery was also apparent during the peace process, while it was the most widely suggested transitional justice measure in the public debate. CSOs, journalists, and commentators engaged with the idea of establishing such a commission. CSOs invited foreign experts to discuss truth commissions from a comparative perspective. Opposition parties addressed the need for a truth commission to resolve the conflict, and even some members of the ruling party expressed support for the idea (Truth Justice Memory Centre 2015).

It was significant when the imprisoned PKK leader, Abdullah Ocalan, called for a truth and reconciliation commission (Agos 2015). During the 2015 *Newroz* celebrations[2] in Diyarbakır, Ocalan's *Newroz* message was read aloud, and it suggested establishing such a commission (Agos 2015). As the most influential figure in Kurdish politics to date, Ocalan has been imprisoned since 1990. He was the leading actor shaping the road map of the peace process on behalf of the

2 *Newroz* is a traditional Kurdish celebration of the spring. It has acquired a political significance and been associated with the resistance of the Kurdish people. Every 21 March, it is celebrated in large demonstrations where political representatives of the Kurdish political movement are also present.

Kurdish side. His message came one month after the Dolmabahçe Declaration by the parties to the peace process, the first time a mutually agreed road map was announced (Çiçek and Coşkun 2016). Although the government did not respond to the justice proposal, it is unlikely that Ocalan's message was sent to Diyarbakır without government approval.

The peace process nevertheless collapsed shortly after, and the agreed road map has never been realised. However, it is remarkable how different non-state actors identified a truth commission as one of the immediate needs of a peace process. Most discussions of transitional justice focused on truth commissions, while other transitional justice measures did not gain as much attention.

Transitional Justice Practices

To get a deeper understanding of Turkey's transitional justice discussions and capture what is missing in the current picture, I will explore in detail two important developments in the last two decades. The driving force behind these developments was the constant activism and advocacy efforts by affected communities, lawyers, activists, and human rights advocates.

The Truth and Justice Commission for the Diyarbakır Prison

One of the most remarkable transitional justice initiatives is the Truth and Justice Commission for the Diyarbakır Prison, as its actors mobilised around the transitional justice discourse and contributed to recognition and accountability. The Diyarbakır Military Prison (DMP) has a central place in the Kurdish collective memory and resistance because of its role in radicalising large numbers of Kurds who later joined the PKK (Zeydanlioglu 2009). It is infamously known for severe human rights violations, including systematic sexualised torture and ill-treatment committed against thousands of Kurdish political prisoners in the aftermath of the 1980 military coup (Yıldız 2016).

The Truth and Justice Commission for the Diyarbakır Prison was established in 2007 by a group of activists supported by academics, lawyers, and psychologists. The intentionality of the commission was in line with transitional justice goals as its main actors explicitly called for justice, recognition, and accountability in defining the commission's objectives. The commission's objectives and the responses it gathered revolved around truth, justice, and memory. The commission members articulated their goals to initiate a judicial process for human rights violations committed between 1980–1983, start a process of revealing the truth and confronting the past, and transform the prison into a museum and that would function as a memory site (CNN Türk 2010). The members of this initiative indicated that they effectively worked like a truth commission for three years (Diyarbakır Cezaevi Gerçekleri Araştırma ve Adalet Komisyonu 2009). Like several unofficial truth projects around the world

(Bickford 2007), it mimicked official truth commissions in its goals and activities, but did not have a similar bureaucratic structure. It collected testimonies from more than 500 ex-prisoners through interviews in different cities of the Kurdish region and the West, held several symposiums across the country, gathered a 7,000 pages-long document, shared its findings with the public, and launched a campaign to turn the prison into a human rights museum with the support of 100,000 signatures (Meryem 2018).

The commission's work attracted several responses from the government. One of them was public acknowledgement of the human rights violations committed in the prison while undermining the widely supported memorialisation demands. In 2010, while the commission was still operating, Erdoğan, who was then prime minister, acknowledged the use of torture in the prison during a speech in Diyarbakır. He said that the government wanted to destroy the premises of the old prison and build a new one to erase the painful memory of the 1980 military coup (Karakaş 2016). Erdoğan's speech was unprecedented in terms of officially recognising the legacy of the prison. However, his approach to memory contradicted the grassroots actors' demands for a memorial site. This speech signified that Erdoğan reluctantly adopted some transitional justice notions that the commission pursued; he recognised the human rights violations committed in the DMP, but wanted to destroy rather than memorialise the prison.

Justice-seeking was another pillar that sparked some responses. In 2010, using the commission's data, 310 ex-prisoners filed a criminal complaint to the Diyarbakır Chief Public Prosecutor's Office. The commission issued a press statement on behalf of the applicants, demanding that the human rights violations committed in the DMP should be treated as crimes against humanity and that the perpetrators should be punished accordingly. Their judicial demands moreover went hand in hand with demands for truth recovery and memorialisation. They called for a parliamentary investigation commission and renewed their call for a human rights museum, arguing that revealing the truth about the violations in the DMP is key to Turkey's dealing with the past. A criminal investigation started the following day, and by 2012 the number of applicants had risen to 1,000 (Sabah 2012).

The truth pillar was also very much present in the commission's work and the responses it generated. The commission released its final report in 2012, revealing the names of the military officers who had allegedly used torture. It also documented torture's physical and psychological effects. In 2015, a parliamentary sub-commission was established under the Human Rights Inquiry Committee to investigate the human rights violations committed in the DMP. It was the first time that the prison was subject to an official public investigation. The sub-commission's mandate included a commitment to dealing with the past, reparations for torture survivors, and truth recovery. Remarkably, parliamentarians from different political parties explicitly committed to transitional justice goals. Activists nevertheless criticised the sub-commission for being ineffective. Moreover, as the peace process collapsed, nothing concrete followed from the sub-commission's report.

Bickford (2007, 995) argues that unofficial truth projects can have an essential contribution to the contexts where official truth commissions are not viable. The Truth and Justice Commission for the Diyarbakır Prison is a vivid example of how civil society actors became vocal about transitional justice objectives, initiated a process to deliver these objectives, and pushed the state actors to take several steps in that direction. These actions were not concrete policy changes. However, they ensured the recording of human rights violations by official bodies and enabled a public discussion about long-neglected issues. The commission brought torture survivors together with experts and civil society practitioners and initiated a judicial process and a parliamentary inquiry.

Apology for the Dersim Massacre

The Truth and Justice Commission for the Diyarbakır Prison is emblematic of public initiatives for dealing with the past. Another attempt of the same era was the Dersim Apology extended by Erdoğan, but in contrast this initiative was top-down. It illustrates the reluctant and pragmatic adoption of transitional justice tools on behalf of the state.

A massive military operation took place in 1937 and 1938 in the Dersim region, populated mostly by Kurdish-Alevi citizens. It resulted in the death of approximately 14,000 civilians and the forced displacement of around 12,000 people (Dinç 2021). According to the official view, the operation was the state's legitimate self-defence against an uprising (Ayata and Hakyemez 2013). In 2009, Erdoğan nevertheless referred to the 'Dersim Massacre' in parliament, symbolising a paradigm shift in the official narrative (Ayata and Hakyemez 2013). Following Erdoğan's speech, a public discussion started about what happened in 1938 and 'the silence about Dersim cracked at the official level' (Ayata and Hakyemez 2013, 137). Several academic and cultural works on Dersim emerged. CSOs organised memorialisation activities, panels, and festivals, gathering a wider audience and more media attention than in previous years (Dinç 2021).

On November 23, 2011, Erdoğan extended an apology for the 1938 Dersim Massacre. He referred to Dersim as the most tragic event in our history and made references to the literature, demonstrating his awareness of state apologies. He said he could, if needed, apologise on behalf of the state if this is what the literature suggests. It was the first time in Turkey's history that a head of state announced that he would apologise for a past atrocity (Ayata and Hakyemez 2013; Bakiner 2013; Dinç 2021).

Erdoğan's apology sparked a mobilisation on the social level. There were public campaigns to remove Sabiha Gokcen from the second busiest airport in Istanbul. She was the first female war pilot in Turkey and participated in the carpet-bombing in Dersim (Bakiner 2013). Hundreds of petitions were sent to the parliament to start an investigation process into the Dersim Massacre, and in 2012 a sub-commission was established to investigate the Dersim Massacre. It was established under the Petition Committee, which raised serious concerns about its effectiveness and capacity to conduct efficient investigations (Truth Justice Memory Centre 2013). It was not mandated to provide any compensation, but to make policy recommendations. However, as Bakiner (2013, 702) points out, this commission could be seen as 'the first truth-commission-like entity in Turkey's human rights history'. The sub-commission collected testimonies from victims, survivors, and the families of the victims, and it started gathering documents from military archives and the prime minister's office (Evrensel 2012). Similarly to the sub-commission on the DMP, this sub-commission's work neither led to a broader attempt at, nor to concrete measures for, dealing with the past.

For a majority of victims to consider an apology complete and satisfactory, it has to be part of a larger package that includes an official commitment to policy changes and legal and other measures to eliminate impunity and guarantees for accountability (Lundy and Rolston 2016, 106). Erdoğan's apology, although followed by a sub-commission, was far from committing to these other elements. As such, it led neither to a fully-fledged truth commission or a parliamentary commission, nor did it have a transformative impact since it was not complemented by other measures such as reparations (Bakiner 2013; Dinç 2021). Dinç (2021) argues that despite this, Erdoğan's apology had a healing impact on the Dersim community. Ayata and Hakyemez (2013) suggest that Erdoğan wanted to be seen as shifting the state discourse from denial to reconciliation by publicly addressing official taboos. However, instead of taking full responsibility on behalf of the state, he pointed to a different perpetrator. In the rest of the speech, he addressed the opposition leader Kemal Kılıçdaroğlu as the real one who must apologise. Kılıçdaroğlu's party is known to be representing the founding ideology of the state, Kemalism, and it was in power during the Dersim Massacre. AKP, at least on the discursive level, built itself against Kemalism. A few months prior to the apology, Erdoğan claimed that his government had ended the denialist politics (Dinç 2021). Erdoğan's half-hearted, reluctant and conditional apology was a calculated political tool to further the state agenda (Dinç 2021) and show how his government was distinct from the official state narrative. The intention was to undermine the political power of his immediate political rival and to challenge Kemalist ideology.

On December 28, 2011, only a month after Erdoğan's apology, another massacre was added to the long list of atrocities. Turkish warplanes bombed 34 Kurdish civilians in the Roboski province of Şırnak. The continued state violence against Kurds made it difficult to believe that the state was ready to reckon with its past. The apology, instead, was seen as an instrumentalised move to convey the message that Erdoğan's government wanted to reconcile with the past and build a new truth regime by rewriting the official narrative (Ayata and Hakyemez 2013).

The official measures, such as the Dersim Apology and the parliamentary sub-commissions, were seen as pragmatic manoeuvres without long-term or a genuine commitment to a fundamental political change. The state failed to recognise the broader political setting, which enabled the conflict to happen and ignored the political responsibility behind human rights abuses. The perpetrators of most crimes committed during the 1990s have not been yet held accountable, and the root causes of the conflict have not been addressed.

The Missing Links

To counter the denial, break the silence, and make the harms recognised by official bodies and then the whole of society, human rights activists have long mobilised to create spaces of truth recovery. It has taken different shapes, from documenting human rights violations to establishing an unofficial truth commission. The quest for truth has always been accompanied by efforts for justice and accountability to overcome the long-lived impunity over conflict-related crimes on behalf of the state's armed forces. CSOs, practitioners, activists, human rights advocates, and grassroots organisations mobilised the transitional justice discourse and pushed for some form of transitional justice in their quest for accountability and recognition. These initiatives were not systematically analysed from a transitional justice point of view. Focusing on such initiatives demonstrates the relevance and usefulness of transitional justice in a broader range of cases, including ongoing conflicts. The analysis of the efforts by grassroots actors to pursue justice provides us with insights into the innovative ways that accountability and recognition could be achieved. This also highlights the value of positioning activists, victim-survivor groups, and CSOs at the forefront of transitional justice activities, including in designing and implementing the transitional justice architecture.

Turkey exemplifies the contexts where transitional justice interventions occur in the absence of a political transition and where the goal is not to consolidate a political transition. Along with the victims and survivors, civil society actors still hold a solid potential to catalyse a transformation and implement transitional justice, at least in small steps. However, there is a need for a new conceptual and analytical framework to amplify that potential and understand the complexities of transitional justice interventions on the ground. The proposed framework in this volume could facilitate such understanding by examining the contestation and co-existence of various realities.

Grassroots actors are still vocal about the demands for justice and engage with truth-seeking efforts through various means. Interestingly, these attempts usually are not translated into the transitional justice terminology. Activists do not necessarily name or consider their practices under the transitional justice umbrella. The absence of a transition from conflict to peace makes it difficult for those actors to label their justice-seeking efforts under the transitional justice banner. It highlights a missing link in the transitional justice literature between the justice-seeking efforts in aparadigmatic cases and the transitional justice framework.

Concerning the missing link, civil society actors are also impacted by the absence of enough guidance on how to use transitional justice in an ongoing conflict. Although they vocally adopt transitional justice goals and objectives in their agenda, they need more tools and capacity to effectively benefit from the transitional justice framework. Getting access to conflict and post-conflict areas and documenting ongoing abuses without being targeted by the conflicting parties or the state surveillance are essential issues that must be researched. One of the interviewees addresses the need to develop a new methodology for transitional justice to be used in ongoing conflicts:

> The discussions in transitional justice literature are precious for me because they provide a basis to think. The only hardship is that I get stuck because the practicalities of transitional justice in ongoing conflicts have not been studied enough. I am a lawyer; this is not my specialisation. We get stuck because we are trying to find the methodology on our own.
>
> (Personal interview, July 2019)

At present, it is not only the Kurdish conflict but also the Turkish state's increasingly authoritarian rule that shapes human rights activism, whether framed as transitional justice or not. As a result of shrinking civic space and oppressive rule targeting human rights activists, there is limited potential for thinking innovatively about transitional justice. Although almost all interviewees agree that it continues to be meaningful to implement transitional justice initiatives also in the context of conflict, there are few concrete suggestions as to what could be done at present. The dynamic grassroots justice movement that existed until a few years ago finds it increasingly difficult to stay active. This means that some earlier discussions and efforts are slowly fading. At the same time, activists insist that when it becomes possible to adopt a more comprehensive transitional justice framework, this framework should be developed by victim and survivor groups, activists, and CSOs to ensure agency-oriented and context-specific approaches.

Concluding Remarks

Grassroots organisations, victim and survivor groups, lawyers, and activists have pioneered efforts to deal with the past and implement transitional justice in Turkey. As stated in the Introduction to this volume, aparadigmatic transitional justice cases tend to have diverse and sometimes ambiguous objectives that raise questions of what is transitional about transitional justice. The attempts in Turkey show how certain elements from the transitional justice 'toolbox' were used to seek accountability and recognition of harm, as well as being part of a broader struggle to disrupt ongoing violent policies. Bottom-up initiatives for accountability, recognition, and social change moved the government to reluctantly adopt a limited transitional justice discourse and take some concrete steps towards recognition. This was arguably for pragmatic reasons, primarily because it suited the political agenda of the time. Therefore, it is crucial to be mindful of the differences between past and present socio-political contexts. While it is true that the conflict was ongoing and there was not an overarching transitional justice agenda by the state, the overall political environment was more favourable towards attempts to bring past atrocities and crimes to the forefront of public debates. Breaking off from the past by condemning a previous regime and challenging the official denial and silence was a useful tool for the government to consolidate its power. In recent years, the changes in the government's priorities moved transitional justice further away from its agenda. Although currently transitional justice is absent, new efforts could be built upon rich knowledge and experience. Learning from those efforts in Turkey can shed light on other aparadigmatic contexts where grassroots organisations pioneer transitional justice in the absence of institutional willingness to adopt it fully.

References

Aboueldahab, N. (2018) 'Writing Atrocities: Syrian Civil Society and Transitional Justice'. Brookings Doha Center Analysis Paper 21, May. Available at: https://www.brookings.edu/research/writing-atrocities-syrian-civil-society-and-transitional-justice/

Agos (2015) 'Öcalan's Newroz Message: I Call Upon the PKK to Hold Congress'. 21 March. Available at: http://www.agos.com.tr/en/article/10963/ocalans-newroz-message-i-call-upon-the-pkk-to-hold-congress

Alıcı, N. (2022) 'Imagining Transitional Justice in the Ongoing Kurdish Conflict: A Victim-Centred Analysis'. PhD Thesis, University of Ulster.

Alıcı, N., G. Bor and G. Daşlı (2020) 'Turkey's Missing WPS Agenda and Implications for the COVID-19 Pandemic'. 28 May. Available at: https://blogs.lse.ac.uk/wps/2020/05/28/turkeys-missing-wps-agenda-and-implications-for-the-covid-19-pandemic/

Ayata, B. and S. Hakyemez (2013) 'The AKP's Engagement with Turkey's Past Crimes: An Analysis of PM Erdoğan's Dersim Apology'. *Dialectical Anthropology* 37(1), 131–143.

Ayata, B. and D. Yükseker (2005) 'A Belated Awakening: National and International Responses to the Internal Displacement of Kurds in Turkey'. *New Perspectives on Turkey* 32, 5–42.

Bakiner, O. (2013) 'Is Turkey Coming to Terms with its Past? Politics of Memory and Majoritarian Conservatism'. *Nationalities Papers* 41(5), 691–708.

Bickford, L. (2007) 'Unofficial Truth Projects'. *Human Rights Quarterly* 29(4), 994–1035.

Bozarslan, H. (2008) 'Kurds and the Turkish State'. In: R. Kasaba, ed. *The Cambridge History of Turkey*. Volume 4. Cambridge: Cambridge University Press.

Budak, Y. (2015) 'Dealing with the past: Transitional Justice, Ongoing Conflict and the Kurdish Issue in Turkey'. *International Journal of Transitional Justice* 9(2), 219–238.

Cengiz, O. K. (2011) '1915, Dersim, yüzleşme …' 25 November. Available at: http://www.radikal.com.tr/yazarlar/orhan-kemal-cengiz/1915-dersim-yuzlesme-1070158/.

CNN Türk (2010) 'Diyarbakır Cezaevi için toplu suç duyurusu.' 11 October. Available at: https://www.cnnturk.com/2010/turkiye/10/11/diyarbakir.cezaevi.icin.toplu.suc.duyurusu/592627.0/index.html

Çalı, B. (2010) 'The Logics of Supranational Human Rights Litigation, Official Acknowledgment, and Human Rights Reform: The Southeast Turkey Cases before the European Court of Human Rights, 1996–2006.' *Law and Social Inquiry* 35(2), 311–337.

Çelik, A. (2015) 'Savaş ve Bellek: Doksanların Zorla Kaybetme Fenomeni Olarak Beyaz Toros'. *Toplum ve Kuram* 10, 41–58.

Çelik, A.B. (2020) 'Agonistic Peace and Confronting the Past: An Analysis of a Failed Peace Process and the Role of Narratives'. *Cooperation and Conflict* 56(1), 26–43.

Çiçek, C. and V. Coşkun (2016) *The Peace Process from Dolmabahçe to Present-Day: Understanding Failure and Finding New Paths*. Istanbul: Peace Foundation.

Dinç, P. (2021) 'Dersim 1937–38: Shifts and Continuities in the State Discourse and Reasoning under Kemalism and Erdoğanism'. In: N. Christofis, ed. *The State of the Kurds in Erdogan's 'New' Turkey*. London and New York: Routledge.

Diyarbakır Cezaevi Gerçekleri Araştırma ve Adalet Komisyonu (2009) 'Diyarbakır Cezaevi Okul Değil, İnsan Hakları Müzesi Olmalıdır!' Birikim15 September. Available at: https://birikimdergisi.com/guncel/773/diyarbakir-cezaevi-okul-degil-insan-haklari-muzesi-olmalidir

Evrensel (2012) 'Dersim belgeleri Meclis'te'. 12 March. Available at: https://www.evrensel.net/haber/24874/dersim-belgeleri-mecliste

Gunes, C. (2013) 'Political Reconciliation in Turkey: Challenges and Prospects'. In: C. Gunes and W. Zeydanlioglu, eds. *The Kurdish Question in Turkey: New Perspectives on Violence, Representation, and Reconciliation*. New York: Routledge.

Human Rights Watch (2016) 'Turkey: State Blocks Probes of Southeast Killings.' Available at: https://www.hrw.org/news/2016/07/11/turkey-state-blocks-probes-southeast-killings

International Crisis Group (2017) 'Managing Turkey's PKK Conflict: The Case of Nusaybin'. Available at: https://www.crisisgroup.org/europe-central-asia/western-europemediterranean/turkey/243-managing-turkeys-pkk-conflict-case-nusaybin

Jongerden, J. (2018) 'Looking Beyond the State: Transitional Justice and the Kurdish Issue in Turkey'. *Ethnic and Racial Studies* 41(4), 721–738.

Göral, Ö.S., A. Işık and Ö. Kaya (2013) *The Unspoken Truth: Enforced Disappearances*. İstanbul: Truth Justice Memory Center.

Işık, A. (2020) 'The Emergence, Transformation and Functions of Paramilitary Groups in Northern Kurdistan (Eastern Turkey) in the 1990s'. Unpublished doctoral dissertation, Utrecht University.

Karakaş, B. (2016) 'Hani Diyarbakır Cezaevi müze olacaktı?' *Platform 24*, 19 December. Available at: http://platform24.org/yazarlar/1922/hani-diyarbakir-cezaevi-muze-olacakti.

Kaya, D.G. (2015) 'Coming to Terms With the Past: Rewriting History Through a Therapeutic Public Discourse in Turkey'. *International Journal of Middle East Studies* 47(4), 681–700.

Kurban, D. (2014) 'Europe as an Agent of Change: The Role of the European Court of Human Rights and the EU in Turkey's Kurdish Policies'. SWP Research Paper 9/2014. Berlin: German Institute for International and Security Affairs.

Kurban, D. (2020) *Limits of Supranational Justice: The European Court of Human Rights and Turkey's Kurdish Conflict*. Cambridge: Cambridge University Press.

Lundy, P. and B. Rolston (2016) 'Redress for Past Harms? Official Apologies in Northern Ireland'. *International Journal of Human Rights* 20(1), 104–122.

Meryem, D. (2018) 'Türkiye'de Yüzleşme Müzeleri ve Yüzleşilemeyen Diyarbakır Cezaevi'. Sivil Sayfalar, 24 May. Available at: https://www.sivilsayfalar.org/2018/05/24/turkiyede-yuzlesme-muzeleri-ve-yuzlesilemeyen-diyarbakir-cezaevi/

Sabah (2012) '12 Eylül'deki işkencelere soruşturma'. 6 April. Available at: https://www.sabah.com.tr/gundem/2012/04/06/12-eyluldeki-iskencelere-sorusturma.

Truth Justice Memory Center (2013) 'Truth Commission for the Mass Killing of Alevis'. 6 January. Available at: https://hakikatadalethafiza.org/en/truth-commission-for-the-mass-killing-of-alevis/.

—— (2015) 'Partiler #90larlaYÜZLEŞMEKiçin ne dedi?' 21 June. Available at: https://hakikatadalethafiza.org/90larlayuzlesmekicin-hangi-partiden-hangi-aday-ne-dedi/.

Uçarlar, N. (2015) *Nothing in Its Right Place: Demands of Justice and Coming to Terms with the Past in the Post-Conflict Period*. Istanbul: DISA Publications.

Yabanci, B. (2019) 'Turkey's Tamed Civil Society: Containment and Appropriation Under a Competitive Authoritarian Regime'. *Journal of Civil Society* 15(4), 285–306.

Yıldız, K. (2012) 'Turkey' s Kurdish Conflict: Pathways to Progress'. *Insight Turkey* 14(4), 151–174.

Yıldız, Y.Y. (2016) 'Forced Confession as a Ritual of Sovereignty: The Case of Diyarbakır Military Prison in Turkey'. *Asia-Pacific Journal on Human Rights and the Law* 17(2), 185–198.

Zeydanlioglu, W. (2009) 'Torture and Turkification in the Diyarbakır Military Prison'. In: W. Zeydanlioglu and J.T. Parry, eds. *Rights, Citizenship and Torture: Perspectives on Evil, Law and the State*. Oxford: Inter-Disciplinary Press.

Türkiye Büyük Millet Meclisi (2013) *Terör ve Şiddet Olayları Kapsamında Yaşam Hakkı İhlallerini İnceleme Raporu*. Ankara: Türkiye Büyük Millet Meclisi Insan Haklarını İnceleme Komisyonu.

Chapter 4

Transitional Justice in Afghanistan

A Hegemonic Power Discourse

Huma Saeed

Introduction

A former official of the Ministry of Planning reported that within three weeks of his appointment in 1980, 25,000 missing persons had been registered (The Afghanistan Justice Project 2005). They were educated and professional people between the ages of 18 and 60: students, medical doctors, government officials, and military and religious figures (Gossman and Kouvo 2013). Today, while most of these people remain missing, we recognise this incident as only the tip of an iceberg in the ocean of mass atrocities in Afghanistan. With over 1 million killed, 1.3 million disabled (ibid.), and tens of thousands forcibly disappeared, Afghanistan has one of the largest internally displaced and diaspora populations – over 4 million and around 6 million, respectively (BBC Persian 2018; UNOCHA 2020). Considering decades of violent conflict with a huge toll on civilians, it is unsurprising that war victims (almost 70% of the population) constitute Afghanistan's biggest constituency.

Yet, gross human rights violations of the last four decades have not been addressed during different periods of transition. Following the collapse of the Taliban regime in 2001, and with the development of the National Action Plan for Peace, Security and Reconciliation (Government of the Islamic Republic of Afghanistan and Others 2005) as a road map to address gross human rights violations, some hoped a small window of opportunity would emerge for a new horizon for justice in Afghanistan. In practice, however, very little was achieved in terms of accountability measures and addressing victims' needs. As a result, many warlords, who had close contact with the previous regimes, became legitimised in the US-backed Hamid Karzai-led interim administration and subsequently in the government and parliament elected in 2004. Twenty years later, Afghanistan is in the midst of another transition, with an additional layer of ongoing war crimes and crimes against humanity that many fear will go unaddressed this time around too. The focus of this chapter, however, remains on the period prior to the return of the Taliban to power in August 2021.

In many post-authoritarian and post-conflict societies, transitional justice has increasingly become a standardised approach for dealing with past violence (Teitel 2003). Afghanistan, however, despite the heavy presence and

DOI: 10.4324/9781003289104-5

influence of the international community, did not follow this trend during its 2001 transition from the first Taliban regime to 'democracy'.[1] Notwithstanding a great demand for justice by Afghan war victims and the intention of some national and international actors to implement transitional justice in Afghanistan, major obstacles occurred at every stage in the process. This chapter argues that we need to examine the failure of the transitional justice process in Afghanistan through a geopolitical lens, reflecting not only on domestic power dynamics, but also, and importantly, on international power dynamics. In particular, the lens through which this chapter examines the (non-)implementation of transitional justice is that of hegemonic power discourse whereby peace and stability arguments took precedence over justice concerns. This has been true for previous regimes as well as for the current Taliban regime. Hegemony in this context can be understood in the Gramscian sense as articulated by Arrighi (2007, 149, emphasis added):

> Gramsci's definition of hegemony [is] something different than sheer domination. According to this definition, hegemony is the *additional* power that accrues to a dominant group by virtue of its capacity to lead society in a direction that not only serves the dominant group's interest but is also perceived by subordinate groups as serving a more general interest.

Significantly, however, as obstacles emerged to the implementation of the more standardised transitional justice process, bottom-up initiatives emerged among civil society and human rights organisations to engage in non-standardised transitional justice practices and to keep victims' quest for justice alive. This chapter will also take a look at some of these initiatives, while proposing the need to engage the large Afghan diaspora in the transitional justice process.

Following a brief country background, part one will present a discussion of a somewhat standardised model of transitional justice in Afghanistan, which was developed after the 2001 transition from the Taliban to the new regime. This section will exhibit the coexistence of the intention to demand accountability and to avoid and resist it at the same time. Part two will examine the responses to the transitional justice implementation through the lens of a hegemonic power discourse, on the one hand, and the response of bottom-up actors, on the other. Part three will propose a transnational perspective that argues for a deeper engagement with refugees and diaspora communities.

1 Examples of multilateral intervention with transitional justice mandates include Kosovo and East Timor. In both cases the United Nations sponsored the International Commission of Inquiry on East Timor and the International Criminal Tribunal for the former Yugoslavia to investigate human rights violations and crimes against humanity (Strohmeyer 2001, 118–119).

Transitional Justice in Afghanistan

Afghanistan has been suffering from war and widespread atrocities since April 1978, when a Soviet-backed coup ended the relatively calm period of President Daud's rule. This was followed by the Soviet Union invasion in 1979, which stirred widespread resistance among Afghans. Following the withdrawal of the Soviet Union forces in 1989, the Kabul regime collapsed in 1992 and a bloody civil war began among the militias and factions of the mainly Islamic parties known as the Mujahideen,[2] who had survived and thrived on the support and funding by the United States, Saudi Arabia, Pakistan, Iran, and other countries during the Soviet invasion. In 1996, the oppressive regime of the Taliban came to power until their removal in 2001. Since 2001, despite a massive international effort to rebuild the country and some progress in doing so, Afghans were caught in a vicious cycle of impunity, ongoing fighting between the insurgents – particularly the Taliban and Al Qaida – the international security forces, and the Afghan government, and a weak and failed state built and 'sustained' on entrenched corruption. Such developments contributed significantly to the sudden collapse of Kabul and the return of the Taliban to power in 2021.

This happened in a context where the US administration had been engaged in intense negotiations with the Taliban since 2018, which culminated in an agreement between the Taliban and the Trump administration in February 2020, followed by the intra-Afghan negotiations in September 2020. Nevertheless, while the US–Taliban agreement gave political legitimacy to the Taliban, subsequent developments related to it did not lead to a political settlement. In mid-2021, the withdrawal of US troops paved the way for a military takeover by the Taliban.

Over the last four decades, during every regime transition, which has often involved a quick agreement to lead to the next phase,[3] the question of addressing past atrocities has been largely ignored by the new leaders. However, in the aftermath of the Taliban regime post-2001, which led to the Bonn Agreement (2001) and a transitional government, a small window of opportunity opened up that led many Afghans to believe that war and their miseries would end and some form of justice and accountability would prevail (Rubin 2003). The

2 *Mujahideen*, literally holy warriors or those who fight *jihad*, was the term commonly used to refer to various factions of the Islamic groups. However, the term also applied to non-Islamist, even secular, freedom fighters during the national uprising against the Soviet occupation. Today, the (ex-)secular freedom fighters no longer label themselves as such. Rather, 'mujahideen' has come to be associated with those who fought the Soviets on religious grounds and committed serious human rights violations during the civil war of 1992–1996.

3 As an example, the 1988 Geneva Accords, which defined the Soviet conditions of withdrawal from Afghanistan, had no references to addressing past crimes (Vigier 2009, 5). On the contrary, an amnesty, adopted by the Supreme Soviet, excluded any possibilities of prosecutions of its forces for 'deliberate or indiscriminate attacks against Afghan civilians' (Gossman 2006, 258).

current chapter, therefore, will largely focus on this phase of transition that demonstrates the different dynamics and intentionality as regards to the transitional justice project in Afghanistan.

The Bonn Agreement

The 2001 Bonn Agreement was a defining moment in a period of transition from Taliban rule to what many hoped would be a peaceful future. Following the overthrow of the Taliban regime at the end of 2001, UN-sponsored talks[4] were held in Bonn, Germany, involving many prominent Afghan personalities and parties as well as regional and international powers in an attempt to establish an interim administration. However, unlike the Dayton Agreement or the El Salvador Peace Accords, which involved all sides of the armed conflict in an effort to end the war, the Bonn Agreement excluded the Taliban, an important party to the conflict, from the negotiations table. While the negotiations were ongoing, the United States was still bombarding Taliban strongholds in the South and South-East of the country (Rubin 2003). As such, the Bonn Agreement was not a peace agreement (Gossman 2006; Rubin 2003; Wisner 2008).

The Bonn Agreement was controversial with regard to addressing questions of justice for past war crimes. In fact, the issue came up only once during the negotiations (Gossman and Kouvo 2013). In an attempt to secure an agreement between different factions, some of whom were accused of gross human rights violations, the UN-lead negotiators avoided the inclusion of any references to the investigation of past human rights violations and war crimes (Rubin 2003). The Bonn Agreement did not contain many standard parts of UN-mediated peace accords, such as disarmament, demobilisation, or reintegration, nor did it address the underlying causes and consequences of the conflict or their effects on Afghan war victims (Winterbotham 2010). Although the United Nations initially had included a paragraph on disarmament, demobilisation, and reintegration in the draft agreement, prominent Mujahideen leaders fiercely objected to it and insisted on its removal (Rubin 2003). Significantly, the Afghan signatories to the agreement included a number of alleged perpetrators of human rights violations, which set the stage for an entrenched culture of impunity to pursue ethnic, factional, and economic interests in the years to come (Mani 2003). The Bonn Agreement did not contain any references to transitional justice apart from the establishment of the Human Rights Commission, 'whose mandate was understood, though not stated, to include coping with past as well as current abuses' (Rubin 2003, 571). Moreover, the initial draft included a paragraph forbidding an amnesty, which the participating warlords also resisted (Rubin 2003); they eventually had it replaced with one that read:

4 Security Council Resolution 1386 (2001).

> Expressing their appreciation to the Afghan mujahidin who, over the years, have defended the independence, territorial integrity and national unity of the country and have played a major role in the struggle against terrorism and oppression, and whose sacrifice has now made them both heroes of jihad and champions of peace, stability and reconstruction of their beloved homeland, Afghanistan.
>
> (UN 2001, para. 6)

The future political and security developments since the Bonn Conference painfully proved Mr Lakhdar Brahimi, the UN special envoy to Afghanistan and a prominent architect of the Bonn Conference, who had repeatedly warned of the danger of a blanket amnesty.

The Action Plan for Peace, Reconciliation and Justice

The most important achievement of the Bonn Agreement with regard to human rights was the establishment of the Afghanistan Independent Human Rights Commission (AIHRC), which played an important role in creating a roadmap for transitional justice in Afghanistan. A Presidential Decree mandated the AIHRC to carry out a national consultation and to propose a 'national strategy for transitional justice and for addressing the abuses of the past' (Government of the Islamic Republic of Afghanistan et al. 2005, 1). The AIHRC conducted consultations among 6,000 participants, including Afghan refugees in Pakistan and Iran, over the course of eight months to gauge citizens' perceptions of justice and dealing with gross human rights violations of the past. The result of the consultation was published in a groundbreaking 75-page document entitled 'A Call for Justice'. The report stated: 'To date, [the] past has not been confronted. This report seeks to explore whether the people of Afghanistan want this to be addressed, and if so, how' (AIHRC 2005, 5). The report established that 69% of the population identified themselves or a close relative as direct victims of human rights violations, and that 45% of the population demanded immediate accountability in the form of trials, and 76.4% believed that trials would help to safeguard peace and security. A majority of respondents (61%), moreover, rejected amnesties for confessions. While 54% of the respondents believed in the culpability of external powers in the country's decades-long violence, including the former Soviet Union, the United States, and neighbouring Pakistan and Iran, 30% were not able to identify the culprit and in general no specific period of different phases of conflict stood out as the worst (ibid., 8–22).

The impact of 'A Call for Justice' was instrumental in setting the stage for the next step, the drafting of the Action Plan for Peace, Reconciliation and Justice (the Action Plan) by the President's Office, the AIHRC, and the UN Assistant Mission to Afghanistan (UNAMA). In December 2005, the Cabinet 'narrowly adopted' it (Winterbotham 2010, 7). The Action Plan identified five key components of justice and reconciliation for Afghanistan, including truth-seeking, symbolic measures, accountability mechanisms involving vetting procedures, institutional reform, and reconciliation. Each key action area entailed different sub-actions allocated to the leadership of a particular government or state agency, the AIHRC, or the international community. The Action Plan emphatically rejected amnesty provisions, stating that neither Islam nor international law allows amnesty for gross violations of human rights, including crimes against humanity. At the same time, the Action Plan promoted a 'culture of forgiveness, affection, brotherhood and sisterhood' as well as strengthening solidarity between the 'country's today and tomorrow generation' as its principal foundation (Government of the Islamic Republic of Afghanistan and Others 2005, 2). While stressing the adoption of measures on the return and reintegration of warring groups in the society, the Action Plan called for 'bold action' against war crimes, crimes against humanity, and genocide as 'a universally accepted moral principle' (ibid.).

Despite being an important document containing significant measures in theory, in practice very little was achieved before the three-year timeline mandate of the Action Plan expired in March 2009 (Winterbotham 2010). This was mainly due to fierce opposition from both within the previous Afghan government and parliament as well as among the donors (Gossman and Kouvo 2013). In the first place, it took President Karzai over a year to officially launch the Action Plan on December 10, 2006, because of significant opposition from his government, including some of his trusted advisors (Winterbotham 2010). A second fierce opposition came from within the Afghan parliament and important sectors of the administration. In March 2007, the parliament passed the National Reconciliation, General Amnesty and National Stability Law (the Amnesty Law) that ensured a blanket amnesty for all perpetrators of human rights abuses of the past regimes, thus turning impunity into law (Kouvo 2010). A modified version was eventually published in the official gazette in 2009. Many national and international human rights organisations condemned the Law, arguing that a blanket amnesty for serious war crimes goes against the standards of international law (International Center for Transitional Justice 2010).

The amnesty law shattered any hope for justice that many Afghans longed to see beyond some small – and mainly symbolic – measures the Action Plan was able to achieve. Moreover, the law further entrenched the culture of impunity and removed virtually all opportunities to legally sanction past and present war crimes. As a result, with well-known perpetrators holding high positions of power, human rights violations continued to be tolerated by the Afghan government and the international community (Wisner 2008), including systematic and widespread land grabbing and other forms of economic state crimes (Saeed and Parmentier 2017). The amnesty law, in particular, demonstrates how an unjust and unaccountable status quo was consolidated as a reaction to the standardised transitional justice measures proposed in the Action Plan by local as well as international political actors. Thus, the transition in 2001 that appeared to 'offer the chance of a break with the past' instead led to two decades that 'replicated patterns of abuse already in place' (Gossman and Kouvo 2013, 49).

Trading Transitional Justice for Stability

This section presents a discussion of how different actors mobilised or resisted transitional justice in Afghanistan. The first part will examine the role of the international community, particularly the United States, in resisting transitional justice initiatives. The second part will shed light on the bottom-up efforts by civil society and victims' groups, supported and enabled by international actors, to keep victims' rights and transitional justice on the agenda.

Understanding the Role of International Political Actors Through a Hegemonic Power Discourse

To understand the role of major international actors, particularly the United States, in relation to the transitional justice process in Afghanistan, one has to examine the issue through the prism of a hegemonic power discourse. When justice demands were so immediate and prevalent among Afghans, as demonstrated by 'A Call for Justice', why were they denied their right to know, to access reparation, and to fair judgement in an era when transitional justice was becoming a norm? As Gossman and Kouvo (2013, 48) note, 'Kabul was burning at the same time when atrocities were committed in Sarajevo, Kigali and Freetown'. Yet only in Afghanistan were justice issues 'completely swept under the carpet' (ibid.). The explanation for this can be sought in a geopolitical framework where the interest of US-led coalition forces triumphed over justice concerns (also see Hansen in this volume). In pursuing its policy to fight against Al-Qaeda and the Taliban, the US-led coalition forces initially and continuously relied on those Afghan factions, often collectively called 'the warlords', who were opposed to the Taliban (Gossman 2006). By backing them militarily, politically, and financially, the United States reinvigorated those warlords who, by 2001, had been militarily defeated and politically relegated to obscurity. Interestingly, while some factional commanders anticipated disarmament after the Bonn Conference (ibid.), they instead became entrenched in the power structure 'due to US pressure to include them' (Gossman and Kouvo 2013, 19). As Mani (2003, 22) argues, there was an implicit agreement in the elite political circles among both domestic and international players that it was not the right time to tackle transitional justice's concerns over accountability or recognition, and that, instead domestic and international stability was to be prioritised. This was most obvious with regard to vetting and documentation procedures.

Vetting Mechanisms

As a transitional justice measure, vetting processes are aimed at 'screening public employees or candidates for public employment' in order to ensure that those whose prior conduct, particularly with regard to human rights, is not fully up to the accepted standards are excluded from public office (Duthie 2007, 17). In many post-conflict countries, as Duthie (2007) argues, the main targets of vetting processes are often security and judicial sectors which are deemed to have been implicated in serious atrocities. Where years of war and political violence eroded trust between people and institutions, vetting processes can be a way to rebuild confidence in public institutions. Yet, vetting is a contested mechanism in the transitional justice toolkit, particularly for reforming the security sector (UNDP 2006).

In 2001 Afghanistan was a country where years of war had physically destroyed the country and its institutions, as well as eroded trust in public institutions, especially the judiciary, police, and security services.[5] Despite the manifest need for rebuilding public trust and Key Action 2 on vetting procedures, little was achieved in this regard (Winterbotham 2010). Unlike in Bosnia and Herzegovina, where the 'international regime turned into a quasi protectorate' and the United Nations were provided with powers to 'impose vetting processes on domestic institutions' (Mayer-Rieckh 2007, 210–2011), the international community in Afghanistan remained at best indifferent to this issue and to those of accountability and recognition because it feared disruption. As Wisner (2008, 4) argues, '[t]he international community has also dragged its feet on accountability, fearful that rising instability in the country could spiral into anarchy if it alienates its main allies in the government'. This view was also confirmed in other research (Gossman and Kouvo 2013; Winterbotham 2010), which found that security and peace arguments trumped concerns over accountability and recognition, since many main allies were among those most responsible for gross human rights violations.

This logic prevailed throughout the transition phase and onwards in Afghanistan. From that point on, at every stage of political development a pattern of not addressing impunity continued (Wisner 2008, 1). For example, during the constitutional Loya Jirga[6] of 2003, a rule existed to prevent those with serious allegations of war crimes and crimes against humanity from participating as delegates. However, this was hardly enforced as UNAMA, and the United States turned a blind eye to the warlords: 'the Loya Jirga represented another moment when US policy interests, fears within UNAMA about not alienating powerful and dangerous political figures, and simply bad

5 As an example, 58% of Afghans responded that they did not trust the country's legal system (AIHRC 2005, 22).

6 Loya Jirga is a traditional Afghan Grand Council where delegates from different parts of the country come together to decide on important issues of national interest such as the country's constitution.

management discredited the political process' (Gossman 2006, 264). The passionate call of Malalai Joya, a young female delegate at the Loya Jirga, who exposed the presence of the warlords in the assembly, boldly sitting in the first row against all legality and dignity, once again fell on deaf ears, and she was abruptly silenced by the chairman Sigbatullah Mojadidi. Such incidents continued during the presidential and parliamentary elections, where the power grip of warlords was further tightened to the extent that they ended up controlling the parliament and eventually passing the amnesty law.[7] It is clear that in this case of contested government, transitional justice was heavily resisted by the most powerful, precisely because of its promise of accountability, recognition, and disruption. This is not only true regarding vetting processes, but also in relation to documentation.

Documentation

The documentation of past violations is considered another important component of transitional justice which often takes place within the official mandate of a truth commission. However, when an official inquiry is not possible – often due to the lack of political will – unofficial documentation can be vital to prepare the ground for a future formal transitional justice process. In Guatemala, for example, the publication by the Catholic Church of an extensive report about the decades of political violence was essential for the subsequent work of the UN-sanctioned Historical Clarification Commission (Hayner 2002, 47). Furthermore, preserving mass graves and documenting war crimes and crimes against humanity is an important step in preventing the possibility of denial by officials.

In Afghanistan, the 2005 Action Plan established a mandate for truth-seeking and documentation, as stated in its Key Action 3 (Government of the Islamic Republic of Afghanistan et al. 2005):

> Through truth-seeking and documentation, evaluate the facts of the conflicts and injustices happened in the past, establish accountability and put an end to the continued state of impunity through acknowledging the oppression and expressing the belief in justice, while supporting reconciliation and recognizing that there are multiple truths.

The AIHRC was mandated to initiate truth-seeking and documentation mechanisms in consultation with civil society, academia, religious leaders, media, and other sectors of society. Moreover, the Office of the High Commissioner

7 Even UN officials who defended the results of the Loya Jirga admitted a year later that a good opportunity to weaken the grip of warlords was 'squandered for the sake of short term stability' (Gossman 2006).

for Human Rights (OHCHR) was also appointed as an additional support to this initiative, in particular to introduce the experiences of other countries to Afghanistan.

Some important documentation projects have been accomplished in Afghanistan. The most noteworthy are the ones by the AIHRC (2005), The Afghanistan Justice Project (2005), and the OHCHR, all of which have mapped Afghanistan's 1978–2001 human rights violations. Apart from these, Human Rights Watch (2005) and a number of local civil society and media outlets have been conducting documentation projects based on interviews with victims and survivors. Another important initiative has been carried out by Physicians for Human Rights (PHR) to preserve sites of mass graves (Winterbotham 2010).

The importance of such projects can hardly be overestimated, particularly in a multifaceted conflict such as that of Afghanistan. Although the discussion about the establishment of a truth commission never gained momentum,[8] even at a time when transitional justice was officially on the agenda, the demand for seeking truth was very high among Afghans. According to 'A Call for Justice', 95% of the people interviewed believed the documentation of wartime violations was important for the establishment of justice (Afghanistan Independent Human Rights Commission 2005). Despite such a high desire for truth-seeking and documentation, the reports of the projects mentioned above were never made publicly available.

This, too, can be explained in a hegemonic power discourse framework where security and stability considerations pushed off the table truth-seeking and documentation efforts aimed at accountability and recognition. Various incidents exist to illustrate this point. For example, a 300-page OHCHR report mapping Afghanistan's major human rights violations of the past decades was never released. According to Gossman (2006, 270), this was primarily due to security and political reasons:

> UNAMA pressed the High Commissioner, Louise Arbour, not to make it public. UNAMA officials argued that a public release would endanger UN staff, and complicate negotiations surrounding the planned demobilization of several powerful militias, including one loyal to [Abudulrab Rasul] Sayyaf.

Furthermore, certain countries, particularly the United States, used their power to block the release (Gossman 2006). An important example is Dasht-i Leili, a location in northern Afghanistan, where several 'sites visited by PHR

8 Apart from the suggestion by the UN Special Rapporteur, Asma Jahangir, to establish an independent commission of inquiry, no other serious proposal was made. Hayner (2002, 266–267) mentions in her concluding remarks that in 2001 there were discussions about the possibility of a truth commission for Afghanistan.

teams contained human remains consistent with their designation as possible gravesites' (Physicians for Human Rights 2008, 15). Several sources linked these findings to the disappearance of around 2,000 Afghan and Pakistani Taliban prisoners who had been captured by the Northern Alliance[9] forces that were then 'receiving assistance from the US Special Forces and CIA operatives' (Rubin 2003, 574). Despite several requests by PHR for a complete forensic investigation, however, an official exhumation was never carried out. This was due to the lack of political will, a view also confirmed by Pierre Prosper, a former US ambassador for war crime issues (Winterbotham 2010, 23–24). First, the Bush administration did not favour an investigation fearing that it could undermine Karzai's government and cause instability. Furthermore, the chief suspect, General Rashid Dostum, was on the CIA payroll at the time, and his militia worked closely with the US Special Forces (Risen 2021). Hence, the US administration was potentially concerned that exhumation could hint at its own complicity (Rubin 2003). As the issue hit the Western media and as the PHR repeatedly demanded an investigation, the Obama administration expressed an initial interest in an inquiry (BBC News 2009).

As Hayner (2002) argues, the international community is often crucial for encouraging and supporting truth-seeking and documentation efforts. This is truer in *de facto* occupied territories, where former perpetrators continue to hold positions of power. However, in Afghanistan, despite a strong public yearning for truth-seeking, the international community actively cooperated with the Karzai government to quietly shelve attempts at accountability and recognition because these could be too disruptive.[10]

Bottom-Up Responses

Against this background, civil society organisations (CSOs) nevertheless developed several bottom-up transitional justice initiatives that continued to the last days before the return of the Taliban in the summer of 2021. Through 'demanding accountability, focusing on documentation, and mobilizing victims' (Kouvo 2009, 2), civil society sought to mobilise transitional justice's disruptive potential and to keep victims' rights on the agenda. The most prominent of such organisations is the Afghanistan Human Rights and Democracy Organization (AHRDO), which was established as a small group of committed individuals in Kabul in 2009. Inspired by Paolo Freire's pedagogy of the oppressed and Augusto Boal's theatre of the oppressed, AHRDO has been

9 The Northern Alliance are those Afghan parties who in the 1990s joined ranks to fight the Taliban, particularly in northern Afghanistan. In 2001, they were among the closest US allies aiming to topple the Taliban regime.

10 This also included Lakhdar Brahimi, the then head of UNAMA, who had rejected both an investigation into the Dash-e Laili incident and Asma Jahangir's proposal for establishing a truth commission (Gossman and Kuovo 2013).

engaged with questions of justice, human rights, victims' rights, and democracy from the bottom up and across different regions in Afghanistan (Saeed 2015). In February 2019, AHRDO's years of persistent and tenacious activism with war victims culminated in the establishment of the Afghanistan Center for Memory and Dialogue. The first of its kind, the Center housed 'memory boxes' of war victims from various phases of violent conflicts in Afghanistan and provided a space where war victims, CSOs, scholars, and other actors came together to preserve memory, promote accountability, and foster peace.

Another groundbreaking initiative of AHRDO was the establishment of the National Victims' Network, inaugurated on December 10, 2020. With a particular focus on the last 20 years, the Network represented victims from various phases of the Afghan conflict, who were harmed by the Afghan government, the Taliban, other insurgent groups, and international security forces. During 42 years of conflict, it was the first time that a national network of war victims was established, particularly at a critical juncture of intra-Afghan peace negotiations. The main purpose of the Network was to ensure representation of war victims at the peace talks and advocacy for a victim-centred justice which recognises the harm done to victims. The Network's demands for victims' representation (Arifi 2020) were further strengthened by the AIHRC's new leadership, which called persistently for the inclusion of victims' rights and victims-centred justice in the Afghan peace process (Afghanistan Independent Human Rights Commission 2021).

In addition to the initiatives undertaken by AHRDO and the AIHRC, since 2009 the Transitional Justice Coordination Group has existed as an umbrella organisation of civil society groups to demand accountability and strengthen advocacy and coordination among different organisations. Apart from issuing statements on various occasions and organising national conferences, one of the most important contributions of the Coordination Group has been the collection of 699 individual and collective applications of war victims to the International Criminal Court. These served as a crucial ground for the prosecutor in her 2017 decision to open an investigation into war crimes and crimes against humanity committed in Afghanistan since May 2003 (Saeed 2019). Such bottom-up initiatives were not only crucial for victims' rights advocacy and mobilisation, but they were also sending a strong message to the Afghan government and the international community that the demand for justice could not be ignored and forgotten.

While certain international actors, as discussed above, played a role in suspending the more standardised transitional justice initiatives, others have either actively supported Afghan civil society or have themselves pursued initiatives. For example, the Swedish International Development Cooperation Agency, the Open Society Foundation, and the International Center for Transitional Justice have provided financial and technical assistance to local civil society actors. Initiatives undertaken by international organisations include the establishment of a documentation centre for war crimes in Afghanistan at the

American University in Washington DC, a national directory of mass graves created by Physicians for Human Rights, and a series of war crimes documentaries made by the Institute for War and Peace Reporting (Gossman and Kouvo 2013). These initiatives suggest that, depending on the intentions of the actors, transitional justice can be considered highly relevant also in contexts where there is no paradigmatic transition, precisely because it can keep issues of accountability and recognition on the agenda, including in ways that are potentially disruptive of the status quo. Interestingly, some of these projects received funding from the US government, despite the country's resistance to transitional justice in Afghanistan (ibid.).

Transnational Transitional Justice

When the implementation of formal transitional justice is resisted in a given country, and that country has significant diaspora communities, transnational transitional justice could be a logical path to explore. This could be conceptualised in two ways.

First, we could think more systematically about the role of diaspora communities in pursuing accountability, recognition, and disruption in their home countries (also see Aboueldahab, and Herremans and Bellintani in this volume). The relationship between transitional justice and diaspora communities has lately gained some attention from human rights activists and transitional justice scholars and practitioners (Koinova and Karabegović 2020; Mefreh 2020). The diaspora community can contribute towards transitional justice by taking initiatives to demand accountability for war crimes, especially when it is difficult and risky to do so inside the country. As an example, the Geneva-based Committee for Justice, established in 2015 by a group of diaspora human rights advocates, aims to support victims of human rights violations in the Middle East and North Africa by assisting initiatives to counter impunity and provide justice to victims (Mefreh 2020). Similarly, a group of Syrian refugees who were either relatives of or victims of torture and enforced disappearance formed the Caesar Families Association in Berlin in 2018.[11] Together with four other groups, this Association formulated the Truth and Justice Charter in February 2021, which advocates for a victim-centred approach in the peace process and in transitional justice.[12] Importantly, through their persistent struggle for justice and supported by European NGOs, Syrian refugees played a significant role in bringing to trial two Syrian perpetrators before courts in Germany applying universal jurisdiction laws.

With over 6 million people abroad, Afghanistan has the second-largest diaspora population globally, which can play an important role in furthering

11 www.caesarfamilies.org/

12 www.impunitywatch.org/truth-and-justice-charter-syria

transitional justice measures. This role has gained further momentum with the mass departure, evacuation, and exile of many human rights and civil society activists and journalists, who played an important role in the bottom-up initiatives inside Afghanistan. In addition to this new diaspora following the 2021 Taliban takeover, the older Afghan diaspora has also undertaken certain initiatives. In Europe, for example, the latter diaspora established the Afghanistan Victims' Rights Foundation, which aims to keep the issue of justice for war victims alive. With more resources and investment, the Foundation could engage more systematically and effectively in supporting initiatives aimed at accountability and recognition, while also learning from other diaspora communities, such as Syrians. Furthermore, the 'new' and the 'old' Afghan diaspora can join forces to interact on such initiatives to mutually reinforce, share, and learn from each other.

Second, diaspora communities escaping from violent conflicts could be seen as victims who deserve to be included in transitional justice initiatives, even if they are no longer in their home countries. Displaced populations, including refugees, are in a state of transition and should be entitled to demand justice for past grievances. A political transition typically refers to a regime change and the establishment of a new legal framework over a certain territory. In the personal transition of a refugee escaping persecution, there is similarly a change of regime and jurisdiction, but this happens spatially rather than temporally. The situation of refugees seeking justice for the crimes of the past is somewhat similar to the challenges faced by the victims of past crimes within their own country after partial political transitions, of which Afghanistan prior to the Taliban return was a case. The experiences of transitional justice practitioners in situations of blocked or partial political transitions may offer important clues for building transnational justice initiatives that move forward the demands of refugees in Western countries. Some transitional justice tools and methods may be suitable for being transposed in trying to address refugees' demands for accountability and recognition, thus extending the scope of transitional justice itself.

Since transitional justice seeks to recognise and address legacies of massive human rights violations and help societies move forward, refugees are an obvious constituency. Even if transitional justice measures are typically applied within the confines of a given country, considering the rapid growth in displacement, it is reasonable to argue that some transitional justice measures should also be applied transnationally. Beyond some individual cases, transitional justice has not developed a mechanism to address the legacy of past crimes and demand justice in a refugee's life. Once granted asylum abroad, refugees seem to disappear from transitional justice's narrative of victim-centredness. Asylum and ancillary services of protection and integration in the new country could arguably be seen as a sort of indirect reparation provided by the host country, yet this does not address any accountability concerns. However, refugees often carry with them grievances related to their past experiences that may require special measures, above and beyond humanitarian support.

Transitional justice scholars and activists could advocate for a number of proactive measures to be included in the life of conflict-affected diaspora communities. For example, truth-telling initiatives could also be undertaken in host countries. The right to truth is an inalienable right for victims of gross human rights violations that includes knowledge about the causes of abuse and violence, the identity of perpetrators, and the whereabouts of the forcibly displaced or disappeared (ECOSOC 2006). Truth-telling could arguably play an important role in the host country as a measure of acknowledgement and host community insights into the circumstances of refugees. Particularly considering the current volatile political situation in relation to the question of refugees, truth-telling initiatives could potentially diminish certain socio-political tensions in host countries.

Another area where transitional justice could contribute is rehabilitation and psychosocial support to war victims in the host country. Rehabilitation is considered an important form of reparation in transitional justice discourse and practice. However, it has so far primarily been implemented in victims' countries of origin. This chapter proposes its application also in their host countries, premising it on the basis that many refugees after all are war victims in need of special support mechanisms and approaches similar to those devised in transitional justice context. Such mechanisms could provide a form of recognition and accountability.

Conclusion

Through the case study of Afghanistan, this chapter has demonstrated the extent to which the role of internal political actors has been shaped primarily by external ones. This was as evident in the aftermath of the events of September 11, 2001, when the US-led international community deployed troops to Afghanistan, as it is today with the Taliban's return to power.

Ongoing war and human rights violations, impunity, entrenched and systematic corruption, as well as political illegitimacy have characterised Afghanistan over the last two decades. This chapter maintains that one important reason for such failure is the lack of implementation of transitional justice mechanisms during the transition in early 2000. The United States and their allies deployed their hegemonic power in an attempt to persuade the Afghans – and themselves – that accountability was a luxury that could be postponed to brighter days. The present was to be left to backroom deals (Gossman 2006) with the same warlords that had terrorised the country, arguing that stability will bring justice in due time. The facts on the ground have proven this assumption wrong. This strategic mistake sits at the core of the failure of the hegemonic project for state-building in Afghanistan, where both domestic and international legitimacy has largely failed. A failure that is increasingly hurting the interests of the United States itself, and one which helped pave the return of the Taliban.

Afghanistan is a good example to show that transitional justice, despite its current status as a 'norm', is not a process that can be taken for granted in post-conflict situations. The nexus between the 'prevailing dynamics of transitional justice' and politics, in particular in an international context, should not be underestimated, an issue that the existing scholarship has not yet captured adequately (Teitel 2003, 85).

Finally, what becomes ever more evident day by day in Afghanistan's political development is the reality that without dealing with past atrocities, without recognising the wounds of 70% of its population, the future is more likely to lead to further revenge and bloodshed; as Mamdani (1996, 23) warns: 'The more justice is delayed, the more people will take matters into their own hands—the more revenge will be the order of the day'. Realising this danger, the Afghan civil society and victims' rights groups engaged in bottom-up initiatives with little resources and at the expense of their own lives to state that a policy of bygones be bygones is morally and politically wrong (Méndez 1997). The return of the Taliban to power has shifted the attention of Afghans and international community towards the humanitarian crisis currently unfolding in Afghanistan. While it is vital to take prompt and concerted action to avoid disaster and further human rights violations, it is equally critical to ensure that victims of Afghanistan's war receive justice (Saeed 2021). After all, the bulk of the same war victims are once again being victimised. We can only hope to break the cycle of violence and the perpetuation of human rights violations by bringing justice to war victims, who make up about 70% of the population, and demanding accountability from national and international perpetrators.

References

Afghanistan Independent Human Rights Commission (2005) 'A Call for Justice: A National Consultation on past Human Rights Violation in Afghanistan'. Available at: http://www.refworld.org/pdfid/47fdfad50.pdf.

—— (2021) 'Second Round of Intra-Afghan Peace Talks: AIHRC's Demands from the Negotiating Parties'. [online]. Available from: https://www.aihrc.org.af/home/press_release/9050.

Arifi, A. (2020) 'قربانیان جنگ باید طرف سوم مذاکرات صلح باشند [War Victims Must Participate as a Third Party to Peace Negotiations]. روزنامه اطلاعات روز'. Available at: https://www.etilaatroz.com/115008/victims-of-war-must-be-third-party-in-peace-negotiations/.

Arrighi, G. (2007) *Adam Smith in Beijing: Lineages of the Twenty-First Century*. London: Verso.

BBC News (2009) 'Obama "Examining Afghan Killings" '. 13 July. Available at: http://news.bbc.co.uk/2/hi/8147383.stm.

BBC Persian (2018) 'شمار مهاجران افغان به 'شش میلیون رسیده است' [The Number of Afghan Refugees "Reaching Six Million"]'. Available at: https://www .bbc .com /persian /afghanistan-44532137.

Duthie, R. (2007) 'Introduction'. In: R.A. Mayer and P. de Greiff, eds. *Justice as Prevention: Vetting Public Employees in Transitional Societies*. New York: Social Science Research Council.

ECOSOC (2006) *Promotion and Protection of Human Rights: Study on the Right to the Truth*. Commission on Human Rights. E/CN.4/2006/91, 8 February. New York: United Nations.

Gossman, P. (2006) 'Truth, Justice and Stability in Afghanistan'. In: N. Roht-Arriaza and J. Mariezcurrena, eds. *Transitional Justice in the Twenty-First Century: Beyond Truth Versus Justice* (pp. 255–277). Cambridge: Cambridge University Press.

Gossman, P. and S. Kouvo (2013) *Tell Us How This Ends: Transitional Justice and Prospects for Peace in Afghanistan*. Kabul: Afghanistan Analysts Network.

Government of the Islamic Republic of Afghanistan and Others (2005) 'Peace, Reconciliation and Justice in Afghanistan: Action Plan of the Government of the Islamic Republic of Afghanistan'. Retrieved from: http://www.aihrc.org.af/media/files/Reports/Thematic%20reports/Action_Pln_Gov_Af.pdf.

Hayner, P.B. (2002) *Unspeakable Truths: Confronting State Terror and Atrocity*. 1st ed. London and New York: Routledge.

Human Rights Watch (2005) 'Blood-Stained Hands Past Atrocities in Kabul and Afghanistan's Legacy of Impunity.' 6 July. Available at: https://www.hrw.org/report/2005/07/07/blood-stained-hands/past-atrocities-kabul-and-afghanistans-legacy-impunity.

International Center for Transitional Justice (2010) 'ICTJ Statement on Afghanistan Amnesty Law'. 17 February. Available from: http://www.ictj.org/en/news/features/3456.html.

Koinova, M. and D. Karabegović (2020) *Diaspora Mobilizations for Transitional Justice*. London and New York: Routledge.

Kouvo, S. (2009) 'Transitional Justice in the Context of Ongoing Conflict: The Case of Afghanistan'. September. Available at: https://www.ictj.org/publication/transitional-justice-context-ongoing-conflict-case-afghanistan.

—— (2010) *After Two Years in Legal Limbo: A First Glance at the Approved 'Amnesty Law'*. 22 February. Kabul: Afghanistan Analyst Network.

Mamdani, M. (1996) 'Reconciliation Without Justice.' *Southern African Review of Books* 46, 3–5.

Mani, R. (2003) 'Ending Impunity and Building Justice in Afghanistan.' December. Afghanistan Research and Evaluation Unit. Available at: http://unpan1.un.org/intradoc/groups/public/documents/APCITY/UNPAN016655.pdf.

Mayer–Rieckh, A. (2007) 'Vetting to Prevent future Abuses: Reforming the Police, Courts, and Prosecutor's Offices in Bosnia and Herzegovina'. In: P. de Greiff, ed. *Justice as Prevention: Vetting Public Employees in Transitional Societies* (pp. 180–220). New York: Social Science Research Council.

Mefreh, A. (2020) 'Combatting Injustice from Abroad: The Diaspora's Role in Transitional Justice in Egypt'. Brookings Doha Center. 24 November. Available at: https://www.brookings.edu/opinions/combatting-injustice-from-abroad-the-diasporas-role-in-transitional-justice-in-egypt/.

Méndez, J. (1997) 'In Defense of Transitional Justice'. In: A.J. McAdams, ed. *Transitional Justice and the Rule of Law in New Democracies* (pp. 1–26). Notre Dame: University of Notre Dame Press.

Physicians for Human Rights (2008) 'Preliminary Assessment of Alleged Mass Gravesites in the Area of Mazar-I-Sharif, Afghanistan: January 16–21 and February 7–14'. Available from: https://s3.amazonaws.com/PHR_other/afghanistan-mass-grave/prelim-assess-afghanistan2002-amend2008.pdf.

Risen, J. (2021) 'A War's Epitaph: For Two Decades, Americans Told One Lie After Another About What They Were Doing in Afghanistan'. The Intercept, 26 August. Available at: https://theintercept.com/2021/08/26/afghanistan-america-failures/.

Rubin, B.R. (2003) 'Transitional Justice and Human Rights in Afghanistan'. *International Affairs* 79(3), 567–581.

Saeed, H. (2015) 'Empowering Unheard Voices through "Theatre of the Oppressed": Reflections on the Legislative Theatre Project for Women in Afghanistan'. *Journal of Human Rights Practice* 7(2), 299–326.

—— (2019) 'A Slap in the Face of Justice: The ICC and Afghanistan'. Security Praxis, 8 May. Available from: https://securitypraxis.eu/afghanistan-icc/.

—— (2021) 'What Happens to the Victims of Afghanistan's War?' Inkstick, 24 May. Available from: https://inkstickmedia.com/what-happens-to-the-victims-of-afghanistans-war/.

Saeed, H. and S. Parmentier (2017) 'When Rabbits are in Charge of Carrots: Land Grabbing, Transitional Justice and Economic-State Crime in Afghanistan'. *State Crime Journal* 6(1), 13–36.

Strohmeyer, H. (2001) 'Making Multilateral Interventions Work: The U.N. and the Creation of Transitional Justice Systems in Kosovo and East Timor'. *The Fletcher Forum of World Affairs* 25(2), 107–128.

Teitel, R. (2003) 'Transitional Justice Genealogy'. *Harvard Human Rights Journal* 16, 1669–95.

The Afghanistan Justice Project (2005) Casting Shadows: War Crimes and Crimes against Humanity, 1978–2001. Available at: https://www.opensocietyfoundations.org/reports/casting-shadows-war-crimes-and-crimes-against-humanity-1978-2001.

UN (2001) 'Agreement on Provisional Arrangements in Afghanistan Pending the Re-establishment of Permanent Government Institutions'. 5 December. New York: United Nations. Retrieved from: https://ihl-databases.icrc.org/ihl-nat/a24d1cf3344e99934125673e00508142/4ef7a08878a00fe5c12571140032e471/$FILE/BONN%20AGREEMENT.pdf

UNOCHA (2020) 'Afghanisan: COVID-19 Multi-sectoral Response'. 22 April. Kabul: UNOCHA Afghanistan. Available at: https://www.humanitarianresponse.info/sites/www.humanitarianresponse.info/files/documents/files/covid_sitrep1_final.pdf.

UNDP (2006) *Vetting Public Employees in Post-conflict Settings: Operational Guidelines*. New York: UN Development Programme Bureau for Crisis Prevention and Recovery.

Vigier, C. (2009) *Conflict Assessment Afghanistan*. February. Philadelphia: American Friends Service Committee. Available at: https://www.afsc.org/sites/afsc.civicactions.net/files/documents/Afghanistan%20-%20Conflict%20Assessment.pdf.

Winterbotham, E. (2010) 'The State of Transitional Justice in Afghanistan: Actors, Approaches and Challenges'. Discussion paper, April. Afghanistan Research and Evaluation Unit. Available at: http://www.areu.org.af/index.php?option=com_docman&Itemid=26&task=doc_download&gid=760.

Wisner, M. (2008) 'Is Time Ripe for Transitional Justice in Afghanistan?' Al Nakhlah: The Fletcher School Online Journal for Southwest Asia and Islamic Civilization (fall). Available at: https://www.ciaonet.org/attachments/10678/uploads.

Chapter 5

Unable to See the Forest for the Trees

Transitional Justice and the United States of America

Brianne McGonigle Leyh

Introduction

In 2020, the United States (US) witnessed the greatest civil unrest the country had seen in decades, largely in response to the rising number of deaths of unarmed Black Americans at the hands of police (National Public Radio 2020). Protesters carried banners calling for justice and demanding change. A June 2020 poll showed that 76% of Americans considered racism and discrimination a 'big problem' – a significant 26% increase from 2015 (Monmouth University Polling Institute 2020). Given that Trump had run both his presidential campaigns on 'often racist and xenophobic' platforms (Sadat 2017), it is little surprise that the racial divisions of the country were put on full show leading up to the 2020 presidential elections. Nevertheless, the challenges facing the country surrounding race did not begin under the Trump administration but rather evidences the country's long history of racism and discrimination (Kendi 2016). What the recent protests made clear is that the United States has never fully grappled with or addressed its exploitative, violent, and traumatic past.

This failure to comprehensively address the past has contributed in many ways to feelings of disillusionment, anger, and frustration on the part of communities who have felt the brunt of systematic discrimination and violence. Demands for accountability, truth, reparation, and change have been continuous, though disjointed, and progress has been slow. Arguably, the United States could benefit from applying the frame of transitional justice to help in transforming its social and legal institutions. The field of transitional justice has evolved significantly over the last few decades, shifting in focus from 'transitions to democracy' to 'transitions to peace' and now 'transitions to social justice' (McGonigle Leyh 2017). This new emphasis on addressing, through transitional justice ideas and processes, social justice harms as well as social justice needs and concerns opens up possibilities for the field to become relevant to so-called aparadigmatic contexts. A country like the United States, a consolidated democracy that is neither transitioning from authoritarian to democratic rule nor from a situation of armed conflict to peace, can profit from transitional justice precisely because of its need to address past institutional and structural harms such as systemic racism (Murphy 2020).

DOI: 10.4324/9781003289104-6

First, this chapter lays out how transitioning to social justice can be a useful frame for the US context. This frame offers a clear vision for where the United States needs to transition to (a more socially just society) and a useful operational framework for doing so (the four pillars of transitional justice). The academic discourses and wealth of practices within the transitional justice field also present an opportunity for individuals and communities in the United States to learn from other experiences in order to take steps that could address not only past violence but violence experienced in the here and now. Using the analytical constructs presented in the Introduction to this volume, this chapter expounds upon the disruptive potential of various initiatives and the intentionality and responses surrounding them, employing the so-called pillars of transitional justice for structuring the analysis. Accordingly, this chapter unpacks a sample of varied and fragmented initiatives that have taken shape—both historically and more recently—across the country that could be labelled as transitional justice measures seeking to address past wrongs and social justice concerns. It touches on their standardised or non-standardised nature as well as on their innovative aspects. There are important initiatives being undertaken in response to a wide array of issues, with most of them taking place at the state or local level. However, the challenges facing these initiatives, which differ from the challenges facing post-authoritarian or post-conflict states, are no less daunting and potentially just as disruptive.

The chapter highlights how the decentralised and disjointed legal system of the United States and its geographic size, with its current cultural and political divisions, hinders any effective, holistic transitional justice approach. To overcome these challenges, the federal government would need to take a more prominent role in espousing a coherent and comprehensive plan of action. States and local governments could then better situate their responses within the broader national narrative to facilitate meaningful change. Civil society actors and activists should drive these processes and continue to use their voices, platforms, and strategy tools to demand action for social justice. Without a more coherent narrative, the piecemeal initiatives taking place across the United States will result in the inability to see the forest for the trees. In other words, without a national transitional justice strategy based on calls for change by civil society, too much attention will be paid to sporadic, localised processes without addressing the broader and common issues across the country. A balance between the two needs to be found. The grassroots efforts are significant in many ways, for example, by opening up spaces for local voices to innovatively impact processes that are directly meaningful to local communities. However, without the national narrative (and financial support), responses will likely remain fragmented and have less of an overall impact on social justice across the country.

Should a Transitional Justice Frame Even Apply to the US Context?

Traditionally, scholarship from the field of transitional justice focuses on societies emerging from conflict, authoritarian rule, and widespread human rights abuses (Sharp 2019). The concept of transitional justice is generally premised on the notion that predominantly temporary and backwards-looking processes, which acknowledge and address harms suffered by victims and victim communities, will help bring about more peaceful and democratic societies (Minow 1998). There is a foundational belief in the field that past harms that go unaddressed often fuel future conflict or, at the very least, contribute to growing inequality (Leebaw 2008).

Although definitions vary, the United Nations defines transitional justice as 'the full range of processes and mechanisms associated with a society's attempts to come to terms with a legacy of large-scale past abuses, in order to ensure accountability, serve justice and achieve reconciliation' (UN Security Council 2004, para. 8). The processes include, for instance, domestic and international(ised) trials, truth commissions, historical commissions, reparation programmes, vetting and lustration practices, and other efforts to promote reconciliation and memorialisation. The United Nations has further identified four main 'pillars' of transitional justice: accountability; truth-telling; reparations; and guarantees of non-repetition (UN Secretary-General 2010), which have later been taken up by other larger, institutional actors (African Union 2019; European Union 2015). These pillars do not fully reflect specific mechanisms but rather are meant to emphasise the wide-ranging objectives of transitional justice more generally. Ideally, there will be multiple measures adopted that address each of the pillar's objectives—though perhaps not all at the same time. Moreover, the measures should be context-dependent and the processes inclusive and participatory.

As noted in the Introduction, the field of transitional justice has grown a great deal in the last few decades, expanding to include new situations and contexts. The field has widened from its origins around 'transitions to democracy' (Arthur 2009) to 'transitions to peace' and, more recently, towards 'transitions to social justice' (McGonigle Leyh 2017). After realising that many post-conflict processes fail to fully address the needs and concerns of victims and victim communities, scholars and practitioners argued that transitional justice needed to embrace a more holistic approach; otherwise, it would remain one-dimensional and prove unsuccessful in preventing future conflict (Cahill-Ripley 2014; Lambourne 2009; Laplante 2008; Sharp 2012). They called for an unqualified shift within the field where 'social justice' would be the ultimate objective. Social justice has since become the conceptual umbrella term for a diverse array of concepts, including past violations of economic, social, and cultural rights, the root causes of structural socio-economic violence, marginalisation, and socio-economic concerns of the future (McGonigle Leyh 2019). The inclination to include social justice as a key objective of transitional justice, and using the language of transformation or radical change that addresses structural causes of inequality and violence, has resulted in the application of a transitional justice frame to situations not originally envisioned by scholars and practitioners in the 1980s and 1990s. They have started to use a transitional justice lens to examine so-called stable, democratic societies if those societies have experienced great social and political traumas that have never been adequately dealt with and there is a need to transition to a more socially just society. The discourses around transitional justice provide an operational language for social movements: for change, for transition to something better, and possibly even for a transformation of social, economic, legal, and political institutions.

There are, however, concerns about extending the reach of a transitional justice frame to cover transitions to social justice. Roht-Arriaza (2006, 2) has noted that expanding the scope of 'transitional justice to encompass the building of a just as well as peaceful society may make the effort so broad as to become meaningless'. Other (related) fields may be better suited to address social justice concerns, such as the field of human rights. In the US context, however, human rights on their own are likely not enough (Miller and Redhead 2019). In the United States, in particular, economic, social, and cultural rights have never been fully recognised as Constitutional or human rights applicable in the domestic sphere (Ward and Flowers 2019). A rights-based language may only go so far. Because transitional justice is defined around the establishment of (disruptive) processes and actions, largely shaped around the four pillars of accountability, truth-telling, reparations, and guarantees of non-repetition, a transitional justice framework may be able to offer both a vision of transitioning to a more socially just society and new methods or measures to specifically address the mass victimisation or harms that have occurred. New, inclusive, and participatory structures can be created where the voices of marginalised or oppressed groups can be heard.

What Types of Transitional Justice Measures Have Taken Shape in the United States?

A number of transitional justice-type measures have taken shape in the United States, sometimes even with state or non-state actors intentionally evoking the transitional justice terminology in their set-up or operation. The below section highlights a few relevant initiatives under the umbrella of the four main 'pillars' of transitional justice. In doing so, it becomes possible to view them from the standardised frames while recognising their disruptive potential and (often) non-standardised setting in the US context. Given the limitations of this chapter, it does not cover all of the initiatives taking shape, but the examples touched upon give a general idea of the situation in the United States. Each sub-section describes and unpacks some of the intentions (or lack thereof) around the initiatives, as well as comments upon the responses to these intentions with special attention paid to time, actors involved, and wider socio-political challenges.

Accountability – Prosecuting Police Violence

Of the range of accountability measures falling under the accountability pillar, criminal justice or retributive processes are often the most popular type of response demanded by victims of serious human rights abuses (McGonigle Leyh 2016). Retributive justice theories stress the link between punishment and moral wrongdoing (Heikkilä 2004). Through criminal accountability and punishment, retribution communicates a society's disapproval of the criminal act and the responsible individual. There is an effort to individualise responsibility, curtailing judgements of collective guilt (Leebaw 2008). It has the potential to express the message that no individual is above the law (Orentlicher 1991).

Recourse to the criminal justice paradigm is a standardised measure within transitional justice scholarship, and there seems to be support for such an approach in the US context for situations of excessive police violence. Prominent social justice movements, like Black Lives Matter (BLM), regularly call for greater police accountability and have made justice reform a key part of their work. A 2020 AP-NORC (2020) opinion poll found that an overwhelming majority of Americans favoured prosecuting officers who use excessive force. Another opinion poll from June 2020 showed that 75% of Americans supported giving civilian oversight boards the power to investigate and discipline officers accused of misconduct (Pew Research Center 2020). And yet, in the United States, prosecuting police officers remains extremely difficult. Under federal law, prosecutors would need to prove beyond a reasonable doubt that a police officer acted willfully to deprive an individual of a federally protected right, such as the right to be free from unreasonable seizure under the Fourth Amendment of the US Constitution.[1] In addition, the prosecutor must show that the force used was objectively unreasonable. This is a very high standard to meet (US Department of Justice 2017), resulting in very few criminal cases being pursued (Morton 2018). There have been various attempts to pass reform legislation to address excessive police violence and provide accountability, but few have been successful (Congressional Research Service 2015).

Beyond the legal obstacles at the federal level, there are also clear political issues involved at the local and state levels. The role played by powerful police unions in fighting reforms is, for example, troubling (Finnegan 2020; Scheiber et al. 2020). But even if changes were made, the individualisation of the criminal justice process also means that the larger institutional structures that contribute to the reoccurrence of excessive police violence may not be adequately addressed. For this and other reasons, scholars have long critiqued retributive justice theories, especially for systemic violence and mass victimisation (Shklar 1963). Nevertheless, trials do have an expressive value (Stahn 2020). They operate as communicative bodies by pronouncing on moral wrongs and producing an official history of the guilt of at least one accused, while underpinning respect for the rule of law (Drumbl 2007). As imperfect

1 See Title 18, US Code, Section 242 (Deprivation of Rights Under Color of Law).

as they are, trials do more than simply adjudicate upon the guilt of an accused. This is why civil society organisations, activists, and other stakeholders have been continuously pushing for legal reforms and a greater number of prosecutions using the standardised language of justice and accountability. Even so, for now, American politicians and prosecutors do not seem prepared to embrace criminal accountability as the appropriate response to excessive police violence used against Black Americans.

Truth-Telling – Community and National Truth Commissions

In contrast with criminal justice processes, scholars have found that truth commissions are especially well suited to delivering on the goals of social justice (McGonigle Leyh 2019; Sandoval 2017). Though definitions vary, truth commissions are generally seen to be officially sanctioned, temporary, non-judicial investigative bodies designed to produce a final report detailing and explaining patterns of violence and abuse, including its causes and its consequences (Hayner 2011). Truth commissions can take, collect, and analyse written and oral statements, hold public hearings, carry out exhumations, and undertake historical/archival research to investigate allegations of wrongdoing (Office of the High Commissioner for Human Rights 2006). More than 40 states, and an even higher number of communities around the world, have adopted truth commissions or truth-telling processes (Aciru 2017; Bakiner 2014).

Unlike South Africa, Peru, Tunisia, or Canada, where truth commissions received greater media and scholarly attention, the few examples of US truth commissions or truth commission-like processes are relatively unknown and either take the form of officially backed commissions or unofficial, civil society-led processes. One of the earliest truth commission-like processes was the Commission on Wartime Relocation and Internment of Civilians. The US Congress created this commission in 1980 to produce an official government study (or report) on the internment of Japanese Americans during the Second World War. The commission was mandated to look at Executive Order 9066 that led to the internment, the underlying issues of racism, and the impact that this had on individuals and their families. The nine-member commission held public hearings in Washington, DC, as well as in nine additional American cities and other locations, receiving testimony from 750 individuals. For many victims, it was the first time they spoke about their experiences. The commission concluded in its report, 'Personal Justice Denied', that internment was not justified by military necessity but was perpetuated by 'race prejudice, war hysteria, and a failure of political leadership' (Nikkei for Civil Rights and Redress Archives 1981). Importantly, the report's recommendations led to the passing of the Civil Liberties Act of 1988, and a related Act in 1992, which formally apologised and provided tax-free compensation payments of 20,000

USD to more than 82,000 Japanese Americans, totalling more than 1.6 billion USD.[2]

In contrast with the nationally-mandated commission on Wartime Relocation and Internment of Civilians, citizens at the grassroots or local level have experimented with other attempts at establishing a truth-telling process. One such example concerns a truth commission that was created by a group of community activists in Greensboro, North Carolina. Citizens created the Greensboro Truth and Reconciliation Commission in 2004 in response to an incident that took place in November 1979 when members of the Ku Klux Klan and the Nazi Party opened fire and attacked a racially mixed group of labour organisers and political activists, murdering five individuals and wounding ten others. After several failed prosecutions, and years of racial tension and continued inequality, community members began to call for a truth commission drawing direct inspiration from the South African model. However, unlike the South African model, the commission did not have government support. Rather, citizens raised funds, agreed on the mandate, and promoted its work.

The Greensboro Commission had seven commissioners who interviewed witnesses and survivors, police officials, former Klansmen and Nazis, and experts. They also held public hearings to listen to fellow community members. In its final report, the commission found that the police had made poor decisions when it came to ensuring the protection and rights of the organisers and that the police and other government representatives deliberately misled the public about the event. They further found that the lack of diversity on the juries contributed to the failed prosecutions. The 500-page report was rejected by the white-majority city council, which at that time only offered a statement of regret (Jovanovic 2012; Souli 2020).

The Greensboro Commission is not widely known within the United States outside of academic circles, but quite significantly at the local level its work has led to further investigations of police discrimination and the installation of a memorial in 2015 (Inwood 2017). And following from the 2020 BLM protests against excessive police violence, in October 2020, the Greensboro City Council voted 7–2 to issue an official apology, acknowledging the failures of the police, and agreeing to annually fund five scholarships in the name of the five murdered activists from 1979 (Green 2020). It took a number of years, but this grassroots attempt to address past racial and social injustice through a disruptive, truth-telling process has resulted in an official

2 US, Civil Liberties Act 1988, 50 USC App. 1989b et seq; see also US Government Archives, Redress Case Files, available at: www.archives.gov/research/japanese-americans/redress, noting that additional funds (5,000 USD) were also paid out to 145 Japanese Latin Americans after a 1996 civil suit filed by four victims in the so-called *Machizuki* case.

apology and forward-looking steps aimed at the reconciliation of community members.

Grassroots activists have pushed for the creation of their own reconciliation and truth-telling processes across different American cities. Unlike in Greensboro, the examples below were able to garner official acceptance at the local level, but they varied significantly in terms of how successful they were at collecting information, producing reports, and seeing concrete results. This highlights the challenges faced by these types of responses. In 2011, a longer-term community truth process called the Boston Busing/Desegregation Project was established to address Boston's systemic racism in its education policies (Boston Project 2012). The Project collects testimonies and other information, facilitates dialogues, and produces reports and action lines for the city to improve its current and future work. Also, in 2011, Detroit established the Metro Detroit Truth and Reconciliation Commission to investigate race-based housing policies and discrimination. However, it had no subpoena powers and commissioners were not paid (Christian 2011). Over a two-year period, it struggled to complete its broad mandate and no official report was made public (Parker 2017). In a more promising example, from February 2013–June 2015, the Maine Wabanaki-State Child Welfare Truth and Reconciliation Commission led a truth-seeking process around child-welfare practices for Maine's Native people (Maine Commission 2015). This commission reviewed state documents and interviewed over 150 individuals. Its work specifically focused on the rehabilitation and healing of Native American peoples. Finally, in 2019, with bipartisan support, Maryland established the Maryland Lynching Truth and Reconciliation Commission. It investigates racially motivated lynchings and holds public hearings to listen to those who are connected to the crimes, either as ancestral victims or perpetrators (Souli 2020).

In many ways, smaller-scale, community or state-driven initiatives like those in Greensboro, Maine, or Maryland have demonstrated that more localised and even grassroots responses can have an impact on key community members. However, the Detroit example shows just how difficult these processes can be to carry out effectively, and they all point to the fact that the localised responses have only limited influence beyond their city or state. A larger, government-backed process at the federal level around violence, racism, and discrimination may be more impactful and meaningful given the widespread and systemic nature of the harms experienced by people of colour in the United States. For this reason, proponents of truth commissions for racial healing are calling for a national truth-telling process to be established (Aboueldahab 2020).

There have been some recent attempts to garner congressional support for two national truth commissions in the 2019–2020 and 2020–2021 terms. The first attempt was a resolution introduced (multiple times) in both the House of Representatives and the Senate for the creation of a Commission on Truth,

Racial Healing, and Transformation.[3] This resolution specifically grounds the US attempt within a broader narrative of global truth-telling and transitional justice. The second is a resolution for a Truth and Healing Commission on Indian Boarding School Policy.[4] Neither of the resolutions have yet made it out of committee discussions. Prior to 2021, in 1997, the closest national response was Bill Clinton's 'One America' initiative that set up a seven-member advisory board, supported by 35 staff, to hold town-hall and congressional meetings, promote community dialogue, and suggest recommendations on race relations such as housing tax credits, scholarships, and money to support civil rights enforcement. While some important steps were taken (Inwood 2017), due to the political scandals at the time surrounding President Clinton, the work of the 4.8 million USD project was largely dismissed (Souli 2020).

Notably, within transitional justice scholarship, truth commissions are generally considered standardised processes due to their increasing popularity and clear relevance to the truth-telling pillar. However, within the US context, they cannot be so easily categorised as standard. It is true that the few initiatives have drawn inspiration from one another, as well as from international examples like South Africa, but in many ways they are unique responses rooted in community demands against failures of the system. As noted by Jovanovic (2012, 49) in her book on the Greensboro process, truth commissions 'can illuminate the shortcomings surrounding the sanctity of legal action'. While the more localised processes are embracing a 'standardised' approach within the field, the local truth-telling processes are in many ways a counter-response to more legalised measures and are not standard at all in the US context. They are focusing on truth, recognition, and social change; even when not immediately resulting in the desired impact, they may have impact years later, as was the case with the Greensboro Commission report. The various local and state initiatives also seem to have had an impact on recent national efforts calling for truth processes. For now, until a national response materialises, perhaps these fragmented, yet specialised, processes can provide scholars and practitioners with insights to inform the creation of more truth-telling initiatives.

Reparations for Slavery, Discrimination, and Other Serious Human Rights Violations

Within the US context, one of the biggest questions in relation to reparations is when and how reparations for slavery and hundreds of years of racial discrimination can take place. Since the emancipation of enslaved people, promises and demands for reparations have always been made but never provided (Coates

3 See H.Con.Res.100, 116th Congress, 2019–2020; S.Con.Res.50, 116th Congress, 2019–2020; H.Con.Res.19, 117th Congress, 2020–2021; S.Con.Res.6, 117th Congress, 2020–2021.

4 See H.R.8420, 116th Congress, 2019–2020.

2014; Kendi 2016). In 2019, and for the first time in over a decade, a House Judiciary subcommittee discussed a bill to create a commission that would have the ability to make recommendations on an official apology and compensation for descendants of enslaved people (US Congress 2019). However, it never went further than discussion. In the current truth commission resolutions submitted before both the House and Senate there are provisions for a reparations protocol to be developed but nothing concrete. For now, the struggle for reparations for historical harms has been more successful locally—at the state, city, or even university level, where community voices have found allies. In June 2021, in response to the lack of any movement at the federal level, California (a state that never formally sanctioned slavery) took steps to create a taskforce to study the harms of slavery and systemic racism, with a view towards providing reparations. Following on from the BLM movement, there is hope that this and other initiatives will provide the impetus for nationally-mandated reparations in the future.

Historically, there are examples of nationally mandated reparation programmes. One example is from the Japanese American Evacuation Claims Act of July 2, 1948. This Act provided compensation to Japanese Americans interned during WWII for losses of real and personal property. Roughly 26,500 claims totalling, on average, 142,000 USD were filed. It was administered by the Justice Department, which awarded a total of 36,974,240 USD. As noted above, the United States later set up reparation processes for individual payments of 20,000 USD to a large portion of Japanese Americans interned. Following the Second World War, the US Congress also set up the Indian Claims Commission to pay compensation to recognised Native American tribes for land that had been seized by the government. The fact that they listened to tribal leaders was significant on many levels, but the process was far from ideal. The commission paid out approximately 1.3 billion USD by the time it dissolved in 1978, but this amount is the equivalent of less than 1,000 USD for every Native American in the United States at the time. Moreover, and significantly, the government never gave the tribes direct control over the funds, believing they were not 'competent to receive such large amounts of money' (Hassan and Healy 2019). Instead, the funds were held in trust accounts administered by others. This exclusionary approach reflects the ways that systemic racism impacts upon the creation and management of the transitional justice process, whether carried out at the federal or more local level, which is why it is crucial to ensure that the harmed communities play a central role in the design and implementation of any reparation process.

In addition to these few federally led reparation processes, there are also a wide variety of state/city/university-led reparation processes. One example concerns a reparations law that was passed by the state of Florida in 1994. It concerned a massacre of Black residents and the burning of their homes and church by a mob of white racists in the town of Rosewood almost 70 years prior. The law set up a fund of 2 million USD for those who survived the attack. Individual payments came to around 2,000 USD and later a scholarship fund was established (Howard-Hassmann 2004; Samuels 2020). Another example concerns the widespread practice of state-sanctioned sterilisations that were closely connected with the eugenics movement from the early 1900s. Top scientists of the day argued that the state and medical profession had a leading role to play in stopping individuals from passing down 'undesirable' traits to offspring. These programmes ran from the early 1900s to as late as the 1970s, affecting over 65,000 individuals (Brightman et al. 2015; Klein 2012; Stern 2005; Stern et al. 2017), predominately women of colour, poor, and uneducated. As with many other examples, attempts at reparations took two routes: (i) through the courts using tort law and (ii) through the political systems to set up administrative processes to make reparation payments. The few surviving victims found very little success through the courts, due in large part to the limits of tort law and what one author called the 'clash of cultures' between the victims and the judges (Stern 2005, 1135). Using the political process to lobby for administrative reparation processes fared a bit better. State legislatures in Virginia and North Carolina have established reparation processes (Klein 2012). The compensation bodies were able to produce official reports, official apologies, suggest educational reforms, launch oral history projects, recommend ethics and human rights training for state employees, and provide limited monetary compensation to a dwindling number of living victims (Brightman et al. 2015).

In 2015, after years of fighting by community activists and lawyers, the city of Chicago took steps to establish a reparations process for victims of police brutality and torture. The city set up a fund of 5.5 million USD to compensate 57 victims, nearly all of whom were Black Americans. But more than the individual payments, the city agreed to finance a Torture Justice Center to provide psycho-social counselling to victims of police violence, supported the erection of a public memorial, and now include information about police violence in the educational curriculum. This handful of successful initiatives, driven by community activists, have spurred on supporters of other activities across the country. Over the years, city councils in New York, Cleveland, Detroit, Washington, DC, and elsewhere have passed resolutions calling for reparations, with Evanston, Illinois, being the first city to fund reparations for Black residents for loss of generational wealth due to slavery and discrimination. Committing 10 million USD, and innovatively paid for by a 3% sales tax on legal recreational marijuana, the city will provide eligible residents up to 25,000 USD to use for housing (Brown et al. 2020).

In addition to these steps taken by cities, well-known universities, like Georgetown and Brown, are beginning to uncover and confront past ties with slavery and their effects on institutional racism and inequalities. In some cases, they have come up with novel ways to provide redress. For instance, in 2016, in addition to a formal apology, Georgetown University agreed to give admissions preference to the descendants of the 272 enslaved people whom the

University had sold in 1833 to secure the school's future (Harris et al. 2019). Additionally, there are now student-supported initiatives to increase tuition by 27.20 USD to raise money for a fund to provide more direct reparations to the descendants (Hassan 2019). This example and others show that sustained attention by students and staff (and the media), coupled with the timing of broader political issues, can result in some concrete institutional changes. But overall, these initiatives will not impact the functioning or finances of the universities or improve the lives of wider segments of society. Beyond these more localised reparation programmes, a national response for broader reparations for slavery has made very little headway. This means that if someone is lucky enough to live in a city that takes steps towards redress, they may benefit. More likely than not, they will not benefit from any reparations for the long-term discriminatory impacts of slavery and racism.

Seeking court-ordered reparations is a standardised approach within transitional justice. This standardised approach is one that seems to be popular among victim communities, primarily because it recognises the harm suffered. Numerous reparation claims at both the federal and state level have been driven by victim communities and their family members or decedents rather than initiated by state actors. But for every successful claim of reparations, there are usually many others that have failed (Howard-Hassmann 2004). Unlike truth commissions, which have often linked their creation to broader transitional justice efforts around the globe, reparations discourses in the United States have not done so to the same extent. Rather, they are linked closely with American perceptions of fairness and legality. It is clear that standard principles of tort law apply—as opposed to more transformational reparations. The standard approach means that the victim group is made up of direct victims and their immediate family members or dependents, and that the reparation awards are not meant to transform the lives of the victims or victim communities but instead place them in a position they would have been in had the harm not taken place. With a few exceptions, like the reparations in Chicago for police torture or in Evanston for housing discrimination, reparation programmes have not sought to address more structural issues causing the violations. However, whether to avoid bad publicity or out of a genuine sense of remorse, cities and universities like Georgetown are slowly crafting responses to their specific contexts and identifying victim groups and doing so in new ways that touch directly on innovations in the field.

Guarantees of Non-Repetition – Police and Memorialisation Reforms

The final pillar of transitional justice involves guarantees of non-repetition. These measures relate to actions taken, usually through larger-scale reforms, to prevent the recurrence of violence, and are at the nexus of human security, democratic governance, human rights, and the rule of law. Scholarship recognises guarantees of non-repetition as offering the highest potential for bringing about real institutional and cultural changes in a society (de Greiff 2015; Mayer-Rieckh 2017). Measures are wide-ranging and include state-sponsored actions such as educational reforms, security sector reforms (police), and justice reforms (criminal law) (UN General Assembly 2005, art. 23). They also include other actions that break with the past and signal 'confidence in a continuing relationship' between the state and society (International Law Commission 2001, 219). Guarantees of non-repetition should be underpinned with a human rights-based approach to reform, which requires the state to view itself as the principal duty-bearer of reform obligations (Sharp 2015). A rights-based approach also entails that reforms adopted by the state should go towards realising the norms and standards espoused in international human rights instruments, including those related to social justice.

Across the United States, there are numerous federal, state, and local government efforts of reform: education initiatives (Alenuma 2009); housing reforms (Landis and Reina 2019); and efforts at criminal justice reform (Beckett 2018; Worden and McLean 2017). Still, very few, if any, of the state actors involved in these reforms seem to adopt the language of guarantees of non-repetition (despite its prominent use internationally), and few overtly adopt a human rights-based approach. This may have to do with the fact that the United States does not recognise a human or Constitutional right to housing, work, or healthcare. The success of the reforms that are taking place has been hindered for two reasons. First, because of the counter responses and reforms targeting anti-racist work. Here, one can think of the state laws enacted to restrict the teaching of critical race theory or the banning of certain study programmes or even books. Second, because the reforms taking shape from the very local level to the national level are disjointed and disorganised. State and local actors are not seen as having a clear obligation to deliver. The federal system in the United States, with decentralised control over education and policing, for example, contributes to the fragmented approach to reforms (Lacey 2020). The multiplicity of actors involved, coupled with regional interests and concerns, result in modest changes that do not go far enough in addressing underlying social justice concerns in any holistic way.

There are nevertheless important non-standardised responses aimed at guaranteeing the non-recurrence of violence and attempting to shed light on larger issues of social justice. Some examples include visual and symbolic steps, such as changing street or school names. Following the BLM protests, the contestations around memorialisation showed that standardised domestic legal routes have often been ineffectual in removing or renaming statues or street names. This is largely to do with the domestic cultural heritage laws passed in each state (American Bar Association 2019; McConnell 2020). Changes were made by city officials frequently in response to acts of outrage and defiance against statues, memorial sites, and street names. The changing memory landscapes that took place across the United States in 2020 highlight the powerful role played by protests (and other disruptive acts) in shaping and reshaping collective memory.

Reflecting on Transitional Justice in the US Context: Innovation and Consolidation of the Field

This new emphasis on addressing, through transitional justice processes, social justice harms, needs, and concerns opens up possibilities for the field to become relevant to so-called aparadigmatic contexts. Using a broad 'transition to social justice' frame aligns with the demands being made by key grassroots actors across the United States, while also allowing both backwards- and forwards-looking processes to complement one another. Adopting such a frame may mean that the original context of transitioning out of authoritarian rule to democratic governance, or its later application to post-conflict peace-building situations, are less useful as comparators. For instance, it may be less about breaking with the past and building new institutions and more about dealing with the past and reforming existing institutions. Regardless, the core components of transitional justice – accountability, truth-telling, reparation, and guarantees of non-repetition – would still be wholly applicable. For instance, 'transitioning to social justice' recognises that a failure to address and redress systemic police brutality, mass incarcerations, or state-sanctioned discrimination in housing, which are all forms of physical violence, institutional violence, or economic violence, will lead to greater inequalities and a heightened chance of conflict.

While the standardisation of the transitional justice field around these four pillars may in many ways negatively impact upon innovation, it also creates a relatively easy-to-understand framework for a more coherent and complete approach that has clearly not taken shape organically in the United States. Moreover, although the approaches called for and initiated by grassroots actors may be viewed as 'standard' within the field, in the context of the United States, they can be seen as disruptive or innovative because they are generally not well-known or institutionally embraced. Disruptive and powerful voices, like the BLM social movement, have been able to claim spaces through protests and other actions. And bottom-up approaches, like the Greensboro Truth Commission, have continued to drive change and have an impact on community responses. Also, in many ways, the so-called standard approaches seem to resonate with all relevant actors, from institutional decision makers to civil society activists, given the very legalised culture in the United States. As noted in the Introduction, the more standard transitional justice framework can still 'open the "justice imagination" by offering new perspectives on what can be expected' as well as what would be possible in terms of transitioning to a socially just society.

Indeed, there are always new ways to do transitional justice and the steps taken by some US universities point in this direction; but, again, the patchwork approach makes these initiatives less impactful for broader communities – at least at the moment. The hope is that each of the smaller initiatives combined can propel the country towards a larger vision. Nevertheless, for now, the fragmented responses signal that there are significant challenges that impede any potential to facilitate real transitioning or social transformation, even if a transitional justice frame were to be adopted. Understanding these challenges, which often include political resistance to these types of responses, is important because it can help shape future demands, responses, and impacts. Just as when transitional justice is applied to post-authoritarian or post-conflict situations, there are challenges to transitioning to a more socially just society in stable states as well.

Like with all transitional justice cases, the challenges faced, and successes won are context-sensitive. The challenges in the United States are structural, geographic, political, and cultural. Structurally, the federal system poses obstacles because it was designed to be fragmented. Some key issues (education, security, justice) remain largely the prerogative of the state, while others fall under the ambit of the federal government. It is messy and complicated, resulting in a multitude of institutional actors. Indeed, the federal system in the United States contributes to resistance where arguments around state rights or local rights vis-à-vis the role of the federal government are often used to push back against any type of national response. In terms of geography, US transitional justice also faces challenges. The size of the country means that issues and concerns facing one state, such as specific massacres or discriminatory programmes, may not be given the attention it deserves by citizens or politicians operating thousands of miles away. Regional resistance often shows via political 'whataboutism' and/or refusal to examine past events that are not directly linked to a specific geographical area. For the reparations processes in particular, there is strong resistance to using government funds to provide individual reparations: Why these victims and not others? This question of course also relates to the political and cultural divisions across the country. These deepening rifts may result in the entrenchment of feelings of distrust towards other citizens and the state – according to Horne (2017), this makes change more difficult to bring about. Yet, these growing divides only solidify the need for a national transitional justice narrative driven by civil society actors.

Conclusions: Seeing the Forest for the Trees

This chapter asserts that the field of transitional justice can assist aparadigmatic cases, like the United States, when dealing with its turbulent and traumatic past. It suggests that when addressing past violations, human rights communities in the United States are already taking steps that can be associated with transitional justice. The examples show that in addition to complexity and messiness, there is currently a disjointed and patchwork approach across the United States. These initiatives are led predominantly by local citizens with the hope that specific communities, cities, or states will react positively to particular, targeted demands. There is little in the way of a coordinated effort (either across cities or state lines; or across responses) evoking transitional justice as a comprehensive framework. A coherent and comprehensive response at the federal level, coupled with the innovative and disruptive potential of state and local-level initiatives, would likely bring about greater social justice transformations than the current fragmented initiatives. Only by adopting this more comprehensive framework of transitioning to a more socially just society will the United States be able to see the forest for the trees.

References

Aboueldahab, N. (2020) 'The United States Needs a Truth Commission. It Should be Televised." Foreign Policy, 24 July. Available at: https://foreignpolicy.com/2020/07/24/united-states-racism-truth-commission-televise-south-africa-tunisia/

Aciru, M. (2017) 'Rethinking Post-Truth Commissions: Empowering Local Capacities to Shape the Post-Truth Commission Discourse'. *Human Rights and International Legal Discourse* 11(1), 71–82.

African Union (2019) 'African Union Transitional Justice Framework'. 12 February. Available at: https://www.legal-tools.org/doc/bcdc97/pdf/.

Alenuma, S.J. (2009) *Race and Educational Reform in America*. Wilmington: David Publishing.

American Bar Association (2019) 'Confederate-monument Removals Slowed by Knot of Legal Issues'. Available at: https://www.americanbar.org/news/abanews/publications/youraba/2019/december-2019/efforts-to-remove-confederate-monuments-slowed-by-knot-of-legal-/.

AP-NORC (2020) 'Widespread Desire for Policing and Criminal Justice Reform'. Article. Available at: https://apnorc.org/projects/widespread-desire-for-policing-and-criminal-justice-reform/.

Arthur, P. (2009) 'How Transitional Justice Reshaped Human Rights: A Conceptual History of Transitional Justice'. *Human Rights Quarterly* 31(2), 321–367.

Bakiner, O. (2014) 'Truth Commission Impact: An Assessment of How Commissions Influence Politics and Society'. *International Journal of Transitional Justice* 8(1), 6–30.

Beckett, K. (2018) 'The Politics, Promise, and Perils of Criminal Justice Reform in the Context of Mass Incarceration'. *Annual Review of Criminology* 1(1), 235–59.

Boston Project (2012) 'Report on Phase One: Can We Talk About Equity, Access, and Excellence?'. Available at: https://bbdplearningnetwork.files.wordpress.com/2012/10/bbdp-phase-1-summary-report-draft-21.pdf.

Brightman, S., E. Lenning and K. McElrath (2015) 'State-Directed Sterilizations in North Carolina: Victim-Centeredness and Reparations'. *British Journal of Criminology* 55(3), 474–493.

Brown, A., E. de Sainte Maresville and A. Young (2020) 'How the 1st US City to Fund Reparations for Black Residents is Making Amends'. ABC News, 1 March. Available at: https://abcnews.go.com/US/1st-us-city-fund-reparations-black-residents-making/story?id=76118463.

Cahill-Ripley, A. (2014) 'Foregrounding Socio-Economic Rights in Transitional Justice: Realising Justice for Violations of Economic and Social Rights'. *Netherlands Quarterly of Human Rights* 32(2), 183–213.

Christian, N. (2011) 'Truth and Reconciliation Comes to Detroit'. WNYC Studios, 21 November. Available at: www.wnyc.org/story/171612-truth-and-reconciliation-comes-detroit/.

Coates, T. (2014) 'The Case for Reparations'. The Atlantic, June. Available at: https://www.theatlantic.com/magazine/archive/2014/06/the-case-for-reparations/361631/.

Congressional Research Service (2015) 'Police Use of Force: Rules, Remedies, and Reforms.' Report R44256, 30 October. Available at: https://www.everycrsreport.com/files/20151030_R44256_f6c3152f4734c1fb057a8d1bb8fe2639fcb3e94f.pdf.

Cummings, S.L. and D.L. Rhode (2009) 'Public Interest Litigation: Insights from Theory and Practice'. *Fordham Urban Law Journal* 36(4), 603–651.

Drumbl, M. (2007) *Atrocity, Punishment, and International Law*. Cambridge: Cambridge University Press.

European Union (2015) 'The EU's Policy Framework on Support for Transitional Justice'. 16 November. Available at: https://www.eeas.edurorpa.eu.

Evans, M. and D. Wilkins (2019) 'Transformative Justice, Reparations and Transatlantic Slavery'. *Social & Legal Studies* 28(2), 137–157.

Finnegan, W. (2020) 'How Police Unions Fight Reform'. The New Yorker, 27 July. Retrieved from: https://www.newyorker.com/magazine/2020/08/03/how-police-unions-fight-reform.

Green, J. (2020) 'Can Greensboro Model a National Truth and Reconciliation Process?' *Sojourners*, 14 October. Retrieved from https://sojo.net/articles/can-greensboro-model-national-truth-and-reconciliation-process.

de Greiff, P. (2015) 'Report of the Special Rapporteur on the Promotion of Truth, Justice, Reparation and Guarantees of Non-recurrence'. A/HRC/30/42, 7 September 2015.

Harris, L.M., J.T. Campbell and A.L. Brophy (2019) *Slavery and the University: Histories and Legacies*. Athens, GA: University of Georgia Press.

Hassan, A. (2019) 'Georgetown Students Agree to Create Reparation Fund'. New York Times, 12 April. Retrieved from https://www.nytimes.com/2019/04/12/us/georgetown-reparations.html.

Hassan, A. and J. Healy (2019) 'American Has Tried Reparations Before. Here is How It Went'. New York Times, 19 June. Retrieved from: www.nytimes.com/2019/06/19/us/reparations-slavery.html.

Hayner, P.B. (2011) *Unspeakable Truths: Transitional Justice and the Challenge of Truth Commissions*, 2nd ed. London: Routledge.

Heikkilä, M. (2004) *International Criminal Tribunals and Victims of Crime*. Turku: Åbo Akademi University Press.

Horne, C.M. (2017) *Building Trust and Democracy: Transitional Justice in Post-Communist Countries*. Oxford: Oxford University Press.

Howard-Hassmann, R.E. (2004) 'Getting to Reparations: Japanese Americans and African Americans'. *Social Forces* 83(2), 823–840.

International Law Commission (2001) *Draft Articles on Responsibility of States for Internationally Wrongful Acts. Report of the International Law Commission on the Work of Its Fifty-third Session*. A/56/10. New York: United Nations.

Inwood, J.F.J. (2017) 'Dealing with Hate: Can America's Truth and Reconciliation Commissions Help?' The Conversation, 1 March. Retrieved from www.theconversation.com/dealing-with-hate-can-americas-truth-and-reconciliation-commissions-help-73170.

Jovanovic, S. (2012) *Democracy, Dialogue, and Community Action: Truth and Reconciliation in Greensboro*. Fayetteville, AR: University of Arkansas Press.

Kendi, I.X. (2016) *Stamped from the Beginning: The Definitive History of Racist Ideas in America*. New York: Nation Books.

Klein, J.M. (2012) 'Compensating Victims of Forced Sterilization: Lessons from North Carolina'. *Journal of Law, Medicine & Ethics* 40(2), 422–426.

Lacey, N. (2020) 'The Fragmented US System Means that the Battle for Criminal Justice Reform must be Fought in Multiple Political Arenas'. LSE American Politics and Policy Blog, 11 June. Retrieved from: https://blogs.lse.ac.uk/usappblog/2020/06/11/the-fragmented-us-system-means-that-the-battle-for-criminal-justice-reform-must-be-fought-in-multiple-political-arenas/.

Lambourne, W. (2009) 'Transitional Justice and Peacebuilding after Mass Violence'. *International Journal of Transitional Justice* 3(1), 28–48.

Landis, J. and V. Reina (2019) 'Eleven Ways Demographic and Economic Change is Reframing American Housing Policy'. *Housing Policy Debate* 29(1), 4–21.

Laplante, L.J. (2008) 'Transitional Justice and Peace Building: Diagnosing and Addressing the Socio-economic Roots of Violence through a Human Rights Framework'. *International Journal of Transitional Justice* 2(3), 331–355.

Leebaw, B.A. (2008) 'The Irreconcilable Goals of Transitional Justice'. *Human Rights Quarterly* 30(1), 95–118.

Maine Commission (2015) 'Maine Wabanaki-State Child Welfare Truth and Reconciliation Commission Final Report. Beyond the Mandate: Continuing the Conversation'. Available at: https://d3n8a8pro7vhmx.cloudfront.net/mainewabanakireach/pages/17/attachments/original/1468974047/TRC-Report-Expanded_July2015.pdf?1468974047.

Mayer-Rieckh, A. (2017) 'Guarantees of Non-Recurrence: An Approximation'. *Human Rights Quarterly* 39(2), 416–448.

McConnell, L. (2020) 'Edward Colston: Listing Controversy'. University of Bristol Law School Blog, 15 June. Retrieved from: https://legalresearch.blogs.bris.ac.uk/2020/06/edward-colston-listing-controversy/.

McGonigle Leyh, B. (2016) 'Nuremberg's Legacy on Transitional Justice: Prosecutions are Here to Stay'. *Washington University Global Studies Law Review* 15(4), 559–574.

—— (2017) 'The Socialization of Transitional Justice: Expanding Justice Theories within the Field'. *Human Rights and International Legal Discourse* 11(1), 83–95.

—— (2019) 'Truth Commissions and Social Justice: 'Wishful Thinking or Not Very Thoughtful Wishing'?' In: J. Sarkin, ed. *The Global Impact and Legacy of Truth Commissions* (pp. 169–188). Cambridge: Intersentia.

Miller, H. and R. Redhead (2019) 'Beyond 'Rights-based Approaches'? Employing a Process and Outcomes Framework'. *International Journal of Human Rights* 23, 699–718.

Minow, M. (1998) *Between Vengeance and Forgiveness: Facing History after Genocide and Mass Violence*. Boston: Beacon Press.

Monmouth University Polling Institute (2020) 'Protestors' Anger Justified Even If Actions May Not Be'. 2 June. Retrieved from www.monmouth.edu/polling-institute/documents/monmouthpoll_us_060220.pdf.

Morton, D.R. (2018) 'Improving Police Transparency and Accountability in Violent Encounters with African Americans'. *Journal of African American Studies* 22(1), 125–138.

Murphy, C. (2020) 'Transitional Justice in the United States'. Just Security, 16 July. Retrieved from https://www.justsecurity.org/71236/transitional-justice-in-the-united-states/.

National Public Radio (2020) 'A Decade of Watching Black People Die'. 31 May. Retrieved from https://www.npr.org/2020/05/29/865261916/a-decade-of-watching-black-people-die?t=1598516948527.

Nikkei for Civil Rights and Redress Archives (1981) 'Redress Hearings: Commission on Wartime Relocation and Internment of Civilians (CWRIC) Hearings'. Retrieved from: https://ncrr-la.org/NCRR_archives/redresshearings81/redresshearings.htm

Office of the UN High Commissioner for Human Rights (2006) *Rule of Law Tools for Post-Conflict States: Truth Commissions*. HR/PUB/06/1. Geneva: United Nations.

Orentlicher, D.F. (1991) 'Settling Accounts: The Duty to Prosecute Human Rights Violations of a Prior Regime'. *Yale Law Review* 100(8), 2537–2615.

Parker, H. (2017) 'Truth and Reconciliation Commissions: A Needed Force in Alaska?' *Alaska Law Review* 34(1), 27–66.

Pew Research Center (2020) 'Majority of Public Favors Giving Civilians the Power to Sue Police Officers for Misconduct'. 9 July. Retrieved from: https://www.pewresearch.org/politics/2020/07/09/majority-of-public-favors-giving-civilians-the-power-to-sue-police-officers-for-misconduct/.

Roht-Arriaza, N. (2006) 'The New Landscape of Transitional Justice'. In: N. Roht-Arriaza and J. Mariezcurrena, eds. *Transitional Justice in the Twenty-First Century* (pp. 1–16). Cambridge: Cambridge University Press.

Sadat, L.N. (2017) 'Whither Human Rights in the Era of Trump'. *Netherlands Quarterly of Human Rights* 35(2), 77–85.

Samuels, R. (2020) 'After Reparations: How a Scholarship Helped — and Didn't Help — Descendants of Victims of the 1923 Rosewood Racial Massacre'. Washington Post, 3 April. Retrieved from https://www.washingtonpost.com/graphics/2020/national/rosewood-reparations/.

Sandoval, C. (2017) 'Reflections on the Transformative Potential of Transitional Justice and the Nature of Social Change in Times of Transition'. In: R. Duthie and P. Seils, eds. *Justice Mosaics: How Context Shapes Transitional Justice in Fractured Societies* (pp. 166–201). New York: International Center For Transitional Justice.

Scheiber, N., F. Stockman and J.D. Goodman (2020) ,How Police Unions Became Such Powerful Opponents to Reform Efforts'. New York Times, 6 June. Retrieved from https://www.nytimes.com/2020/06/06/us/police-unions-minneapolis-kroll.html.

Sharp, D.N. (2012) 'Addressing Economic Violence in Times of Transition: Toward a Positive-Peace Paradigm for Transitional Justice'. *Fordham International Law Journal* 35(3), 781–814.

—— (2015) 'Security Sector Reform for Human Security: The Role of International Law and Transitional Justice in Shaping More Effective Policy and Practice'. In: Saul, M. and J.A. Sweeney, eds. *International Law and Post-Conflict Reconstruction Policy* (pp. 198–217). New York: Routledge.

—— (2019) 'What Would Satisfy Us? Taking Stock of Critical Approaches to Transitional Justice'. *International Journal of Transitional Justice* 13(3), 570–589.

Shklar, J. (1963) *Legalism: Law, Moral and Political Trials*. Cambridge, MA: Harvard University Press.

Souli, S. (2020) 'Does America Need a Truth and Reconciliation Commission?' *Politico*, 16 August. Retrieved from: www.politico.com/news/magazine/2020/08/16/does-america-need-a-truth-and-reconciliation-commission-395332.

Stahn, C. (2020) *Justice as Message: Expressivist Foundations of International Criminal Justice*. Oxford: Oxford University Press.

Stern, A.M. (2005) 'Sterilized in the Name of Public Health: Race, Immigration, and Reproductive Control in Modern California'. *American Journal of Public Health* 95(7), 1128–1138.

Stern, A.M., N.L. Novak, N. Lira, K. O'Connor, S. Harlow, and S. Kardia (2017) 'California's Sterilization Survivors: An Estimate and Call for Redress'. *American Journal of Public Health* 107(1), 50–54.

UN General Assembly (2005) 'Basic Principles and Guidelines on the Right to a Remedy and Reparation for the Victims of Gross Violations of International Human Rights Law and Serious Violations of International Humanitarian Law'. A/RES/60/147, 16 December.

UN Secretary-General (2010) 'Guidance Note of the Secretary-General. United Nations Approach to Transitional Justice'. DPA/UNSG/2010-00904, 10 March.

UN Security Council (2004) 'UN Secretary-General Report to the UN Security Council. The Rule of Law and Transitional Justice in Conflict and Post-Conflict Societies'. S/2004/616, 23 August.

US Congress (2019) 'Commission to Study and Develop Reparation Proposals for African-Americans Act'. In: 116th Congress, H.R.40 –House Judiciary Subcommittee, hearing held on 19 June 2019.

US Department of Justice, Office of Public Affairs (2017, May 3). Federal Officials Close Investigation into Death of Alton Sterling. Retrieved from https://www.justice.gov/opa/pr/federal-officials-close-investigation-death-alton-sterling.

Ward, J.K. and C.C. Flowers (2019) 'How the Trump Administration's Efforts to Redefine Human Rights Threaten Economic, Social, and Racial Justice'. *Human Rights Law Review Online* 4, 20–54.

Worden, R.E. and S.J. McLean (2017) *Mirage of Police Reform: Procedural Justice and Police Legitimacy*. Oakland: University of California Press.

Chapter 6

Transitional Justice in the North Atlantic

The Greenland Reconciliation Commission and the Role of Political Authority

Line Engbo Gissel

Introduction

Denmark is a consolidated democracy and not a transitional state, but Greenland perceives itself as transitioning to full independence (Kielsen 2021). While transitional justice in Denmark is seen as relevant mainly for the Global South, in Greenland it is understood as a post-colonial project of defining and reckoning with the past in order to understand and take responsibility for a troubled present. Contemporary Greenland sees itself as struggling with alienation, diversity, and divisions springing from colonial and post-colonial modernisation policies and differentiated experiences with these. This chapter analyses the expansion of transitional justice to the North Atlantic, where the ideas of justice and reconciliation in Danish–Greenland relations have been met with both resistance and embrace. It explores the role of political authority in shaping the parameters and processes of justice and applies the concept of transitional justice as recognition, accountability and disruption to an empirical case.

This volume conceptualises transitional justice as practices that involve a potential for accountability, reconciliation, and disruption. Whether this potential is realised in particular situations is an empirical question; there should be no *a priori* assumption that transitional justice in fact meets these goals. In Denmark–Greenland relations, transitional justice centres on questions of recognition, while accountability is largely perceived as irrelevant both in Denmark and Greenland. The potential for disruption is, however, an element of transitional justice that likely accounts for both the explicit resistance to transitional justice by the Danish government and, conversely, Greenland's embrace of it.

The Introduction to this volume theorises formal transitional justice as an increasingly standardised field comprising a set of largely state-centric mechanisms. The state centricity derives partly from the fact that transitional justice addresses types of violence and wrongs which were possible only because the state either perpetrated them or failed to protect against them. Therefore, state acknowledgement of past harm implies that civilians ought to have been protected by their state. This aspect of transitional justice is illuminated by the politics of recognition in Denmark–Greenland relations. The Danish government

DOI: 10.4324/9781003289104-7

declined to participate in the Greenland Reconciliation Commission and thereby influenced the scope, making it one-sided and focused on intra-Greenlandic matters. The decision reflects a longer tradition in the Danish political establishment of refusing to deal with the past. At times, however, this strategy has been punctuated by inquiries into and apologies for specific historical and harmful policies followed by compensation to specific individuals.

Where the state has the monopoly on violence, civil society is not tasked with protecting against atrocity, but it may contribute to realising the potential for accountability, recognition, and disruption. The Greenland Reconciliation Commission, due to its internal focus, had a strong focus on civil society relations in Greenland, particularly between East and West Greenland. The Commission illustrated the importance – and limits – of civil society recognition, and the potential for civil-society-led disruption, while calls for official apologies and the defacing of colonial statues represent bottom-up recognition and disruption. It is possible that the Danish government declined to participate in reconciliation efforts because it feared the Commission's disruption of Danish–Greenland relations, which could end in a call for independence and de facto decolonisation.

The chapter is structured as follows. The first part situates transitional justice in Denmark and Greenland. It provides a historical background to the question of justice and identifies three narratives that inform intentions and responses to transitional justice. The second part describes and analyses the Greenland Reconciliation Commission and the intentions and responses animating involved actors, such as the Greenland and Danish governments, the commissioners, and the wider public.

Transitional Justice in Denmark and Greenland

In Denmark, transitional justice is generally considered a paradigm that applies to others, particularly those in the Global South. The official development agency, Danida, funds transitional justice projects and initiatives in bilateral partner countries affected by conflict, such as Nepal, South Sudan, Syria, and Uganda and supports NGOs involved in transitional justice, such as the Danish Human Rights Institute and the International Center for Transitional Justice (Ministry of Foreign Affairs of Denmark 2011, 2013, 2016). It also provides multilateral funding to bodies that organise and finance justice programmes in the Global South, such as the UN Office of the High Commissioner for Human Rights (Ministry of Foreign Affairs of Denmark 2019).

Dealing with the past is in principle as relevant for Denmark as for other post-colonial societies. As an imperial power, Denmark colonised islands in the North Atlantic and the West Indies, as well as coastal territories in eastern India and the Gold Coast (now Ghana). Denmark's tropical possessions were taken in the 17th century and included a fortified trading post in Tharangambadi, south of Pondicherry, a trading post in Serampore, north of Kolkata, and a series of fortified villages on the eastern coast of the Gold Coast. Colonisation of the Danish Virgin Islands (now St. Thomas, St. John, and St. Croix) began in 1665, where Denmark established plantation societies based on enslaved African labour. In the 1840s, Denmark sold its African and Indian possessions to the UK, while it completed the sale of the Danish Virgin Islands to the United States in 1917.

Denmark's presence in the North Atlantic has been longer and deeper, beginning with explorations in the 15th century. Iceland, the Faroe Islands, and Greenland were brought under Denmark–Norway in 1536.[1] Iceland gained de facto independence in 1918 and formal independence in 1944. The Faroe Islands and Greenland have continued to be part of the Danish Realm. The Faroe Islands gained home rule in 1948, after a referendum returned a slim majority in favour of independence, while Greenland ceased to be a colony in 1953 and transited to home rule in 1979 and autonomy in 2009.

Historical Background: Colonisation, Home Rule, and Self-Government

Between the 10th and 15th centuries, Norsemen from Iceland settled in southern Greenland. In 1721, a Danish-Norwegian missionary, Hans Egede, sailed to Greenland to find and christen the Norse settlers, apparently worrying that they had missed the Reformation (Johnstone 2020, 2). He found instead thriving Inuit communities and established a mission to convert them to Lutheranism. Colonialists from Denmark–Norway then settled and claimed sovereignty over what was considered *terra nullius*, legally uninhabited land (Johnstone 2020, 2). They established trading posts and monopolised trade through the Royal Greenland Trading Department, primarily exporting train oil and wildlife tusks, skin, and fur. The Department was responsible for administration in Greenland until 1908, while its trade monopoly was lifted only in 1950.

The United States explored northern Greenland around the 1900s but renounced any claim to Greenland as part of the agreement to buy the Danish West Indies in 1916. In 1946 the United States tried to buy Greenland and in 1951 Denmark agreed to the establishment of a US military airbase in northern Greenland near Uummannaq (Thule). Norway declared sovereignty over a large part of East Greenland in 1931, a claim rejected by the Permanent Court of International Justice, which held that sovereignty could be demonstrated by

1 The kingdom of Denmark–Norway came into being in 1380 when the child king Olaf IV inherited the throne of Norway. Between 1397–1524 Denmark–Norway and Sweden formed the Kalmar Union. During the Napoleonic Wars, as Britain (allied with Sweden) in 1807 bombarded Copenhagen and took the Danish fleet, Denmark–Norway allied with France. The 1814 Kiel peace treaty gave Norway to Sweden, while Iceland, the Faroe Islands, and Greenland remained Danish crown possessions.

Denmark. When co-founding the United Nations in 1945, Denmark listed Greenland as a non-self-governing territory and had to report to the UN Secretary-General on the wellbeing and development of the Greenlanders. Denmark became obliged to prepare Greenlanders for self-rule and faced pressure to decolonise (Hermann 2021; Johnstone 2020). Colonialism had become an embarrassment to the Danish state (Jensen 2015).

The government transcended the problem by integrating Greenland into the Danish commonwealth, *Rigsfællesskabet*, in 1953, ostensibly decolonising it. Greenland formally became a Danish county and was removed from the UN's list of trust territories, while Greenlanders became full and equal citizens with the right to elect two MPs to the Danish parliament (*Folketing*). The new status was legitimised by a constitutional referendum in 1953, in which Greenlanders paradoxically could not vote because at the time they were not citizens. To justify its North Atlantic possession internationally and transform a people perceived to be backwards and primitive, in the half-century following UN membership and straddling the trustee and county periods, Denmark implemented a rapid modernisation programme involving forced relocation, urbanisation ('concentration'), linguistic and cultural Danification, Danish expatriation, and welfarism. Natives and settlers were institutionally differentiated by laws governing education and labour. For instance, between 1964–1989 a Greenlandic-born public employee had to earn less than his or her Danish-born counterpart (Lidegaard 2009).

In 1979, Greenland opted for home rule and in 1985 it left the European Economic Community chiefly to protect its fishing rights.[2] Following a 2008 referendum on enhanced home rule, the Greenland Self-Government Act (2009) gave the Greenlandic government, *Naalakkersuisut*, authority to govern Greenlandic affairs with the exception of justice, defence, foreign and security affairs, and monetary matters. Contemporary Greenland is postcolonial yet not decolonised, and exists in an asymmetric relationship with Denmark, sometimes termed a 'confederacy' (Rezvani 2007, 117). Due to Greenland's place within a unitary Danish state, *Naalakkersuisut's* leader is the 'chairperson', while its ministries are termed 'departments'.

Most political parties and members of the political elite envisage a future independent Greenland (Kielsen 2021), although they disagree about the nature of the transition. Questions about the future are linked to questions about the past, including its wrongs and injustices. Although the term 'transitional justice' is rarely used, debates and initiatives suggest that the global field of transitional justice has expanded to include Greenland–Denmark relations: historical commissions, calls for public apologies, the Greenland Reconciliation Commission (2014–2017), and debates about colonial statutes in public spaces. Transitional justice in Denmark–Greenland relations is

2 Denmark joined the European Community in 1973.

characterised by being focused on the *recognition* of harm, rather than *accountability* for its occurrence. It also has a *disruptive* potential, which is arguably key to the Danish government's resistance to reconciliation initiatives. Greenlandic civil society activists and politicians have regularly called for apologies and reparations for Greenland's painful colonial past, but these have generally not been well received by the Danish population. At the same time, there have been some fact-finding initiatives and two public apologies for specific acts. To understand transitional justice in Greenland-Denmark affairs, it is useful to dwell on several ideas and narratives that inform intentions and responses in Greenland and Denmark.

The Ideational Context of Transitional Justice

Transitional justice initiatives exist within an ideational context. Ideas such as group identities, understandings of political history, causal beliefs, and notions of justice and appropriateness shape the intentions of and responses to transitional justice. They may be analysed as narratives, perspectives, or discourses that shape transitional justice (Little 2011). In relation to transitional justice in Greenland and Denmark, there are three conflicting narratives about the colonisation and modernisation of Greenland, which inform how people respond to transitional justice.

Benevolent Colonialism and Modernisation

The most dominant narrative regarding Denmark's involvement in Greenland is a narrative of benevolent colonialism (Andersen 2019; Bjørnsson 2016; Thisted 2014). Many in the Danish political establishment and in wider society argue that past imperial activities have been, on the whole, benevolent. It follows that even manifestly harmful policies were developed with good intentions (Bryld 1998; Hermann 2021). This narrative developed during the Danish democratisation process from the late 18th century onwards, as the country transited from imperial autocracy to an inwards-oriented nation-state (Andersen 2010). As colonisation gradually lost its profitability and prestige, official narratives about Danish presence in the North Atlantic came to emphasise civilisation and enlightenment. For instance, the Danish prime minister, Thorvald Stauning (quoted in Bjørnsson 2016, 124), argued in 1930 that Greenland's closed economy protected its population against exploitation by capitalists and prevented the destruction of its 'ancient, free, hunting culture'. In 1948, in the new context of international pressure to decolonise, Prime Minister Hans Hedtoft argued that Danish policy in Greenland was marked by 'humanism and idealism', although mistakes had been made (Bjørnsson 2016, 124). Indeed, to Hedtoft, Denmark's greater role was moral and educational: to show other nations how to lead a primitive people to a modern stage of development (Bjørnsson 2016, 124).

According to the Greenlandic historian and former member of the Reconciliation Commission, Jens Heinrich (2014), the Danish national identity still rests on the myth of the benevolent colonial master. Danes struggle to acknowledge that their forefathers were colonisers, slave traders, and imperialists (see also Hermann 2021). Greenland's former psychiatric chief physician, Fatuma Ali (2006), has observed psychological 'barriers' to admitting colonial wrongs. To her, Danes become defensive about colonialism or argue that although Danes did not always do good in Greenland, they were much better than, for example, the British (Bjørnsson 2016). Given the narrative's place in Denmark's self-identification, the Danish government is vulnerable to public shaming around colonial wrongs. Indeed, the threat of this shaming is a 'bargaining chip for Greenland', which its leaders have used to gain more influence in foreign policy matters (Jacobsen and Gad 2018, 17).

Damaging Colonialism and Modernisation

Against the narrative of benevolent stewardship, there is a narrative of damage. It holds that although Danish colonialism was not as violent as elsewhere, wrongs and injustices were committed and the relationship of Greenland to Denmark was – and continues to be – marked by fundamental inequality. The injustices relate to policies carried out both before and after 1953, when Greenland formally ceased being a colony, such as the forced relocation of communities, the laws distinguishing natives from settlers (e.g. the 'birthplace criteria'), and the Danification of culture and language (Andersen 2019; Jacobsen and Gad 2018; Thisted 2014).

Involuntary resettlement programmes are highlighted as having been particularly damaging and demonstrate to Greenlanders that Danish policy was carried out not to civilise or protect people, but to serve Danish (as opposed to Greenlandic) interests. For instance, in 1925, residents from Ammassalik in south-east Greenland were relocated to the newly-established Scorebysund in the remote and unpopulated north-east to secure Danish claims to north-east Greenland (Andersen 2019); in 1953 an Inughuit settlement in Uummannaq was relocated 160 kilometres to the north to enable the United States to establish the Thule Air Base (Jacobsen and Gad 2018); and in 1972 Qullissat, the third-largest town, was closed and its population dispersed across 2,000 kilometres because its main source of livelihood, a government-owned mine became unprofitable (Andersen et al. 2016).[3] The Qullissat closure became a symbol of Danish administrative malpractices, and even 'triggered the Greenlandic autonomy movement', which fought for home rule (Andersen et al. 2016, 97).

3 Andersen et al. (2016) question whether the mine was objectively unprofitable. It would be more correct to state that it became considered unprofitable by the Danish government.

The critical narrative about Danish involvement in Greenland developed as a response to the Danification policy, a growing critique by Greenlanders, and the 1970s anti-authoritative youth revolt in Denmark (Thisted 2014). It is present in both Greenland and Denmark. The focus on Denmark's good intentions, it argues, under-acknowledges Denmark's role in Greenland's contemporary challenges.[4] Still, Greenlandic governments have invoked the narrative to different degrees. Aleqa Hammond's government, which initiated the Reconciliation Commission, appears more nationalistic than its predecessors and successors. The current government articulates a wish for independence, while planning to celebrate the tercentenary of Hans Egede's fatal arrival (Kielsen 2021).

Historical Responsibility and Change

Denmark has a strong rule-of-law tradition and its foreign service routinely advocates justice processes in the wake of atrocity. However, when it comes to both its distant and recent past in the North Atlantic, there is a sense that accountability is irrelevant because 'one should not judge the past with the standards of today'. There are two arguments against formalising any form of justice claims. First, a progress argument holds that society develops, values change, and the actions of the past were marked by different values. For instance, former minister Claus Hjort Frederiksen (quoted in Scherrebeck 2015), the liberal party's spokesperson for Greenland, argued with reference to Greenlandic reconciliation that it is 'very difficult' to 'assess the societal values on which decisions 50–100–200 years ago were based. Danish citizens were also treated differently 100 years ago than they are today, so should we also apologise to past generations here in Denmark?' Second, the idea of apologising for something that one had no direct responsibility for is alien to many and likely relates to the positivism of the Danish law tradition. As the Greenland spokesperson for Denmark's social-liberal party, Christian Friis Bach (quoted in Gaardmand 2014, 2), has argued, it 'does not make sense to apologise for things that have been carried out in a different era by other people under different conditions'. This narrative about historical responsibility and change reconciles and transcends the other narratives about Danish colonialism and modernisation: Even if Denmark's influence in Greenland was damaging and not primarily benevolent, it is meaningless to apologise for or deal with it because the past is in the past. Accordingly, the idea of reconciliation met with government resistance.

The Greenland Reconciliation Commission

The Greenland Reconciliation Commission was established in July 2014 by Greenland's coalition government, *Naalakkersuisut*, led by Aleqa Hammond

4 Interview, Jens Heinrich, July 2016.

of Greenland's social-democratic party, Siumut. The agreement binding the party coalition had committed its members to make an 'action plan' to pursue reconciliation and forgiveness, stating that '[i]n order to create a distance to the colonisation of our country, it is necessary to have reconciliation and forgiveness' (Greenland Naalakkersuisut 2013, 13).[5] The coalition agreement does not specify actors, but is understood to refer to both Greenland and Denmark. The government appointed five commissioners and an honorary member of the Reconciliation Commission (four women and two men), while the Greenlandic parliament, *Inatsisartut*, nominated members to a political oversight committee. Hammond and the commissioners drew inspiration from the field of transitional justice and particularly the South African Truth and Reconciliation Commission, the Canadian Truth and Reconciliation Commission on Indian Residential Schools, and Australia's official apology to Aborigines and Torres Strait Islanders (Andersen 2019; Søndergaard 2013).

Before the Commission's establishment, Greenland's *Naalakkersuisut* imagined that reconciliation would pertain to both intra-Greenlandic and Greenland–Denmark relations (Søndergaard 2013; Hannestad 2013a; Greenland Naalakkersuisut 2013). The long history between Denmark and Greenland was to be 'investigate[d]' ('*kulegraves*') (Hannestad 2013b). But when Hammond communicated the idea to the Danish prime minister in August 2013, Helle Thorning-Schmidt, a fellow social-democratic party leader, declined to participate in this process. Speaking on behalf of Denmark, Thorning-Schmidt (quoted in Forsoningskommissionen 2017, 16) stated that 'We do not have a need for reconciliation, but I respect that it is a discussion that occupies the Greenlandic people. We will observe the discussion carefully from here'. She explained later that the establishment of the Reconciliation Commission:

> is a Greenlandic initiative. And the [Greenlandic] government has clearly suggested that it should be a Greenlandic project with terms of reference developed in Greenland. I respect that fully. On the Danish side, we are most taken up by the challenges of the present and the future and that we continue our good collaboration.[6]
>
> (Thorning-Schmidt 2014)

Importantly, the Danish refusal to participate resulted in a narrowing of scope (Forsoningskommissionen 2017, 16). The Commission became an 'internal commission' and was now to focus solely on intra-Greenlandic reconciliation.

5 The original text reads, 'For at lægge afstand til koloniseringen af vort land, er det nødvendigt at der finder forsoning og tilgivelser sted. Der udarbejdes en handlingsplan for dette'. Own translation.

6 The quote is translated by the author.

The Greenlandic term for reconciliation is *saammaatta*. It means to let go: to hear and see each other and thereafter to move on.[7] The Commission conceptualised reconciliation as both an 'overall process' and a 'goal' that includes making the population conscious of Greenland's history and how it affects the present; creating an understanding of the past in order to move towards a common future; a process for long-term societal change; the (re)building of relations; and the acknowledgement of remembrance and learning from the past (Forsoningskommissionen 2017, 17). Reflecting the Danish refusal to participate, the Commission's terms of reference took a point of departure in the Greenlandic people's 'shared responsibility for contributing to a positive development' and the idea that a 'diverse society' must have respect for its citizens' different historical memories and perceptions (Forsoningskommissionen 2017, 8). Moreover, it stressed the importance of discussing the past and building the understanding that the past shapes present societal relations and conditions of life. 'This will benefit the self-conscience of individuals and the Greenlandic people' (Forsoningskommissionen 2017, 8, 48). The Commission was therefore to initiate activities that would enable ordinary people to deal with the colonial heritage, create dialogue and reflection on that history, build an understanding of society's diversity, and foster reconciliation.

The Commission worked for three years, from 2014 to November 2017, and focused on the lived experiences of the general population as well as the policy-making field. Its terms of reference did not specify a temporal focus, but the substantive focus aimed at 'internal sociological problems' and 'the historical development and cultural interaction in Greenland as well as between Greenland and Denmark' (Forsoningskommissionen 2017, 48). It held 33 public meetings, nine focus group meetings for professionals, and a conference, and conducted 58 narrative interviews across Greenland. It issued a short story competition and commissioned a play, seven art pieces, and a popular song about reconciliation. It produced videos about its work, aims, and findings. It commissioned historical reports. The Commission report, published in 2017, entails many recommendations to *Naalakkersuisut*: To develop a national strategy for how to tell Greenland's history 'from our perspective',[8] using historical artefacts, citizen participation, and oral history; establish a centre for history and reconciliation; expand the vocabulary for both the colonial heritage and methods for reconciliation; establish a foundation to support research and other activities that aid reconciliation; develop a common set of values for Greenlandic society; strengthen the Greenlandic language; and ensure free, prior, and informed consent to large projects that affect individual lives. The Commission did not recommend material reparations or general apologies, but recommended a public debate about official apologies since

7 Interview with former commissioner, Jens Heinrich, July 2016.
8 In Danish, 'set med vores øjne'.

this wish was expressed by 'some citizens, particularly of the older generation' (Forsoningskommissionen 2017, 46). However, there was 'clear wish' for apologies by the Danish and Greenlandic governments for the harm produced by the many forced resettlements (Forsoningskommissionen 2017, 37).

The idea of reconciliation was not new in Greenland but had been spearheaded by civil society. A decade earlier, a group of citizens and professionals – politicians, psychologists, teachers, journalists, and businessmen – acting in their private capacity had initiated a reconciliation society that held monthly meetings and town-hall discussions in Nuuk (Kalaallit Nunaata Radioa 2005). Their first activity was a week-long 'reconciliation retreat' for 18 Greenlanders and Danes in Toscana in September 2004, hosted by Greenland's psychiatric chief physician, Fatuma Ali (2006; Thisted 2017). Highly educated Greenlanders there spoke of a low self-esteem deriving from the colonial past. The psychologist linked the problem to Greenland's high incidence of passion crime and suicide and saw Greenland as 'being at war with itself'. This understanding was echoed by the Reconciliation Commission, which diagnosed an 'inner war' (Forsoningskommissionen 2017, 8). Ali's early ideas about Greenlandic reconciliation were, however, controversial in Denmark because they challenged the narrative of benevolent colonialism (Ali 1998b, 1998a; Lidegaard 1998a, 1998b).

Intentions and Responses

The narrative context shaped the intentions and responses of different actors to the Greenland Reconciliation Commission. The idea and scope of the Commission changed, as we saw, in response to the Danish decision to be an external observer rather than a participant. For *Naalakkersuisut*, the Commission was all along a post-colonial project linked to Greenland's future independence, but it became unilateral in implementation and internal in scope. It was to build a Greenlandic narrative in order to help Greenlanders deal with their past and accept themselves and each other. Commissioners were thus selected from different communities with different experiences and perspectives (Andersen 2019, 222).[9] Hammond articulated the narrative of damaging colonialism and modernisation described above (see, e.g. Hammond in Andersen 2014). Dealing with the past would enable social and societal repair. The Danish refusal to participate disappointed Greenland's members of the Danish *Folketing* (Ritzau 2014; Gaardmand 2014), suggesting that they had envisaged a bilateral project with participation from Denmark.

The government-appointed Commission shared this understanding, while stressing the social dimension. The report opens with the observation that

9 The composition changed during the three-year period, as several commissioners resigned for professional and personal reasons. A total of nine commissioners and an honorable member were involved.

'post-colonial tensions' mark society, while its development 'as a former colony' is 'to a great extent shaped by a pattern of thought that stems directly from the colonial history' (Forsoningskommissionen 2017, 8). The effects of colonialism, according to the Commission, are an 'inner war' at the individual level, which is expressed through substance or sexual abuse, violence, suicide, and the lack of responsibility for oneself (Forsoningskommissionen 2017, 8). The Commission was established in the hope that awareness of the past would create the conditions of possibility for an inclusive and respectful society and secure development. In addition, a fuller history may create a more equal relationship between Greenland and Denmark.[10] According to Commissioner Jens Heinrich (quoted in Scherrebeck 2015), 'Greenland must tell its own story. Its history is primarily written from the outside, so some important dimensions and angles are missing'. In line with the narrative of colonial and modernising damage, Greenlanders have 'national traumas that stem from having been a colony' (Heinrich, in Scherrebeck 2015). But where does the past lead to? Andersen (2019) identifies a tension in the direction of the Commission's work: towards full modern statehood and future equality with Denmark or towards a traditional modernity that rekindles the indigenous worldview? Both strands aimed at 'mastering the past' but spoke to different audiences and were not always reconciled (Andersen 2019, 226). The tension between tradition and modernity is also identified in Greenlandic foreign policy discourse (Jacobsen and Gad 2018).

The post-colonial intentions, however, went beyond the right to define and historicise. The Commission involved an element of taking responsibility for the present, as reflected in the title of the Commission report, 'We Understand the Past, We Take Responsibility for the Present, We Work for a Better Future' (Forsoningskommissionen 2017). The Commission (2017, 8) quotes Aviâja Egede Lynge for suggesting that in order to take responsibility for the past and the life of the people, Greenlanders must study their colonial and post-colonial history, stop blaming others and themselves, and understand that their present feelings relate to their past. This discourse of responsibilisation responds to the idea that Greenland is not yet ready to assume statehood as it relies on budget support from Denmark and has many social problems; it involves agency and a vision for national sovereignty. Hammond's successor, the more moderate and pragmatic Kim Kielsen, continued the discourse of responsibilisation (see, e.g. Kielsen 2021; Egede 2021). It constitutes a nationalist response to the narrative of benevolence and dependence prevalent in Denmark.

Although inspired by transitional justice in South Africa, Canada, and Australia, the Reconciliation Commission sought recognition rather than truth or accountability. The Commission's website explains that truth commissions often aim to achieve reparations and apologies, while the Greenlandic

10 Interview with former commissioner, Jens Heinrich, July 2016.

Commission would 'not demand apologies or [raise] legal claims'.[11] It was thus more akin to a historical commission (see also Pallí-Asperó in this volume).[12] The report states that the commissioners agreed with this intention to not have a truth mandate (Forsoningskommissionen 2017, 17). To former commissioner Jens Heinrich, as the Commission did not have an investigative mandate, it could not have a truth focus.[13] Processes of accountability, which Denmark supports and promotes internationally, were also not intended. This was partly because the Commission had 'insufficient knowledge about who the responsible are', but also due to the more ambiguous issue of Greenland's own role in some of the harmful policies.[14] Greenland's governing council (*Landsrådet*), the main political body until home rule in 1979, formally supported some of the harmful modernisation policies. To Heinrich, therefore, the fact that the political elite had some responsibility complicates Greenland's victim role. 'Can one be a victim if one has part of the responsibility?'[15] This question of culpability may have influenced the Commission's mandate, although others suggest that the role of *Landsrådet* in harmful modernisation policies was constrained by Danish deceit and misinformation (Hermann 2021).

The Commission was controversial in Greenland and Denmark among both experts and the wider population. The mere idea of reconciliation in Greenland or with Denmark was upsetting to those who felt it was a waste of money, unnecessary, or implied an unfair or inappropriate critique of Denmark. Thorkild Kjærgaard (2014, para. 1), a Danish historian who espouses the benevolence narrative, felt that Denmark has 'nothing to regret, nothing to apologise for, and nothing to reconcile'. Thorning-Schmidt acted 'honourably' by refusing to participate in the 'ridiculous' Commission (Kjærgaard 2014, para. 1). Others associated the Commission with its founding politician, Hammond, who was implicated in a corruption scandal shortly after establishing it. Hammond's successor, Kim Kielsen, has arguably paid little attention to the final report.

There is nothing to suggest that Hammond's government initially planned to include an investigation, accountability, or reparations mandate in the Reconciliation Commission, yet the Danish government early on declined to participate in the process. It shared this stand not with young Western countries (Australia, Canada, and New Zealand), but with Europe's older states (see also Destrooper in this volume). To the Greenlandic Broadcasting Corporation, the prime minister stated, 'I do not think it is the intention that Denmark should contribute to this work. I would like to emphasise that it is completely up to

11 The Commission's website *saammaatta.gl* is no longer active, but a copy of the text is available from the author. Accessed May 3, 2021.

12 Ibid.

13 Interview with former commissioner, Jens Heinrich, July 2016.

14 Ibid.

15 Ibid.

the Greenlandic people to start such as discussion' (quoted in Kalaallit Nunaata Radioa 2013a, para. 2). The decision was legitimised with reference to respect for Greenland and equality in the Danish commonwealth (Thorning-Schmidt 2014). Respect and equality, however, could equally justify compliance with Greenland's wish to involve Denmark in a bilateral commission. Perhaps the Danish government feared the disruptive potential of a broad-based inquiry into and discussion of past policies on Greenland, as this could lead to far-reaching changes in the relationship between Greenland and Denmark. A few months earlier, a poll had suggested that 31% of Greenlanders preferred a future collaboration with Canada, while only 22% looked to Denmark. There was a sense in the Danish political establishment that Hammond's government was confrontational and too nationalist (Haslund 2014). In the Danish political establishment, a conflict with Greenland was 'of course' a source of 'constant worry' (Rasmus Jarlov MP, quoted in Sørensen 2017a). To avoid any disruption, perhaps, the government wanted to avoid a general inquiry into Danish policy in Greenland. Indeed, the political establishment succeeded in making the Commission's work relevant mainly for Greenland. The Social Democratic Party saw the Commission report as an 'internal matter' on which it would be inappropriate to comment (Sørensen 2017b); for instance, Karin Gaardsted MP (quoted in Sørensen 2017b) praised the recommendations for 'pointing to what one can do internally in Greenland'. Other MPs with a Greenland portfolio found the report internal in scope (Sørensen 2017a).

The Role of Political Authority

Truth and reconciliation commissions are by definition 'sanctioned by the state', authorised typically by the executive branch of government (Kochanski 2020, 116). They are often viewed as part of a larger state-building project, whereby a regime aims to signal a break with the past by advancing goals associated with the Commission's work, such as reconciliation. In Greenland, this project is the future of Greenlandic independence. The Greenland Reconciliation Commission illuminates the role of political authority in transitional justice by showing how political decision-making enables and constrains the conditions of possibility for particular transitional justice institutions.

Given the self-government of Greenland, the Danish government could not prevent the Commission's establishment. It was sanctioned and funded by Greenland's government *Naalakkersuisut* and sat within the confines of the constitutional structure of the Danish Realm, whereby Greenland has authority over most internal matters. This structure may explain why the Commission had no accountability or reparations mandate. Greenlandic self-government does not cover justice affairs, including police, prosecutors, courts, and prison services, and this likely explains the Commission's focus on recognition rather than accountability and truth. Some forms of resource extraction (e.g. uranium mining) are considered foreign and security related and thus controlled by Denmark. Given Greenland's economic dependence on Denmark, material reparations could only be realised with funding from Denmark, and this would have been difficult without Danish participation. The disruptive intentions behind the Commission, and its challenge to the status quo, informed the Commission's work, although Denmark's place outside the Commission made it intra-Greenlandic and less focused on Denmark's role (Forsoningskommissionen 2017, 16). Had there been Danish government support for a bilateral commission, it may have had a broader scope and involved the Danish public. As it turned out, Danish newspapers hardly wrote about the Commission's report, while Danish MPs generally approached it as an internal matter. Thus, the Commission's post-colonial politics became a social project.

The politics of public apology in Denmark sheds further light on the nature and role of political authority in shaping transitional justice in Greenland–Denmark relations. In particular, it demonstrates a limited government willingness to recognise, but rarely to compensate and never to be held accountable for harmful policies. This recognition does not aim to disrupt, but rather to maintain the status quo in Denmark-Greenland relations. At the same time, Greenlanders harmed by Danish modernisation or their political representatives have since the 1990s sought recognition and accountability.

Public Apologies

Individuals and organisations have called for official apologies for the harm done by Danish colonial and modernisation policies in Greenland since the 1990s, but Danish governments have generally resisted these suggestions. They have, however, issued two apologies for *particular* state policies and thereby officially recognised the wrong done to *specific* individuals. The apologies came in the wake of official investigations, which were preceded by civil society documentation and advocacy. They were accompanied by monetary compensation to the victims. The public apologies for specific policies may be contrasted with the refusal to apologise for the more general phenomenon of harmful colonisation and modernisation of Greenland. Greenland members of the Danish parliament have over the years – and so far unsuccessfully – called for apologies for 'the obvious injustices' done to Greenland (Quass 2014, para. 6).

The first instance of a public apology was given in 1999 by the Danish and home rule governments for the forceful relocation of the Inughuit of Thule in 1953, particularly for the manner in which this was done. It was given reluctantly, following litigation by an organisation of Greenland hunters against the Danish state.[16] The Danish High Court ordered the government to pay

16 For analysis of *Hingitaq 53, Qajutaq Petersen, and Others v. Prime Minister's Office* see Spiermann (2004) and Wulff (2005).

individual and collective reparations for the forced removal, and in 2001 the latter took the form of partial funding of an airport in Qaanaaq. In contrast, in 2008, the Danish prime minister refused to apologise for the general phenomenon of forcible relocation in Greenland when asked to do so by the head of Greenland's home rule. According to Prime Minister Anders Fogh Rasmussen (quoted in Ritzau 2008, para. 7) of the Liberal Party, 'Denmark and the Danes have not the least to feel ashamed about in Greenland, rather the opposite'.

Greenlanders received their second official apology two decades later, in 2020. Again, it concerned the implementation of a specific government policy with identifiable victims: 22 Greenlandic children aged 5–8 and their families. In 1951, the government, in collaboration with Save the Children Denmark and Danish Red Cross, removed the children from their families to place them in the care of Danish families in Denmark. The aim was to Danify the children, creating a modern elite that would return to Greenland and grow up to modernise society. Upon their return after 1 and a half years, however, the majority were placed in an orphanage in Nuuk rather than back with their families, while six children were adopted by their Danish foster parents. The children were so badly affected by this so-called modernisation 'experiment' that many of them died prematurely.

Civil society actors and Greenlandic MPs had asked successive Danish governments to apologise for the policy since the late 1990s, when non-fiction books and films generated public awareness of the child 'experiment' (Bryld 1998). The refusals to apologise[17] articulated the narrative about historical responsibility and change: The children's experiences were unhappy, but the policy was done with the best intentions and in an era governed by different norms and values. We cannot change the past, but today the relationship between Greenland and Denmark is characterised by mutual respect. This position was shared across the political spectrum by centre-left and centre-right parties but was harder to maintain by the two involved NGOs. The Danish Red Cross Society and Save the Children Denmark accordingly apologised for their role in the programme in 2010 and 2015 (Sørensen 2015).

The Greenlandic Reconciliation Commission also sought to illuminate the issue, having met survivors at its public meetings. It highlighted the widespread use of child relocation programmes, argued that no overview existed of how many children were sent to Denmark, how long they stayed, and how the policy later affected them, and recommended the establishment of a register of such relocated children (Forsoningskommissionen 2017, 47). Even then, the Danish *Folketing* rejected a motion committing the government to apologise

17 These refusals were issued by political actors such as Prime Minister Poul Nyrup Rasmussen (the Social Democratic Party) in 1998; Prime Minister Lars Lykke Rasmussen (the Liberal Party) in 2009 and 2010; Karen Ellemann (the Liberal Party), Minister for Social and Internal Affairs, in 2015; and Mai Mercado (the Conservative Party), Minister for Children and Social Affairs, in 2019.

for the 1951 experiment, initiated by Greenlandic MP Aaja Chemnitz Larsen in 2019. However, unbeknown to parliament, the heads of the Danish government and *Naalakkersuisut* had agreed to initiate a joint historical investigation of the 1951 programme and the subsequent fate of the 22 children (Jensen et al. 2020).

A month after the historical investigation was published in November 2020, the government issued an official apology to the 22 Greenlanders who, as children, were sent to Denmark. Prime Minister Mette Frederiksen stated that 'I have followed the case for many years, and I continue to be deeply affected by the human tragedies it contains. Concerns for the children were set aside. So they lost the ties to their families and lineages, their life story, to Greenland and thereby their own people' (Statsministeriet 2020). At the time, only six participants were still alive. The apology was not accompanied by compensation, however; in 2021 the government declined a request for compensation, arguing that 'the actual recognition of past errors' was the important part (Astrid Krag MP quoted in Ritzau 2021). The survivors were compelled to litigate, but the case has not yet been decided.

The two Greenlandic apologies remain exceptional and have required considerable efforts by victims, civil society, and Greenlandic MPs. Victims of other child relocation policies did not receive an official apology, while comparable harmful policies have never been officially recognized. For instance, in 1995 the government provided monetary compensation without an apology to Thule Air Base workers who in 1968 were deployed to remove the remains of a crashed nuclear-armed military aeroplane. At the time, the Danish and US governments withheld information that the material was radioactive and did not provide any protective clothes and equipment to the workers. The Association for Radiation-affected Thule Workers, whose members allegedly suffer from radiation-related diseases and mortality following the clean-up operation, gave up their pursuit of accountability and further compensation in 2013, having lost all court cases against the Danish government at the national and European levels (Kalaallit Nunaata Radioa 2013b). Accountability and apology were not a political priority.

Conclusions

This chapter has analysed transitional justice in Danish–Greenlandic relations, focusing particularly on the Greenland Reconciliation Commission. Transitional justice has been understood as recognition rather than accountability, and even so only minimally. The Greenland government, Greenlandic MPs, and relevant civil society actors pursued a politics of recognition by Denmark, which was at times reluctantly provided and limited in scope. This recognition was to be part of a larger post-colonial project of defining one's past and taking responsibility for the present and the future. The question of accountability, however, has been largely absent in relations between

Greenland and Denmark. Harmful policies in Greenland – whether relating to relocation, child experiments, or the concealment of nuclear material – were authorised formally and officially. In a few cases, therefore, the government provided compensation and/or apologies. The refusal in 2013 to participate in the Greenland Reconciliation Commission is in line with the general Danish approach to transitional justice in Greenland, which is informed by the narrative of benevolent colonialism and modernisation. If that narrative is impossible to defend, actors resort to that of historical responsibility and change. The official apology in 2020 to the surviving participants of the 1951 child relocation scheme did disrupt this narrative, while the subsequent refusal to compensate partly restored it.

Greenlandic actors pursued disruption insofar as reconciliation with the past was an important element on a path towards sustainable independence. The narrative of damaging colonialism and modernisation, which informed the initiative, would have been empowered by Danish participation in the Commission. Instead, however, the refusal to participate in the Commission likely sought to maintain the status quo.

The Greenland Reconciliation Commission highlights the role of political authority in shaping transitional justice. The Danish government's refusal to participate and its rejection of the need for reconciliation made the Commission unilateral as well as intra-Greenlandic in scope. Without Greenlandic authority over justice affairs, it could only have a soft mandate, pursuing neither truth, accountability, nor reparations. The parliamentary reception of the Commission's report framed Greenland's post-colonial problems as internal to Greenland, in line with the general Danish resistance to recognise official Danish harm in Greenland.

The Danish Realm is a consolidated democracy, yet *Naalakkersuisut* and the Reconciliation Commission claimed that transitional justice was a relevant paradigm for Greenland. Actors in Greenland took early inspiration from South Africa's Truth and Reconciliation Commission (Ali 1998b), and later looked to Australian and Canadian efforts to deal with past harm against indigenous communities. The field expanded from settler democracies to a self-governing dependency in the North Atlantic after 2009, when Greenland attained increased autonomy. In Denmark, however, the field is still associated with post-conflict societies and considered relevant for the Global South.

References

Ali, F. (1998a) 'Når fortiden fejes ind under gulvtæppet'. *Information*, 26 February. Retrieved from: https://www.information.dk/debat/1998/02/naar-fortiden-fejes-gulvtaeppet?lst_cntrb.

—— (1998b) 'Grønlandske sår på sjælen.' *Information*, 13 April. Retrieved from: https://www.information.dk/debat/1998/02/groenlandske-saar-paa-sjaelen?lst_cntrb.

—— (2006) 'Traumer i relation til Grønland.' Blog entry, Fatuma Ali: Skønne oplevelser fra Sydgrønland til Toscana. Available at: http://www.fatumaali.dk/?Artikler.

Andersen, A.N. (2010) 'Vore gamle tropekolonier?' *Slagmark: Tidskrift for idéhistorie* 57, 81–91.

——. 2019. 'The Greenland Reconciliation Commission: Moving Away from a Legal Framework.' *The Yearbook of Polar Law* XI, 214–244.

Andersen, A.N., L. Jensen, and K. Hvenegård-Lassen (2016) 'Qullissat: Historicising and Localising the Danish Scramble for the Arctic.' In: G. Huggan and L. Jensen, eds. *Postcolonial Perspectives on the European High North* (93–116). London: Palgrave Macmillan.

Andersen, M.K. (2014) 'Koloniale sår.' Weekendavisen, 10 January.

Bjørnsson, I. (2016) "Vi har ikke behov for forsoning...' Det danske selvbillede i relation til Grønland 1953–2015.' *Temp: Tidskrift for historie* 7(13), 117–150.

Bryld, T. (1998) *I den bedste mening*. Copenhagen: Gyldendal.

Egede, M.B. (2021) 'Formanden for Naalakkersuisuts åbningstale ved Inatsisartuts efterårssamling 2021.' Retrieved from: https://naalakkersuisut.gl/~/media/Nanoq/Files /Attached Files/Taler/DK/EM2021_Mute_B_Egede_DA.pdf.

Forsoningskommissionen (2017) 'Vi forstår fortiden, vi tager ansvar for nutiden, vi arbejder sammen for en bedre fremtid: Betænkning." Nuuk. Retrieved from: https:// naalakkersuisut.gl/~/media/Nanoq/Files/Attached Files/Forsoningskommission/ Endelig betænkning DK.pdf.

Gaardmand, N.G (2014) 'Vi har ikke behow for forsoning, men jeg har fuld respekt for, at det er en diskussion, der optager det grønlandske folk'. Jyllands-Posten, 13 April.

Greenland Naalakkersuisut (2013) 'Et samlet land - et samlet folk. Koalitionsaftale 2013–2017.' Nuuk. Retrieved from: https://naalakkersuisut.gl/~/media/Nanoq/Files/ Attached Files/Naalakkersuisut/DK/Koalitionsaftaler/Koalitionsaftale 2013–2017 endelig version dansk.pdf.

Hannestad, A. (2013a) 'Grønlands nye regering vil undersøge kolonitiden.' Politiken, 28 March.

—— (2013b) 'Etnisk uheld vi beklager.' Politiken, 7 April.

Haslund, E.A. (2014) 'DF: Aleqa skader Rigsfællesskabet.' Berlingske Tidende, 29 April. Retrieved from: https://www.berlingske.dk/politik/df-aleqa-skader-rigsfaellesskabet.

Heinrich, J. (2014) 'Forsoningskommissionen og fortiden som koloni.' *Baggrund*, 28 Nov.

Hermann, A.K. (2021) *Imperiets børn: Da Danmark vildledte FN og Grønland for at beholde sin sidste koloni*. Copenhagen: Lindhardt & Ringhof.

Jacobsen, M. and U.P. Gad (2018) 'Setting the Scene in Nuuk: Introducing the Cast of Characters in Greenlandic Foreign Policy Narratives.' In: K.S. Kristensen and J. Rahbek-Clemmensen, eds. *Greenland and the International Politics of a Changing Arctic: Postcolonial Paradiplomacy between High and Low Politics* (pp. 11–27). Abingdon: Routledge.

Jensen, E.L., S.A. Nexø, and D. Thorleifsen (2020) *Historisk udredning om de 22 grønlandske børn der blev sendt til Danmark i 1951*. 15 November. Copenhagen: Statsministeriet.

Jensen, L. (2015) 'Postcolonial Denmark: Beyond the Rot of Colonialism?' *Postcolonial Studies* 18(4), 440–452.

Johnstone, R.L (2020) 'The Impact of International Law on Natural Resource Governance in Greenland.' *Polar Record* 56(e21), 1–11.

Kalaallit Nunaata Radioa (2005) 'Nutiden skal forstås gennem fortiden'. 12 May. Retrieved from: https://knr.gl/da/nyheder/nutiden-skal-forstås-gennem-fortiden.

—— (2013a) 'Danmark på sidelinjen i forhold til Forsoningskommission'. 29 August. Retrieved from: https://knr.gl/da/nyheder/danmark-på-sidelinjen-i-forhold-til-forsoningskommission.

—— (2013b) 'Tre Thulearbejdere kæmper fortsat'. 23 October. Retrieved from: https:// knr.gl/da/nyheder/tre-thulearbejdere-kæmper-fortsat.

Kielsen, K. (2021) 'Nytårstale 2021'. Nuuk: Naalakkersuisut. Retrieved from: https://naalakkersuisut.gl/~/media/Nanoq/Files/Attached Files/Taler/DK/Nytårstale 2021.pdf.

Kjærgaard, T. (2014) 'Forsoningskommissionen: En grønlandsk folkekomedie'. Kamikposten, 25 December. Available at: http://www.kamikposten.dk/global/maskinrum/rutine/leksikon.aspx?adgang=bruger&menutekst=Indsigt&tag=nyesteartikler&indgang=fraforside&folder=hvadermeningen&sprog=da&punkt=&udvalgt=20141225120802b26.

Kochanski, A. (2020) 'Mandating Truth: Patterns and Trends in Truth Commission Design.' *Human Rights Review* 21(2), 113–137.

Lidegaard, M. (1998a) 'Grønlandsk selvmedlidenhed'. *Information*, 20 February. Retrieved from: https://www.information.dk/debat/1998/02/groenlandsk-selvmedlidenhed?lst_cntrb.

—— (1998b) 'Grønland er ikke Sydafrika.' *Information*, 4 March. Retrieved from: https://www.information.dk/debat/1998/03/groenland-sydafrika?lst_cntrb.

—— (2009) 'Fødestedskriterium'. In: J. Lund, ed. *Den Store Danske*. Online encyclopedia entry. Available at: https://denstoredanske.lex.dk/fødestedskriterium.

Little, A. (2011) 'Disjunctured Narratives: Rethinking Reconciliation and Conflict Transformation'. *International Political Science Review* 33(1): 82–98.

Ministry of Foreign Affairs of Denmark (2011) *Governance for Development: Five Years Support to Democracy, Human Rights, Justice, and Peace in Uganda*. Kampala: Danida's Human Rights and Good Governance Office in Uganda.

—— (2013) *Joint Evaluation of The International Support to the Peace Process in Nepal, 2006–2012*. Copenhagen: The Government of Denmark.

—— (2016) *Denmark - South Sudan: Interim Country Policy Paper 2016-2018*. Copenhagen: The Government of Denmark.

—— (2019) *Strategy for Denmark's Engagement with the United Nations Office of the High Commissioner for Human Rights, 2019–2022*. Copenhagen: The Government of Denmark.

Quass, L. (2014) 'Danmark vil ikke ind i opgør om Grønlands kolonitid." Berlingske Tidende, 12 April. Retrieved from: https://www.berlingske.dk/politik/danmark-vil-ikke-ind-i-opgoer-om-groenlands-kolonitid.

Rezvani, D.A. (2007) 'The Basis of Puerto Rico's Constitutional Status: Colony, Compact, or 'Federacy'?' *Political Science Quarterly* 122(1), 115–140.

Ritzau (2008) 'Slut med undskyldninger til Grønland'. Berlingske Tidende, 13 June. Retrieved from: https://www.berlingske.dk/politik/slut-med-undskyldninger-til-groenland.

—— (2014) 'Sara og Doris efterlyser dansk deltagelse'. Sermitsiaq, 13 April. Retrieved from: https://sermitsiaq.ag/node/166134.

—— (2021) 'Eksperimentbørn får afvist erstatning - Vil nu stævne staten.' Sermitsiaq, 27 December. Retrieved from: https://sermitsiaq.ag/node/234337.

Scherrebeck, E.E. (2015) '"Forsoning handler sjældent bare om en pose penge"'. Information, 4 April. Retrieved from: https://www.information.dk/moti/2015/04/forsoning-handler-sjaeldent-bare-pose-penge.

Søndergaard, B. (2013) 'Hammond: Jeg håber på et selvstændigt Grønland'. Kristeligt Dagblad, 18 April. https://www.kristeligt-dagblad.dk/danmark/hammond-jeg-håber-på-et-selvstændigt-grønland.

Sørensen, H.N. (2015) 'Red Barnet beklager og undskylder grønlandsk børneeksperiment'. Kalaallit Nunaata Radioa, 20 October. Retrieved from: https://knr.gl/da/nyheder/red-barnet-beklager-og-undskylder-grønlandsk-børneeksperiment.

—— (2017a) 'Danske politikere: Forsoningskommissionens anbefalingerne er for generelle'. Kalaallit Nunaata Radioa, 26 December. Retrieved from: https://knr.gl/da/nyheder/forsoningskommissionens-anbefalingerne-er-generelle.

—— (2017b) 'Røde partier roser anbefalinger i Forsoningskommissionen'. Kalaallit Nunaata Radioa, 27 December. Retrieved from: https://knr.gl/da/nyheder/røde-partier-roser-anbefalinger-i-forsoningskommissionen.

Spiermann, O. (2004) 'Hingitaq 53, Qajutaq Petersen, and Others v. Prime Minister's Office (Qaanaaq Municipality and Greenland Home Rule Government Intervening in Support of the Appellants).' *The American Journal of International Law* 98(3), 572–578.

Statsministeriet (2020) 'Undskyldning til de 22 grønlandske børn, som blev sendt til Danmark i 1951'. Press release, 8 December. Retrieved from: https://www.stm.dk/presse/pressemeddelelser/undskyldning-til-de-22-groenlandske-boern-som-blev-sendt-til-danmark-i-1951/.

Thisted, K. (2014) 'Gamle og nye fortællinger om Rigsfællesskabet mellem Danmark og Grønland'. Baggrund, 6 December. Available at: https://baggrund.com/2014/12/06/gamle-og-nye-fortaellinger-om-rigsfaellesskabet-mellem-danmark-og-gronland/

—— (2017) 'The Greenlandic Reconciliation Commission: Ethnonationalism, Arctic Resources, and Postcolonial Identity.' In: L.A. Körber, S. MacKenzie, and A.W. Stenport, eds. *Arctic Environmental Modernities: From the Age of Polar Exploration to the Era of the Anthropocene* (pp. 231–246). Cham: Springer.

Thorning-Schmidt, H. (2014) 'HTS Et ligeværdigt samarbejde i Rigsfællesskabet'. Berlingske Tidende, 29 April. Available at: https://www.stm.dk/statsministeren/indlaeg/hts-et-ligevaerdigt-samarbejde-i-rigsfaellesskabet/.

Wulff, S. (2005) 'The Legal Bases for the Inughuit Claim to Their Homelands'. *International Journal on Minority and Group Rights* 12(1), 63–92.

Chapter 7

Transitional Justice and the British Military in Iraq

Thomas Obel Hansen

Introduction

This chapter provides an analysis of justice responses relating to crimes allegedly committed by British military forces during the Iraq war. Drawing on the author's previous research on justice for crimes in Iraq (Hansen 2018a, 2020, 2021), the chapter examines the nature, progress, and obstacles to these justice processes through the lenses of transitional justice. This is with a view to understanding how the core concepts addressed in this volume – in particular, the intentions and responses of relevant actors to justice processes covering serious crimes – can help us understand the complexities of this case, and in turn what this case can tell us of more general significance about transitional justice. The chapter thus seeks to draw on contemporary transitional justice discourse to understand justice processes in a non-paradigmatic case covering a so-called 'consolidated democracy', which is also a major military power and allegedly responsible for widespread war crimes in an armed conflict abroad.

The chapter does not argue that justice for war crimes in Iraq is necessarily best viewed as an example of transitional justice; rather, it seeks to understand what we can learn by analysing these justice processes through the lenses of transitional justice, specifically the key concepts addressed in this volume. It focuses on understanding how pro-justice actors approach advocacy, litigation, and other tools familiar to transitional justice practitioners when attempting to create momentum for accountability, truth, redress, and reform, and, in contrast, how actors opposed to justice (or at least certain forms of justice) impact the operations and outcomes of justice processes. In this sense, the chapter uses transitional justice concepts to identify and understand opportunities as well as obstacles to justice for crimes by major military powers such as the United Kingdom.

This analysis connects to a broader theme of 'expansion' in the transitional justice field, involving a tendency whereby cases that would have traditionally fallen outside the ambits of transitional justice discourse, referred to in this volume as 'aparadigmatic' cases, are increasingly subject to analysis (Hansen 2013). Transitional justice scholars have recently made a series of claims as to why justice measures aimed at addressing serious violations should be utilised

DOI: 10.4324/9781003289104-8

not only in contexts of paradigmatic transitions, but beyond that, including in cases involving violations by consolidated democracies in the Global North. While such analyses have tended to focus on 'historical' abuses, typically relating to groups in their own population (Winter 2014), there is merit in also asking what lessons such countries may learn from transitional justice in their approaches to accountability, redress, and reform for violations by their armed forces in military campaigns abroad. Or perhaps rather, how domestic and international non-state actors seeking to promote justice for such abuses can best achieve that objective in the face of government resistance.

The chapter observes that despite the persistent efforts of civil society actors and lawyers and a series of court rulings that have compelled the British government to take action it was unlikely to have otherwise taken, achieving criminal accountability for crimes committed in Iraq has proven difficult, not least due to persistent opposition by British decision-makers. Part of the explanation for the relatively successful resistance by these actors has to do with the resourcefulness of the British government compared to the states where transitional justice has historically occurred.

Indeed, meaningful justice has become increasingly implausible due to steps taken by British authorities, coupled with the limited reach – and sometimes inefficiency – of specific legal processes and regimes. Domestic investigative measures appear to have been deliberately framed in such a way as to give the appearance of accountability, while in reality proving an obstacle to this. Certain international legal regimes, specifically the International Criminal Court (ICC), have proven unable to adequately address the situation. Arguably, attempts to pursue justice for crimes in Iraq may even have proven counter-productive, in the sense that the threats of credible justice have led British decision-makers to launch a broader campaign against human rights lawyers and instated measures aimed at protecting the military from legal oversight and accountability. All of this raises questions about the core assumptions made in the literature about the opportunities and challenges to securing justice in difficult political contexts.

The chapter proceeds with a brief overview of developments in transitional justice discourse, focusing on the expansion to address non-paradigmatic cases, including situations involving consolidated democracies and major military powers. The chapter next provides an analysis of justice measures in the UK/Iraq case.

Transitional Justice as an Analytical Framework to Address Violations by Major Military Powers?

The field of transitional justice emerged in the context of the so-called third wave of democratisation, taking a point of departure in the question of how the new democracies of Latin America and East and Central Europe could and should address violations committed by previous authoritarian or totalitarian regimes. At the time, scholars argued that these fundamental political transitions created a 'window of opportunity', permitting the new democracies to adopt justice tools seen as special or extraordinary (Teitel 2003). The field thus focused on one particular form of transition, namely 'the move from less to more democratic regimes' and the justice processes that occur in these so-called paradigmatic transitions (Teitel 2000, 5).

While transitional justice was understood to hold potential for promoting the rule of law and democratic consolidation, it was also suggested that these justice processes could potentially jeopardise democratisation, in so far as they did not properly take account of the conditions set by the political transition itself. In this sense, transitional justice was seen to require a delicate balance between the demands for justice and the realities or limitations of transitional politics. A confined window of opportunity, the 'transitional moment', allowed for novel justice responses, but how far-reaching these responses could be (and when they could be put in place) was thought to depend heavily on the transitional political context. In that sense, transitional justice is based on the assumption that there is a repressive and violent past (often long-lasting); a (brief) transitional moment; and a (never-ending) peaceful and democratic future, at least when transitional justice mechanisms are used appropriately (Hansen 2021).

However, transitional justice practice and scholarship has developed significantly since then. The perception of relevant forms of transition and actors has changed radically. The paradigmatic transitions that shaped the early field are now seen to be only one type of transition where transitional justice potentially comes into play. Moreover, the three-phase perception of time outlined above is no longer taken for granted. Contemporary studies of transitional justice are preoccupied with examining justice processes in various contexts that are not best characterised as liberalising political transition, including situations where justice processes are put in place to address violations by consolidated democracies.

Further, it is now recognised that justice processes addressing serious abuses are often created both long before and after a transition takes place (Venema 2021). As some scholars have argued, transitional justice therefore appears to have lost its connection to 'an exclusive "moment" in time' (McEvoy and McGregor 2008, 6). New questions have emerged pertaining to when a transition commences and ends; how and when transitional justice tools can and should be applied; and, more generally, when it makes sense to refer to justice processes that address serious violations as a matter of transitional justice and what is the significance of such framing.

In light of these developments, it is perhaps not so odd to study what we can learn from analysing a case involving alleged war crimes by a major military power, such as the United Kingdom, in an armed conflict abroad from a transitional justice perspective, even if no fundamental political transition has occurred or is likely to happen.

It is important to note that even if transitional justice increasingly focuses on justice processes relating to abuses committed by consolidated democracies, the focus so far has mainly been on state-driven processes covering so-called *historical* abuses committed *within* that society, such as past abuse and wrongdoing towards indigenous populations in countries such as Canada (Matsunaga 2016). In contrast, justice for crimes committed by major military powers in recent (and sometimes still ongoing) armed conflicts abroad tend not to be framed as a question of 'transitional justice' and has by and large avoided scrutiny in the transitional justice field. Accountability for these types of abuses by major powers is now slowly emerging as a theme in related discourses, in particular international criminal justice.[1]

However, some of the points made in contemporary transitional justice discourse relating to consolidated democracies may be relevant also to these war-related crimes committed by invading and occupying powers. For example, scholars such as Winter (2013; see also Winter in this volume), who seek to develop a more general theory of transitional justice in established democracies suggest that 'structural injustices embedded in established democracies require more prolonged and substantive efforts than the time-limited models borrowed from paradigmatic cases'. As we shall see in the case analysis below, in the case of the United Kingdom, justice processes have indeed been extremely prolonged. At the same time, some argue that the passage of time and a change in attitudes or prevailing norms *within* a liberal democratic order is a pre-condition for achieving a level of justice for these types of abuses, partly because pressure from civil society groups may in some cases build up over the years and ultimately prove a key determinant for the state's decision to eventually support justice tools (Sharp 2015).

This chapter suggests that in the absence of fundamental political change, state opposition to justice for military abuses should not come as a surprise and almost inevitably results in slow and often inefficient justice processes, especially if the government is resourceful. The political leadership's attitudes to justice for these crimes do not necessarily become more progressive as the justice processes unfold; indeed, state officials and political leaders, especially right-wing or conservative ones aligned with the military, may harden their opposition as the 'threat' of meaningful justice becomes more real. As early transitional justice discourse tended to assume that (newly democratic) states would be *supportive* of justice, the field's expansion to aparadigmatic contexts has resulted in many situations characterised by state *opposition* to justice for serious crimes, as is the UK/Iraq case.

Moreover, the state, which has historically been the main actor in transitional justice, is now viewed as one among several actors relevant for promoting

1 This is of course connected to the ICC's interventions in Iraq and Afghanistan (see, respectively, Hansen 2018a; Ferstman 2018).

and implementing transitional justice. It is now accepted that justice for serious crimes can occur at various levels other than the state and that multiple actors play a role in the policy formation and operation of justice processes. Beyond interrogating how lawyers, human rights NGOs, and other civil society actors approach relevant justice tools in such cases, for the purposes of this chapter, it is also significant to examine what role regional and international courts play in terms of addressing serious crimes. Accordingly, we need to understand who supports and resists specific types of accountability measures covering serious crimes – and how and why they do this. This requires awareness that stated and actual intentions are not necessarily identical and that these processes can be highly dynamic, partly because actors change their rationale and behaviour over time.

Another important observation is that in cases involving major military powers, the kinds of justice processes that are most 'successful' do not involve criminal justice, but rather inquiries, redress, and other forms of justice over which the state has less control. Whenever criminal justice processes are put in place, they tend to face significant challenges in producing the desired accountability outcomes, partly because this form of justice tends to be most fiercely contested by pro-military actors (Hansen 2019). While criminal justice is a core component of justice for serious crimes, this does bring into question the feasibility of the 'prosecution preference' (Aukerman 2022, 47) in contexts involving resourceful states such as the United Kingdom. At the same time, however, processes of criminal justice, especially at the ICC, carry with them stigma and may add pressure on the state, at least as long as the scrutiny remains ongoing.

Equally important, this chapter suggests that speaking about 'the state' as an entity that has clear and coherent policy preferences may be inaccurate or even misleading. Whereas transitional justice discourse tends to assume the existence of some form of unified state preference, rationale and behaviour, the analysis in this chapter points to a messier picture, where policy and decision-makers across a broad spectrum of state bodies, including government ministries, parliamentary committees, and the military may indeed have quite diverging preferences. Consequently, they may adopt distinctive, sometimes even conflicting, strategies and behaviour.

The Intentionality Orbit: How Civil Society Groups and Lawyers Have Pushed for Justice for Crimes in Iraq

The attempts to promote accountability, truth and redress for violations committed by British forces in Iraq have been driven not by the state, but mainly by lawyers and civil society groups in and outside the United Kingdom, often acting in tandem. These actors have made use of various strategies and tools familiar to transitional justice in other countries, including documentation of violations; litigation before domestic and international courts; identification of, consultation with, advocacy for, and representation of victims; and engagement with policy and decision-makers at different levels. The steps taken have focused both on advancing criminal accountability for those allegedly responsible for the crimes and a range of non-criminal measures, in particular, providing a remedy for Iraqi victims and establishing state responsibility for the violations. As we shall see, the latter category of efforts has often proven more successful than the former; this begs the question of the extent to which the 'prosecution preference' (Aukerman 2022, 47) in transitional justice will necessarily lead to the desired justice outcomes in cases involving major military powers.

The pursuit of accountability is thus driven by human rights NGOs and lawyers, some of whom have worked on transitional and international justice in other contexts. Their agenda and goals appear partly to be informed by conceptions of criminal justice and strategies familiar from other contexts, although with some innovation.

Human rights organisations quickly took up the task of investigating and documenting crimes by British forces in Iraq, in particular ill-treatment of detainees and killings that were allegedly unlawful (e.g. Amnesty International 2004). Some of this documentation was eventually passed on to Public Interest Lawyers (PIL), a UK-based law firm which gathered victims' statements in Iraq, initially with a view towards litigation before domestic courts. Due to ineffective criminal investigations in the United Kingdom (detailed below), the legal strategies soon involved engagement with international criminal justice mechanisms.

On January 10, 2014, PIL and the European Center for Constitutional and Human Rights (ECCHR), a Berlin-based justice NGO, submitted a comprehensive communication to the ICC Prosecutor, detailing alleged abuses perpetrated by British troops during the Iraq war (ECCHR and PIL 2014). On this basis, they asked the Prosecutor to open a preliminary examination.

In a sense, this action by lawyers and civil society groups created a 'window of opportunity' for justice for crimes in Iraq. With clear references to the January 2014 PIL/ECCHR submission, in May 2014 the Chief Prosecutor of the ICC, Fatou Bensouda, announced that her Office had decided to re-open the preliminary examination into alleged war crimes committed by British soldiers in Iraq (a previous examination had been terminated by former Chief Prosecutor Luis Moreno-Ocampo on the grounds that the allegations of UK abuses in Iraq were not sufficiently grave because only a limited number of incidents could be substantiated (Office of the Prosecutor 2006)). Following the submission of additional material and sustained engagement with the ICC Prosecutor by PIL, ECCHR, and other groups, in November 2017, the ICC Prosecutor concluded that there was a reasonable basis to believe that crimes within the Court's jurisdiction had been committed by British forces (with respect to the treatment of persons in UK forces' custody) and hence that the requirements of subject-matter jurisdiction therefore appeared to be satisfied (Office of the Prosecutor 2017).

This was seen by many commentators as a major victory and raised hope that finally there was a feasible avenue towards (criminal) justice for British crimes in Iraq. Taken together with the ICC's Afghanistan probe (involving allegations against US armed forces and the CIA) and the Court's examination of the situation in Palestine (involving allegations against Israeli armed forces), the decision was also seen by some, including this author, to suggest the possible emergence of a stronger and more confident international criminal justice system, where even the most powerful could be subject to scrutiny – and, in the best event, ultimately held to account (Hansen 2020).

Yet, it was clear to even the most optimistic observers that the road to justice for crimes in Iraq would be long and complex, and many in civil society grew wary as the ICC Prosecutor continued to delay her decision on whether to proceed with a formal investigation of the situation in Iraq. In December 2020, following a review of domestic proceedings in the United Kingdom in light of the complementarity principle, the Prosecutor decided to close the preliminary examination without requesting a formal investigation. The Prosecutor published a detailed report setting out the reasons for this, essentially observing that while war crimes seemed to have been committed on a substantial scale and only minimal accountability for those responsible had been facilitated by Britain's justice system, the Prosecutor could not reach a conclusion that British authorities had been unwilling to carry out investigations 'genuinely' within the meaning of the Rome Statute (Office of the Prosecutor 2020).

ECCHR representatives and other civil society groups who had worked on the case profoundly questioned these conclusions and noted that the Prosecutor had failed to adequately address the dynamics at play in the United Kingdom. As the ECCHR's Andreas Schüller (2020) argued, the ICC Prosecutor's 'strong findings on the commission of international crimes by UK troops and on the failure of the UK's domestic justice system do not correspond at all with the [Prosecutor's] final decision to close the preliminary examination'. Clive Baldwin, a senior legal advisor with Human Rights Watch who had worked intensively on the case, observed that the Prosecutor's decision 'will doubtless fuel perceptions of an ugly double standard in justice, with one approach for powerful states and quite another for those with less clout' (Human Rights Watch 2020). Amnesty International (2020), in equally disappointed remarks, noted that the closure of the UK/Iraq examination 'provides a road-map for obstructionism [as] it rewards bad faith and delays brought about by the failure of the UK military and authorities to conduct independent and impartial investigations' of crimes in Iraq. The disappointment is understandable, as civil society groups and others had come to view the ICC as the last viable option for criminal justice for crimes in Iraq. To understand why, we need to take a look at how domestic justice processes have operated – and how lawyers and civil society groups have engaged in these processes.

British lawyers and civil society groups have worked intensively to inform domestic investigative mechanisms, in particular the Iraq Historic Allegations

Team (IHAT), the domestic body originally tasked with criminal investigations of the Iraqi claims.[2] Simultaneously with engaging the ICC, PIL submitted thousands of cases to IHAT for review. However, only a very small number of these cases were ultimately referred to the Service Prosecution Authority for further review – and even for those, prosecutors decided not to proceed (Ferstman et al. 2018).

As will be detailed below, due to political pressure and claims of inefficiency, IHAT was terminated in 2017, leaving a smaller team of investigators – referred to as the Service Police Legacy Investigation – to complete the investigation of the remaining cases. Civil society groups reacted to IHAT's closure with dismay, some further noting allegations of government interference in the work of this investigative body (Human Rights Watch 2019).

Despite rigorous campaigning and engagement with relevant criminal justice tools, the attempts by lawyers and civil society groups to promote criminal justice for war crimes in Iraq have thus so far proven almost entirely fruitless from an outcome perspective. As will be detailed below, to understand the outcome of domestic and international criminal justice processes, one needs to consider the actions of pro-military actors.

British lawyers also played an important role in promoting non-criminal justice for crimes in Iraq. This includes pursuing judicial reviews, which aim, as Rachel Kerr (2018) notes, 'not at ensuring *individual* criminal responsibility but at ensuring *institutional* accountability at the level of the state'. These cases, brought by PIL acting for Iraqi civilian claimants, sought to compel the government to conduct inquiries into the alleged unlawful killing, abuse, and mistreatment of Iraqi civilians. Altogether, 13 judicial review cases relating to abuses in Iraq have been brought before British courts, and these have contributed significantly to shedding light on shortcomings in the military's approach to prisoner-of-war handling and other crucial issues, often raising serious critique of how the authorities conducted legal and investigative processes (Kerr 2018).

Other British law firms, in particular Leigh Day, brought numerous civil suits seeking compensation for Iraqi victims, leading to settlements in hundreds of cases whereby the government has paid out millions of pounds to Iraqi victims. This is significant from the perspective of victims' redress, but less so in terms of establishing government liability and public awareness of military misconduct since these settlements are not available to the public.

2 Preceding IHAT, criminal investigations by the Royal Military Police led to a limited number of court martials, but these investigations have been deemed flawed and led only to minimal accountability, which is a key reason for the subsequent investigations by IHAT and the Service Police Legacy Investigation. Altogether four courts martial relating to the situation in Iraq have been completed, leading to the conviction of seven soldiers, out of which only one concerned a war crime. Most defendants have been acquitted or the cases discontinued by the Advocate General (Kerr 2018).

The UK government has also initiated two public inquiries relating to allegations of ill-treatment and unlawful killing by British troops in Iraq, one concerning the killing of Baha Mousa (a 26-year-old Iraqi hotel receptionist who was beaten to death while in British custody), which pointed to 'corporate failure' by the British Army as a reason for the use of banned interrogation techniques (Gage 2011). Lawyers and civil society groups have often referred to the findings, especially in the *Baha Mousa* case in their submissions to the ICC and in other contexts, pointing to a level of innovation whereby Britain's own legal processes were effectively utilised against the government in international justice processes.

There is thus no shortcoming of legal processes covering violations in Iraq, and civil society groups and lawyers have substantially engaged many of these in innovative ways. What is clear from the analysis so far is that from an outcome perspective, non-criminal justice processes, including civil suits, have tended to be more successful compared to their criminal counterparts. This has to do both with the level of control the government exercises over criminal and non-criminal justice processes, respectively, and the relative weakness of the ICC regime in terms of confronting a major military power (which in the case of the United Kingdom has also historically been a strong supporter of the Court).

The Response Orbit: How British Authorities Have Created Obstacles to Justice

Despite a normative commitment to the rule of law and accountability principles, British authorities have taken a series of steps aimed at complicating or even undermining the prospects for justice for crimes in Iraq, sometimes with far-reaching consequences beyond this specific case. As a narrative of 'ambulance-chasing' and greedy 'left-wing' lawyers was devised in policy circles, Conservative government ministers and other 'pro-military' actors, notably the Commons Defence Committee, have consistently opposed legal scrutiny of crimes in Iraq, often with reference to a perceived need to enhance 'legal protection for the armed forces' (Hansen 2021). This has involved, among other measures, efforts to end the ICC's preliminary examination; attempts to undermine the credibility of involved lawyers and targeting of specific domestic legal processes, and, most recently, efforts to reform applicable legal frameworks and systems with a view towards minimising legal oversight of the armed forces. As we shall see, the response orbit has been remarkably successful in capturing the agenda and creating obstacles to justice processes.

British authorities have taken a hostile attitude towards criminal accountability options covering crimes in Iraq. As regards the ICC, authorities have responded in multiple, sometimes seemingly conflicting, ways to the Court's activities. On the same day that Chief Prosecutor Bensouda publicly announced that the preliminary examination of the situation in Iraq was re-opened, then

Attorney General Dominic Grieve stated that the United Kingdom remains 'a strong supporter of the ICC' and will 'co-operate with the Court on the examination' (Cobain 2014). At the same time, however, Grieve rejected the idea that British armed forces in Iraq carried out systematic abuses, implying there was no point in the ICC taking an interest in the case. The Director of the UK Service Prosecution Authority, Andrew Cayley, further suggested that ICC prosecutors would be unlikely to move ahead with an investigation due to the existence of domestic accountability processes, thus intimating that the so-called complementarity principle would render potential ICC cases inadmissible (Cobain 2014). Government officials also made it clear that they believed the preliminary examination should be closed because the information on which it is based is not credible (Hansen 2018a).

As the ICC's preliminary examination proceeded, government officials increasingly grew impatient with the Court and intensified their pressure to see the examination closed. With a not-so-subtle reference to the UK's Iraq examination, during the 2018 ICC Assembly of State Parties meeting, British authorities stressed that the Court 'is not there to second guess, still less to review, the decisions of competent, functioning national systems of justice' (Murdoch 2018). It demanded that the Court 'must urgently adopt a closure strategy for its cases, including timelines and targets for preliminary examinations [...]' (Murdoch 2018). Once the ICC Prosecutor announced the termination of the examination, British officials were quick to suggest that this 'vindicates our efforts to pursue justice where allegations have been founded' (Bowcott 2020).

Policy and decision-makers, most expressively the House of Commons Defence Committee, have continuously voiced concerns about IHAT's operations, ultimately resulting in its closure in 2017. IHAT was created by the Ministry of Defence (MoD). It was initially intended as a response to rulings by the European Court of Human Rights and British courts concerning the need to conduct independent investigations in cases involving articles 2 and 3 of the European Convention of Human Rights (ECHR), rather than a mechanism of complementarity in the context of the ICC's jurisdiction.[3] However, once the ICC Prosecutor re-opened the preliminary examination in 2014, IHAT was portrayed by British authorities as facilitating a process that ought to lead the ICC Prosecutor to terminate the preliminary examination with reference to the complementarity principle (Hansen 2018a). Accordingly, this investigative

3 Decisions by the European Court of Human Rights have significantly impacted the way British courts have approached questions relating to IHAT's independence and structure. Notably, in *Al-Skeini v United Kingdom* the Court held that human rights law applies to the Iraq war and occupation in situations where UK forces were an occupying force or when they had custody over an individual and, moreover, that the Royal Military Police investigations were not sufficiently independent to satisfy the standards in the Convention. See European Court of Human Rights (Grand Chamber), *Al-Skeini and Others v The United Kingdom*, Appl. no. 55721/07, July 7, 2011.

process and its rationale have changed substantially over the years, partly in response to the demands of international justice processes (and the convenience of British authorities).

Although created by the MoD, many Conservative politicians soon started criticising IHAT for a case backlog, the manner in which investigators approached service personnel deployed in Iraq, the financial costs of operating it, and not least the reputational damage and threat of prosecution it inflicted on the armed forces. Bob Stewart, a Conservative member of parliament who sits on the Defence Committee, stated these sentiments in clear terms: 'IHAT is irksome, irritating and upsetting for the Armed Forces' (Greenhill 2017).

The Defence Committee (2017, para. 122) ultimately concluded that IHAT, a 'seemingly unstoppable self-perpetuating machine, deaf to the concerns of the armed forces, blind to their needs, and profligate with its own resources', had proven 'unfit for purpose'. Arguing that IHAT had focused on 'satisfying perceived international obligations and outside bodies, with far too little regard for those who have fought under the UK's flag', the Committee recommended it be dissolved (Defence Committee 2017, summary section). This happened soon thereafter.

Importantly, perceptions regarding the likelihood of an ICC investigation were a major factor for British decision-makers that considered the fate of IHAT. Initially, this played out in favour of keeping IHAT alive. For example, the then Secretary of State for Defence argued that the ICC's preliminary examination required the continuation of the IHAT investigations because 'if we were unable to demonstrate that these [criminal allegations] were being properly investigated, we could have ended up [...] opening the way to the International Criminal Court. That would have got us into a far more difficult situation' (Defence Committee 2017, para. 117). Later, the threat of ICC prosecutions seemingly became less credible and the political costs associated with keeping IHAT alive grew for the Conservative government. IHAT was thus seen by many in the British establishment as a 'necessary evil' to satisfy the procedural requirements under the ECHR and later to 'keep the ICC away'. Once the threat of foreign judicial intervention diminished, IHAT was terminated.

Justice processes for crimes in Iraq have thus not occurred in a confined window of opportunity, but have dragged on for years, often with little tangible outcome. One key reason for this, which is under-explored in the literature, is national decision-makers' interest in maintaining domestic justice measures to avoid activation or escalation of international justice mechanisms. In other words, by keeping in place domestic investigative bodies and portraying some form of investigatory activity, Britain has been able to utilise (some would say manipulate) the ICC's complementarity principle to its advantage. This has, however, not led to accountability.

In her decision not to proceed with an investigation the ICC Prosecutor did not consider the *intention* of British decision-makers. Evidently, their intention has not been to promote credible and efficient accountability mechanisms, but rather to avoid accountability processes altogether. These arguments must be viewed in light of the attacks launched on the legal profession in Britain and the legislative moves towards creating combat impunity, discussed in the following.

Given lawyers' involvement in both criminal and civil Iraq-related cases, the approach taken by government officials and other pro-military actors towards the legal profession in Britain has been hostile, at times even aggressive, and it raises serious concerns from a rule of law perspective. The response orbit, driven by political leaders, has created a narrative of service personnel being chased by greedy, left-wing lawyers. For instance, former Prime Minister Theresa May (quoted in Hansen 2018b) stated, 'We will never again – in any future conflict – let those activist left-wing human rights lawyers harangue and harass the bravest of the brave, the men and women of our armed forces'. While her predecessor, David Cameron (quoted in Hansen 2018b), promised to 'crack down on spurious legal claims' and protect British troops from 'being hounded by lawyers over claims that are totally without foundation'. Bob Stewart MP (quoted in Hansen 2018b), a member of the Defence Committee, observed that 'Not only do we have civilian battlefield ambulance chasers, we now have MoD battlefield ambulance chasers [...] I'm fed up with our soldiers being chased and harassed and intimidated after they have put their lives on the line'.

This narrative gained ground as the lead lawyer for PIL, Phil Shiner, was convicted by the Solicitors Disciplinary Tribunal for misconduct relating to paying Iraqi middlemen to find claimants in Iraq, which is prohibited under UK law. British authorities quickly took advantage of this, arguing that the cases before IHAT and the ICC were vexatious due to Shiner's misconduct (Hansen 2018b). This claim ignored the fact that the cases filed were not necessarily without merit simply because middlemen helped locate victims and witnesses and, moreover, not all cases under review had been brought by PIL.

In fact, the government has been remarkably skilled and successful in turning the narrative from one of justice for crimes in Iraq to one of justice for soldiers wrongly accused of crimes. As then Defence Secretary, Michael Fallon (quoted in Bowcott 2017a), stated after Shiner's conviction: 'Justice has finally been served after we took the unprecedented step of submitting evidence on [Shiner's] abuse of our legal system'.

The most recent move to challenge legal oversight and accountability for the armed forces involves the government's introduction of the so-called Overseas Operations (Service Personnel and Veterans) Bill in 2020. The Bill introduces a statute of limitations-like proposal, referred to as a 'presumption against prosecution', which would substantially limit the possibilities for investigating and prosecuting crimes committed by British soldiers abroad. The Bill also includes a duty for the Secretary of State to consider derogation from the ECHR in the context of overseas operations; amendments to the United Kingdom's legislation domesticating the ECHR, the Human Rights Act; and a so-called 'civil litigation longstop', which, if implemented, is likely to severely limit civil litigation arising from the actions of the UK military when operating abroad (Hansen 2021).

According to the Secretary of State for Defence, Penny Mordaunt MP, these measures were justified given the internal 'lawfare' by British lawyers and civil society groups (Ministry of Defence 2019, 3). To Michael Fallon MP, her predecessor, they were a response to the United Kingdom's legal system having been 'abused to level false charges against our troops on an industrial scale' (quoted in Bowcott 2017b). Critics note that these measures would 'dent soldiers' respect for international law by undermining the part of their training which reminds them that investigations and accountability will follow for violations of international law in armed conflict' (Bates 2020). They could 'entrench flawed investigatory practices, and create incentives either to close investigations without a prosecution, or to leave investigations incomplete for five or more years' (Bates 2020). Others note that by adopting these proposals, the United Kingdom would 'effectively decriminalis[e] torture' (Alistair Carmichael MP, cited in House of Commons Library 2020, 40); and that the limitations for prosecutions 'would encourage a culture of delay and cover-up of criminal investigations' (Baldwin 2020). Whereas the response by government is to limit legal oversight of the armed forces, members intending for transitional justice refer to international obligations and victims' rights when arguing that accountability and legal oversight of the armed forces should be enhanced.

Another important point is that the transitional justice literature tends to assume that legal reforms are introduced in the wake of serious human rights and humanitarian law violations with a view towards enabling *more* or *improved* forms of accountability, truth, redress, non-recurrence of violations, and other goals of transitional justice. Of course, this assumption is associated with the field's origins in examining paradigmatic transitions where a new democratic leadership is a partner in transitional justice: it replaces an authoritarian regime responsible for the violations and therefore would tend to implement legal reform with a view towards promoting justice. However, the UK/Iraq case illustrates that legal reform can also serve the opposite purpose: to limit the prospects for justice for state violations by putting in place new 'justice barriers'. While transitional justice as a field provides some relevant tools for engaging the UK/Iraq case, for example, in terms of potential disruption (see the Introduction in this volume), the case also brings into question a range of assumptions in the field highlighted in this chapter.

Conclusions

A wide range of justice processes have been put in place to address claims of war crimes by British soldiers in Iraq. Overall, these have been slow-moving, are generally resisted by government actors, and have so far produced relatively limited justice outcomes, especially regarding criminal justice. Yet, even if outcomes are limited, these processes have caused disruption in the United Kingdom, due to the awareness of crimes the processes have created and the additional scrutiny that goes with being subject to the ICC's examination regime. Court rulings in and outside of the United Kingdom have forced the government to take action it was unlikely to have otherwise taken.

It is critical to keep in mind that these processes have unfolded, not because the government has actively sought to promote justice and behavioural change, but rather because lawyers and civil society groups have engaged and creatively utilised justice tools intending to pursue accountability for British crimes in Iraq. However, while we have seen some redress to victims, mainly through out-of-court settlements of civil suits, criminal accountability to date has been extremely limited. The response by government authorities and other mainly Conservative political actors has been to take various steps to undermine the justice processes, including by creating a narrative of 'ambulance-chasing lawyers', seeking to undermine some of the justice processes in place, and more recently inventing new legal obstacles to justice. Justice for British crimes in Iraq has not been associated with a political or normative transition at the leadership level, though without the justice processes that we have seen unfolding, there would have been less awareness and acknowledgement that serious crimes were committed by British forces in Iraq, and victims would have been left entirely without a remedy.

References

Amnesty International (AI) (2004) 'Iraq: One Year on the Human Rights Situation Remains Dire'. AI Index: MDE 14/006/2004.

—— (2020) 'ICC Decision on UK Military in Iraq Rewards Obstructionism'. 10 December 2020. Retrieved from: https://www.amnesty.org/en/latest/news/2020/12/icc-decision-on-uk-military-in-iraq-rewards-obstructionism/

Aukerman, M.J. (2002) 'Extraordinary Evil, Ordinary Crime: A Framework for Understanding Transitional Justice'. *Harvard Human Rights Journal* 15, 39–97.

Baldwin, C. (2020) 'UK Bill a License for Military Crime?' New York: Human Rights Watch. Retrieved from: https://www.hrw.org/news/2020/03/20/uk-bill-license-military-crimes.

Bates, E.S. (2020) 'Legislating by Soundbite: The Overseas Operations (Service Personnel and Veterans) Bill'. Blog entry. EJIL:Talk!, 18 September. Retrieved from: https://www.ejiltalk.org/legislating-by-soundbite-the-overseas-operations-service-personnel-and-veterans-bill/.

Bowcott, O. (2017a) 'Phil Shiner: Iraq Human Rights Lawyer Struck Off over Misconduct'. The Guardian, 2 February.

—— (2017b) 'Plan to Opt Out of Rights Accords in Future Wars Dangerous, Inquiry Hears'. The Guardian, 24 April.

—— (2020) 'ICC Abandons Inquiry into Alleged British War Crimes in Iraq'. The Guardian, 9 December.

Cobain, I. (2014) 'ICC to Examine Claims that British Troops Carried Out War Crimes in Iraq'. The Guardian, 13 May 2014. Available at: www.theguardian.com/law/2014/may/13/icc-to-investigate-alleged-british-war-crimes-iraq.

Defence Committee (2017) *Who Guards the Guardians? MoD support for former and serving personnel, Sixth Report of Session 2016–17*'. 9 February. London: House of Commons. Available at: https://www.publications.parliament.uk/pa/cm201617/cmselect/cmdfence/109/10909.htm.

ECCHR & PIL (2014). 'The Responsibility of Officials of the United Kingdom for War Crimes Involving Systematic Detainee Abuse in Iraq from 2003–2008'. 10 January 2014.

Ferstman, C. (2018) 'The International Criminal Court Prosecutor's Preliminary Examination on Afghanistan and Possible Impacts on Accountability for Secret Detention and Rendition'. In: E. Guild, D. Bigo, and M. Gibney, eds. *Extraordinary Rendition: Addressing the Challenges of Accountability*. London: Routledge.

Ferstman, C., T.O. Hansen, and N. Arajärvi (2018) 'The UK Military in Iraq: Efforts and Prospects for Accountability International Crimes Allegations'. Discussion Paper, October. Colchester and Belfast: University of Essex School of Law and Ulster University Transitional Justice Institute. Retrieved from: https://www.ulster.ac.uk/__data/assets/pdf_file/0018/317502/THE-UK-MILITARY-IN-IRAQ-1Oct2018.pdf.

Gage, W. (2011) *The Report of the Baha Mousa Inquiry*. HC 1452–1, 8 September. London: House of Commons.

Greenhill, S. (2017) 'Five Years of Lawyers Sifting Through Abuse Claims... and ONE Guilty Soldier: Allegations Team has Completed just 18 Cases'. The Daily Mail, 11 January. Available at: http://www.dailymail.co.uk/news/article-3393193/Five-years-lawyers-sifting-abuse-claims-ONE-guilty-soldier-Allegations-team-completed-just-18-cases.html

Hansen, T.O. (2013) 'The Vertical and Horizontal Expansion of Transitional Justice: Explanations and Implications for a Contested Field'. In: S. Buckley-Zistel, T.K. Beck, C. Braun, and F. Mieth, eds. *Transitional Justice Theories* (pp. 105–124). Abingdon: Routledge.

—— (2018a) 'Accountability for British War Crimes in Iraq? Examining the Nexus between International and National Justice Responses. In Bergsmo, M. & Stahn, C. (eds.) *Quality Control in Preliminary Examinations*, Vol. 1. Brussels: Torkel Opsahl Academic EPublisher.

—— (2018b) 'Complementarity in(action) in the UK?' Blog entry. EJIL: TALK! 7 December. Available at: https://www.ejiltalk.org/complementarity-inaction-in-the-uk/.

—— (2019) 'Opportunities and Challenges Seeking Accountability for War Crimes in Palestine'. *Notre Dame Journal of International and Comparative Law* 9(2), 1–32.

—— (2020) 'The Role of Great Powers within the Court'. Conference paper, *The International Criminal Court in Crisis?* Conference, 27–28 February. Århus: The Danish Foreign Policy Society and the University of Southern Denmark. Available at: https://papers.ssrn.com/sol3/papers.cfm?abstract_id=3546847

—— (2021) 'The Multiple Aspects of 'Time' Rendering Justice for War Crimes in Iraq'. *International Criminal Law Review* 21(1), 878–904.

House of Commons Library (2020) 'Overseas Operations (Service Personnel and Veterans) Bill 2019–21'. Briefing Paper No. 8983, 22 September. Available at: https://researchbriefings.files.parliament.uk/documents/CBP-8983/CBP-8983.pdf.

Human Rights Watch (2019) 'Joint Letter on UK War Crimes Cover-Up Allegations'. 25 November. Retrieved from: https://www.hrw.org/news/2019/11/25/joint-letter-uk-war-crimes-cover-allegations

—— (2020) 'United Kingdom: ICC Prosecutor Ends Scrutiny of Iraq Abuses'. 10 December. Retrieved from https://www.hrw.org/news/2020/12/10/united-kingdom-icc-prosecutor-ends-scrutiny-iraq-abuses

Kerr, R. (2018) 'The UK in Iraq and the ICC: Judicial Intervention, Positive Complementarity and the Politics of International Criminal Justice'. In: M. Bergsmo, and C. Stahn, eds. *Quality Control in Preliminary Examination* Volume 1. Brussels: Torkel Opsahl Academic EPublisher.

Matsunaga, J. (2016) 'Two Faces of Transitional Justice: Theorizing the Incommensurability of Transitional Justice and Decolonization in Canada'. *Decolonization: Indigeneity, Education & Society* 5(1), 24–44.

McEvoy, K. and L. McGregor (2008) 'Transitional Justice from Below: An Agenda for Research, Policy and Praxis'. In: K. McEvoy and L. McGregor, eds. *Transitional Justice from Below: Grassroots Activism and the Struggle for Change*. London: Hart.

Ministry of Defence (2019) 'Legal Protections for Armed Forces Personnel and Veterans Serving in Operations Outside the United Kingdom'. Consultation paper, 22 July.

Murdoch, A. (2018) 'Statement to the International Criminal Court Assembly of States Parties, at its 17th session in The Hague'. UK statement to the ICC Assembly of States Parties, 17th session. Retrieved from: https://www.gov.uk/government/speeches/uk-statement-to-icc-assembly-of-states-parties-17th-session.

Office of the Prosecutor (2006) 'OTP Response to Communications Received Concerning Iraq'. 9 February. The Hague: The International Criminal Court. Retrieved from: http://www.legal-tools.org/doc/5b8996/.

—— (2017) *Report on Preliminary Examination Activities 2017*. The Hague: The International Criminal Court. Retrieved from: https://www.icc-cpi.int/news/report-preliminary-examination-activities-2017.

—— (2020) *Situation in Iraq/UK: Final Report*. 9 December. The Hague: The International Criminal Court. Retrieved from: http://www.icc-cpi.int/sites/default/files/itemsDocuments/201209-otp-final-report-iraq-uk-eng.pdf.

Schüller, A. (2020) 'The ICC, British War Crimes in Iraq and a Very British Tradition'. Blog entry. Opinio Juris, 11 December. Retrieved from: https://opiniojuris.org/2020/12/11/the-icc-british-war-crimes-in-iraq-and-a-very-british-tradition/.

Sharp, D. (2015) 'Emancipating Transitional Justice from the Bonds of the Paradigmatic Transition'. *International Journal of Transitional Justice* 9(1), 150–169.

Teitel, R. (2000) *Transitional Justice*. Oxford: Oxford University Press.

—— (2003) 'Transitional Justice Genealogy'. *Harvard Human Rights Journal* 16(1) 69–94.

Venema, D (2012). "Transitions as States of Exception: Towards a More General Theory of Transitional Justice". In Palmer, N. et al. (eds.), *Critical Perspectives on Transitional Justice*. Cambridge, UK: Intersentia.

Winter, S. (2013) 'Towards a Unified Theory of Transitional Justice'. *International Journal of Transitional Justice* 7(2), 224–44.

Chapter 8

Divergent Ambitions

Bracketing the Disruptive Potential of Transitional Justice in Belgium[1]

Tine Destrooper

The Relevance of Transitional Justice in Belgium

Belgium is one of the countries which – reluctantly – adopted some elements of standardised transitional justice in an attempt to deal with the legacy of a violent past. In the summer of 2020, the Belgian parliament established a special parliamentary commission to investigate the 'Belgian colonial past in the Congo (1908–1960), and Rwanda and Burundi (1919–1962), the impact thereof and the appropriate response to this' (Belgische Kamer 2020).[2] The establishment of this commission, which soon came to be labelled the Belgian Truth and Reconciliation Commission (Cessou 2020), illustrates (standardised) transitional justice travelling to aparadigmatic contexts that see the potential of these mechanisms and their claim that recognising past harm is a precondition for more peaceful and inclusive societies.

In the first section of this chapter, I examine this truth commission as an external observer (who was also consulted). I argue that the truth commission's ambition is not, *a priori*, out of sync with the core intentionality of transitional justice (i.e. accountability and recognition), but that the process adopted intentionally or unintentionally by the truth commission hampers its capacity to substantially work towards these goals or to have any kind of disruptive effect. In the second section, I contrast this commission with an initiative in the domain of education, in which I was involved as a researcher discussing a new research project with educational stakeholders. The project posited that forward-looking mechanisms developed under transitional justice's fourth pillar (guarantees of non-recurrence) to deal with conflict transformation could also be relevant to transform and prevent societal conflict in consolidated democracies. Specifically, the project highlighted the wealth of information and expertise amongst transitional justice practitioners in the Global South regarding how educational and pedagogical initiatives can contribute to defusing societal

1 This research was partly funded through ERC-StG-804154 VictPart.

2 Author's translation.

DOI: 10.4324/9781003289104-9

polarisation, and how this could also be relevant for consolidated democracies facing increased societal polarisation. Responses to this proposal demonstrated a significant reluctance and sometimes outright rejection on the side of institutionalised experts to engage with the intentionality or mechanisms of transitional justice, whether formulated conservatively or in a more far-reaching manner.

Both initiatives have been proposed in the context of a state that is not per se looking to question its own identity as a liberal rule-of-law state, and that does not seek to fundamentally change anything to the basic make-up of its core state institutions or discourse about justice. As such, initiatives from the domain of transitional justice could be considered too disruptive (see the Introduction in this volume), entailing a risk of delegitimising and disrupting the very discourses that make up the backbone of how national identity, legitimacy, and justice are constructed.

Contrasting these two cases brings out questions and possibilities about which dimensions of transitional justice are rejected and which ones are embraced, and by whom. The establishment of the commission, in that sense, should not unequivocally be read as a progressive or pro-active embrace of transitional justice or its emphasis on accountability. I argue that in Belgium what gets adopted more easily are those standardised forms of transitional justice whose rhetoric of ensuring accountability and recognition of past harm neatly fit the normativity of those in decision-making positions, without posing too much risk of disrupting the status quo. This becomes clear if we consider the narrative, temporal structuring and mandate of the current commission, all of which can be characterised as top-down and managerial, which in turn explains the negative response by many civil society actors. It also becomes clear if we consider institutional actors' rejection of transitional justice in the case of educational reform. The chapter thereby illustrates the argument put forward in the Introduction to this volume, namely that in consolidated democracies transitional justice mechanisms are adopted in ways that minimise disruption of the status quo.

I conclude this chapter by considering what these observations mean for the broader transitional justice picture and comparing the contestation of institutionalised actors (regarding more innovative or far-reaching forms of transitional justice) with that of non-institutionalised actors (regarding the process currently adopted in the context of the commission).

A Truth Commission on Belgium's Colonial Past

Truth-Seeking in 'Consolidated Democracies'

Parliamentary commissions of inquiry are not a new phenomenon in consolidated democracies. They can cover a broad range of issues, some of which are not related to the domain of transitional justice at all (e.g. commissions investigating tax fraud),[3] while others arguably move more explicitly into the realm of transitional justice without using that label per se. An example of the latter type is the Belgian parliamentary commission established in 1999 to research the circumstances of the murder of Patrice Lumumba (Verdoolaege and Kerstens 2004). Yet others, like the current commission, move more explicitly into the domain of transitional justice and engage more explicitly with its notions.

The latter form part of a recent tendency to increasingly and explicitly position these commissions within transitional justice's normative framework of accountability and reconciliation. This can be observed in their naming, as well as in their mandates. Australia, Canada, New Zealand (see Winter in this volume), and the United States (see McGonigle Leyh in this volume) are examples of consolidated democracies that installed commissions of inquiry whose naming and/or mandate followed the logic of classic truth commissions. This is arguably because the transitional justice discourse and label refer to widely recognised mechanisms and normativity that seem appealing.

These examples are cases of settler democracies using commissions to investigate crimes against first nations or indigenous peoples. Belgium, on the contrary, was the first (and, at the time of writing, only) country to establish a commission to deal with its *overseas* colonial legacy within its own institutions and to reflect on the question of reparations (see also Gissel in this volume).[4]

A Special Parliamentary Commission to Deal With the Colonial Legacy

While not officially called a truth commission, the mandate of Belgium's special parliamentary commission follows the method of a truth commission and inscribes itself in the rhetoric of truth commissions. It combines historical research with collecting testimonies obtained in hearings and refers to reconciliation in its mandate. It also adopts the rhetoric of transitional justice in its outreach to consulted experts, which was explicitly structured along the lines of the four transitional justice pillars. I therefore use the denominator 'truth commission' in the remainder of this chapter, which is also what the commission is commonly referred to in the public debate (e.g. Cessou 2020).

The commission was established in the summer of 2020, when Belgium was ruled by a caretaker government of liberals and Christian democrats following

3 The Tunisian Truth and Dignity Commission is an exception where a truth-seeking body explicitly linked tax fraud to human rights violations in the context of transitional justice (e.g. Vatthauer and Weipert 2017).

4 Several truth commissions in former colonies had already opened up the black box of colonial legacies. Think of the temporally extended mandate of the Tunisian truth commission, for example, or the unilateral Greenlandic initiative regarding the Danish colonial period. None of these had the official support of the former colonial power however.

resolutions by the two Green parties and the Christian-Democratic Party. The swift decision came as a surprise to many observers, given that diaspora organisations and CSOs over the past half a century had had little success in pushing the Belgian government to deal with its colonial past in a systematic manner. Moreover, a 2017 bill on a memorial workplan to establish the facts about official Belgian involvement in the Congo, Rwanda, and Burundi had fallen on deaf ears. Ongoing vested interests and a lack of political will had dimmed the prospects of an official truth-seeking body. This was often complemented by the argument that we already knew the truth, and that what was needed now was acknowledgement and repair, not truth-seeking.

The decision to establish a commission can be understood in light of the momentum created by protest against the continued uncontextualised and glorifying presence of Leopold II in the public domain, the growing visibility of the Black Lives Matter movement in Europe, and the 2020 official letter from the Belgian king expressing 'deep regret' over the atrocities in the Congo under Leopold II (Vergauwen 2020). Furthermore, the September 2019 report of the UN Working Group of Experts on People of African Descent explicitly called for the instalment of a truth commission (Human Rights Council 2019, para. 75l).

Within its initial 12-month mandate, the commission was tasked with focusing on truth and reconciliation, which the mandate broadly and ambitiously conceptualised as (a) providing clarity about the Congo Free State (1885–1908) as well as the colonial past of the Belgian state (1908–1960/1962); (b) investigating the impact of Belgian state and non-state actors in the Congo, Rwanda, and Burundi (1885–1962); (c) examining the economic impact of the colonisation on Belgium as well as the three countries; (d) formulating recommendations about how to deal with this past; (e) proposing reconciliation initiatives; and (f) making recommendations about how to better deal with this past in the future (Belgische Kamer 2020).

To work towards these goals, the commission was supported by ten affiliated experts, who were tasked with presenting the first report to the commission two months after their appointment. This report was to cover state-of-the-art scientific research on all the matters mentioned in the mandate, across the four countries (including the historical truth, the effect of colonialism on the postcolonial period, racism, xenophobia, and intolerance); a mapping of the archives in the four countries; a mapping of the scientific consensus; the identification of knowledge gaps and proposed research to be carried out by the commission during the remainder of its mandate to fill these gaps; a status of divulgation activities for existing knowledge; a mapping of all the symbolic and other actions regarding the colonial past that have been undertaken, both in Belgium and in other three countries; and a mapping of all the actors relevant from a reconciliation point of view (Belgische Kamer 2020, para. 7). The immensity of this task combined with the breakneck speed at which the commission aimed to work, met with great resistance from diaspora members and CSOs, who had been mobilising around this topic for decades but were now deprived of any kind of meaningful participation. The broadness of the mandate along with the way in which the process was organised also raised questions of intentionality.

Embracing Transitional Justice to Deal with Belgium's Colonial Legacy

Intentionality

The denomination and mandate of the commission neatly fit the intentionality of transitional justice laid out in the Introduction to this volume. The mandate, for example, expresses an explicit concern with recognition of past violence as a means to work towards a more peaceful and cooperative future. On the day of the commission's establishment, its chairperson, Wouter de Vriendt, cited the need for an 'official discourse in which we condemn the exploitation of colonialism and acknowledge Belgium's responsibility' as one of the main reasons for establishing the commission. He gave further reasons for the need to 'write history', 'acknowledge the past', issue a formal apology, engage in a conversation about reparations, and 'be an example for other former colonizers' in terms of how they can deal with their past (Verberckmoes 2020). In terms of intentionality, the commission thus seemed to rely on a standardised transitional justice rhetoric revolving around certain limited forms of accountability and recognition.

This reliance on standardised transitional justice rhetoric was also observed in the outreach of the expert group to non-affiliated experts. In preparation for its first report, the expert group sent a survey to non-academic experts, which would feed back into its suggestions regarding the commission's operational model, the topics to be dealt with, and the persons to be heard.[5] This survey covered the topics of history, reconciliation, reparation, the relation between colonialism and racism, divulgation and education, and participation. It contained mostly closed questions that explicitly adopted a standardised transitional justice rhetoric. The 'reconciliation' section, for example, asked what would be needed to arrive at reconciliation: truth, justice, reparation, institutional reforms, apologies, and/or acknowledgement of suffering. The 'reparation' section, too, reflected the transitional justice logic, listing as possible reparation measures: the restitution of goods, (psychological) rehabilitation, financial compensation, symbolic reparations, or regulations addressing root causes of ongoing harm. At the same time, the survey was also exploring several non-standardised transitional justice approaches or topics, for example, when asking

5 The initial survey was sent to experts at the end of the working day on September 21, for a report that was due October 1. Following an extension granted by the commission, non-affiliated experts were given four additional weeks to respond to the survey.

about the relation between colonialism and racism or about what could be the role of education. The latter was considered important and was surveyed in a more open-ended Socratic manner, rather than through a highly-scripted checkbox approach.[6] The commission thus relied predominantly on standardised transitional justice approaches and to a lesser extent on non-standardised approaches to arrive at some form of accountability and recognition of past harm.

A more critical reading of the commission's intentions, however, suggests that this transitional justice rhetoric – both in its standardised and non-standardised form – belied some of the ways in which the stated aim of accountability and reconciliation could be undermined by the processual aspects of the commission's work. More specifically, while the mandate of the commission may overlap with a classic transitional justice intentionality of accountability and recognition, the process was organised in a way that arguably challenged the extent to which these outcomes could materialise, notably by initially paying little to no attention to stakeholder involvement. This lack of attention to inclusive processes, as well as the commission's temporal structuring, could explain the responses to the commission's first months of operation, which is the focus of the next section. It also raised the question about the extent to which these processual aspects were, in fact, indicative of institutional actors' seeking to avoid the disruptive potential of such a commission by paying lip service to transitional justice's focus on recognition, but not in fact leading to recognition.

Response

The truth commission did not mean that institutional actors also automatically embraced other elements of transitional justice, such as victim-oriented or inclusive approaches. Instead, the truth commission was a stand-alone, fast-paced, top-down initiative. As a result, responses to the commission were mixed, notably due to the non-inclusion of key stakeholders and its temporal structuring, which challenged the credibility of the commission's intentions.

The proposal in the Introduction of this volume to spatialise responses to transitional justice allows us to visibilise the normative positionality that characterises various positions in the debate. For the purpose of this chapter, the most interesting response came from diaspora organisations, Belgo-African CSOs, and experts with roots in the Congo, Rwanda, or Burundi, who had long been mobilising for more sincere and comprehensive ways of dealing with Belgium's colonial legacy. These groups have been amongst the most notable critics of the commission, and their responses have ranged from scepticism to

6 The question was not 'Should we turn to education?' but, rather, 'Can you propose three ways to turn to education?'

outright rejection.[7] One of the most vocal critics of the commission's approach has been Olivia Rutazibwa, who refused the invitation to join the expert team of the commission. In an open letter, Rutazibwa (2020) problematised the extent to which 'the timeline, pace, agenda and sequence of the proceedings' endangered its core objectives and argued that 'this initiative and those who took it, suffer from a huge deficit of legitimacy, competence and insight'. As an academic, former journalist, and public intellectual, her critique of the commission's composition, timeline, and focus came to shape much of the public discourse.[8]

This critique overlapped with that of Nadia Nsayi (2020), who also refused to join the expert group, citing the commission's lack of legitimacy among diaspora groups, who were initially insufficiently represented in the expert group and not given the same status as the academic experts. The involvement of critical Black experts was crucial, she argued, not just because they put the issue on the agenda, but also because they would ensure that the commission's mandate would be operationalised in ways most relevant to victims, diaspora, and relevant stakeholders, i.e. as an opportunity to bring the existing knowledge together in a way that allows for 'historical conclusions' (Nsayi 2020). Nsayi also problematised the lack of clarity over the commission's mandate, arguing that this challenged its support and legitimacy.[9]

Both experts critiqued the virtual absence of diaspora representatives at the time of initiating the commission and shaping its mandate, and the extent to which these groups – who are expert witnesses of the consequences of colonisation in their daily lives (both in Belgium and in the former colonies) – have been invisibilised and excluded from the various constitutive steps of

7 I do not engage extensively with the attacks coming from the far-right party: these are analytically less relevant because they reflect populist rhetoric for quick political gain, and as such, say little about the practice of transitional justice or how it is perceived. Moreover, the commission was relatively absent from the rhetoric of the far-right party, which found itself caught between its anti-monarchist and anti-Wallonian rhetoric (which would logically have to lead them to endorse this commission because of its narrative that Belgium's colonial past is, in essence, the past of French-speaking Belgium and of the royal family) and its racist, anti-leftist, anti-'political correctness' rhetoric. The latter dominated but this tension made this an uneasy theme to mobilise against in any full-blown manner. Also in the discourse of mainstream political parties the commission has been relatively absent, and it never gathered the kind of public attention or debate as it did in some other countries like Canada.

8 Rutazibwa is lecturer at Portsmouth University, a former full-time journalist at *Mo*Magazine*, and a regular commentator in newspapers.

9 The discussion over whether the focus should be on historical research or on reconciliation also stirred the academic community with 58 academics pleading for more historical research before even considering a public debate or reconciliation (Balace et al. 2020). Others responded to this call by arguing that it would only further delay the process, and that, on the contrary, there should be a political and public debate first to determine what we need more research on, before embarking on that research (Willems et al. 2020).

the commission.[10] Their focus on the process and on who was (allowed to be) engaged in it also touches upon the potential outcomes: by making the process inclusive and opening it to a broad range of stakeholders, a new range of outcomes becomes imaginable.

This goes to the heart of both intentionality and normativity. More specifically, the critique inscribes itself in a transformative transitional justice discourse, which argues that transitional justice should not only be about accountability for and recognition of past harm, but also, and essentially, about changing the epistemic and socio-economic foundations that facilitated that harm's occurrence in the first place (Gready and Robins 2014, Tarusarira 2019). By highlighting the extent to which the initiators failed to 'launch an open call to the communities concerned about whom they would like to put forward for an expert group and what they think the sequence and content of this decolonial initiative should be' (Rutazibwa 2020),[11] the commission's critics called into question its potential to disrupt in any significant way both the epistemic bedrock and the socio-economic conditions underlying the historical and ongoing harm related to decolonisation and the eradication of racism. Indeed, several organisations concurred that the legitimacy and usefulness of this commission should not and could not lie in its uncovering of a historical 'truth' (which is already known), but that it would only be able to gain legitimacy and relevance if it were to (a) move beyond this truth-seeking function and also relate its work to the present day, and (b) ensure 'a radical shift and dislocation of power in this conversation and the initiatives that will follow' (Rutazibwa 2020).

This critique was thus rooted in the way in which the process was organised and the ensuing perception that the intentions of the commission were neither inclusive nor sufficiently far-reaching. The critics also questioned the extent to which the process interfered with the aim of contributing to accountability and recognition of past harm, given that it generated a risk of invisbilising or erasing certain topics or dimensions that were important to stakeholders.

10 To select these experts, rather than consult diaspora or civil society organisations, the commission of Foreign Affairs initially sought the advice of the directors of the (contested) Africa Museum and the Royal National Archive. Their advisory note was leaked, which led 30 diaspora organisations who felt bypassed to write an open letter to the commission, lamenting (a) the problematic track record of the Africa Museum itself in dealing with matters related to truth, reparation, justice, restitution, and even racism, (b) the note's absence of diaspora actors or experts from Congo, Rwanda, or Burundi, (c) the fact that victims were overlooked, and (d) the focus on historical research (Grymonprez 2020; RTBF 2020). Their intervention pushed the final composition of the expert panel in the direction of better representation of diaspora groups and experts with Congolese, Rwandan, or Burundian roots (although no experts *from* the region are included). Several organisations still lamented the extent to which the expertise of Belgo-Congolese organisations was given less weight than that of other academic experts (Belga 2020).

11 These types of consultations have been and are already ongoing within and amongst the concerned communities.

The analytical framework proposed in the Introduction in this volume constitutes a conceptual lens able to analyse the positions of the concerned actors in a more insightful manner than classic binaries would. Specifically, it offers us a way to understand why – after a long period of resistance – some institutional actors have embraced this standardised transitional justice mechanism (i.e. offering a means to pay lip service to transitional justice's ideals of recognition and accountability, without necessarily engaging in disruptive policies), while others contest this because of the way in which the process is organised (i.e. turning the commission into a legitimating add-on that reinforces the status quo and the legitimacy of those in power without supporting any kind of transformative change). At the same time, the commission's focus on – limited forms of – accountability and recognition also prompt us to think about potential, unforeseen disruptive or transformative effects of standardised transitional justice interventions. Indeed, given the commission's relative absence from the public debate and its non-inclusion of key stakeholders, relative isolation from other policy initiatives or reforms, and limited temporal mandate combined with an extensive substantive mandate, it is hard to imagine a genuine concern with transformation or disruption amongst those who established it. Nevertheless, the work of the commission might spark a societal and political debate and create a discursive space for more far-reaching initiatives, initiating a dynamic of rhetorical entrapment whereby the publicly adopted norms and rhetoric of those in power are strategically used by the ones outside of the institutions to push for further steps in their direction (Risse, Ropp, and Sikkink 1999; Schimmelfennig 2001; Winston 2020). This potential, however, should not overshadow the extent to which the exclusion of key stakeholders themselves is inherently problematic from a processual or structural point of view or the extent to which it is unacceptable from these stakeholders' own point of view. This challenges the legitimacy of the intervention and its ability to achieve its stated intentions. It also pushes us to engage in a more critical reading of those stated intentions.

Education

The previous section described an instance of standardised forms of transitional justice being adopted in a consolidated democracy because transitional justice's central intention of ensuring accountability and recognition of harm fit the normativity of those in decision-making positions, while at the same time not posing too much risk of disruption to the status quo. But what could a disruptive transitional justice in Belgium look like?

This section discusses an initiative in the domain of education, which does not propose a standardised 'model' transitional justice approach. Interventions in the domain of education have increasingly been relied upon by transitional justice practitioners, partly because of the role they can play in terms of recognition of past harm, but mostly because of the potential of education to defuse societal polarisation, develop democratic attitudes, and increase civic trust (Ramírez-Barat and Duthie 2017). These functions align closely with a transformative strand of transitional justice that has a forward-looking perspective and relies more readily on non-standardised approaches, both within and beyond state institutions. In this section, I consider how interventions in the domain of education could be relevant for consolidated democracies and reflect on the responses of key stakeholders to a proposal exploring this kind of intervention in the Belgian context. Empirically, it builds on 21 conversations I had with educational stakeholders and experts in Flanders, Belgium, while conceptualising a research proposal.[12] I use the model proposed in the Introduction to this volume to better understand their responses to the idea of learning from transitional justice when conceptualising educational reform in Belgium.

Education as a Tool to Defuse Societal Polarisation

As consolidated democracies are increasingly facing challenges related to polarisation, social tensions, and latent societal conflict, they have started to explore, amongst other things, the role that education can play in defusing these tensions (Lepianka 2018). In doing so, insights are often drawn from critical pedagogy and peace education, which have both paid increasing attention to the relationship between education and conflict transformation (see, for example, Van Alstein 2018). Transitional justice is a field of practice and scholarship that has been left mostly untapped when conceptualising these educational interventions.

This is remarkable given the recent increased attention to what education can do in this regard in the domain of transitional justice itself (under the pillar of guarantees of non-recurrence), and the expertise developed in these contexts where the tensions – and stakes – are often significantly higher than in consolidated democracies.[13] In post-conflict contexts, educational initiatives have mostly focused on empowering individuals emotionally, economically, and socio-politically to become active members of society, thus facilitating their overall reintegration into society and the development of democratic attitudes (Ramírez-Barat and Duthie 2017, 11). This is rooted in the idea that when confronted with certain kinds of social polarisation, people's micro-level attitudes prove to be crucial in explaining the evolution from latent towards violent conflict.

In consolidated democracies, too, formal education is commonly 'charged with the task of enhancing the capacity of citizens, especially – but not only

12 These conversations took place between April and October 2019, which is before the truth commission was established. No follow-up interviews were carried out. Yet, at the time of writing, the public discourse surrounding these matters had not significantly shifted.

13 In the research proposal I developed, I argued that, for such lesson learning to work, we need measurement tools that allow us to make empirically grounded assessments of what works when and how, rather than normative claims, and that we need to better understand how we can translate these insights to the context of consolidated democracies, since there are many handbooks to transpose North-based models to the Global South, but the opposite pathway for lesson learning is much less explored, meaning that we are leaving entire pools of experience and expertise untapped.

– adolescents and children, to think critically about the present and the past, so they can foresee and construct a better future' (Frisancho and Réategui 2009, 421). As Ramírez-Barat and Duthie (2017, 15) argue, at the social level, education policies can contribute to reshaping the public sphere on the basis of knowledge about the past and by creating opportunities and tools for political interaction with young citizens, while more broadly contributing to the establishment of a culture of human rights and peace. Especially when specific capabilities connected to so-called life skills are integrated into education programmes aimed at conflict prevention and transformation, these approaches can be highly relevant, also beyond post-conflict settings, to disrupt polarisation processes (Dubois and Trabelsi 2007).

Belgium's Educational Initiatives in the Domain of Societal Polarisation

Around 2017–2018, the concept of societal polarisation increasingly surfaced in public and political discourse, while various initiatives aimed at defusing and countering polarisation were established. Given the structure of the Belgian federal system, most of these initiatives were developed and implemented at the sub-state level (in this case, Flanders).[14]

Like several other countries in Europe, Flanders revised its educational curricula and explicitly mainstreamed elements of polarisation management, democratic dialogue, and conflict transformation into the standard course offering for elementary and high school pupils. Reforms to educational curricula now constitute 16 key competences, including historical awareness and civic competences, as the leading principles for secondary education. These involve a specific focus on human rights, (de- and neo-)colonisation, discrimination, democracy, enslavement, and crimes against humanity (Human Rights Council 2019). Furthermore, several organisations, such as *Kleur Bekennen* and the Committee on Remembrance Education, received additional subsidies to develop educational initiatives. Many of these initiatives, in line with insights from critical pedagogy, seek to move beyond the teaching of rational-cognitive programmes and instead focus on group dynamics, skills development, and polarisation management. Around the same time, several research institutes published handbooks on the topic of polarisation. As director at the time of one such institute, I engaged in several round tables and bilateral conversations on this topic and was involved in the dissemination of a handbook on how to deal with polarisation in the classroom. The handbook relied on critical pedagogy, citizenship studies, and peace education to present best practices relevant to the Flemish attempts to deal with polarisation in the domain of education.

14 Sub-national institutions have authority over policy areas such as education or culture, within which most of these initiatives are developed. This section focuses on the Flemish (Dutch-speaking) region and community.

Markedly absent from the initiatives and the conversations surrounding them were references to expertise developed in the Global South in the context of transitional justice. Virtually non-existent were references to the expertise of organisations working in post-conflict countries to defuse polarisation through educational reform.

In the wake of conversations and extensive stakeholder consultation, I formulated a research proposal about how consolidated democracies, like Belgium, could learn from transitional justice's experiences in the domain of education. The proposal started from the reality that consolidated democracies are increasingly confronted with the need to defuse latent conflicts and societal polarisation, often around (collective) identity issues, to avoid them from degenerating into violent conflict, and to protect democratic principles and human rights. These challenges are in several ways similar to those being addressed – in non-standardised ways – in several paradigmatic transitional justice settings under the forward-looking pillar of guarantees of non-recurrence. As such, this dimension of transitional justice could be relevant to consolidated democracies. In the development of the proposal, I explored together with Belgian educational stakeholders what the relevance of this expertise could be within the context of educational initiatives developed at the time in Belgium.[15] The next section builds on conversations I had with educational stakeholders, as a researcher and initiator of a project exploring the relevance of this dimension of transitional justice for consolidated democracies.

Pushbacks Against Transitional Justice in the Domain of Education

Intentionality

Education lies at the heart of a regime's efforts to legitimise itself and consolidate its authority. The stakes of intervening in this domain are, therefore, naturally high. Depending on the content of the proposed change, it may be perceived as disruptive of the state's authority and legitimacy. As argued above, the context in which the current depolarisation programmes are implemented in Belgium, is that of a state which does not (wish or seek to) question its own identity as a liberal rule-of-law state. As such, proposals to borrow insights

15 The project proposed to (a) develop a measurement toolkit/empirical approach that allows us to identify what worked where and why; (b) create an overview of best practices in post-conflict societies, focused on the contextual dynamics that facilitated positive impacts to emerge; (c) establish avenues for integrating these best practices into the educational policies of established democracies. The central objective of the project was thus to understand how established democracies could learn from transitional justice with regard to how educational programs can play a role in the transformation of conflict and the management of societal polarisation.

from the domain of transitional justice to develop educational programmes could potentially be read as too disruptive.

On the contrary, dealing with polarisation through a managerial approach that mostly proposes hands-on conversational strategies and pedagogical tools that require skill on the side of the teacher (e.g. Brandsma 2018), but no genuine acknowledgement of societal or historical dynamics that might nourish polarisation, may be perceived as much less disruptive of the status quo than explicitly relying on the transitional justice framework with its – potentially disruptive – emphasis on accountability and recognition of past harm.

Genuinely engaging with the *problematique* of polarisation requires that the various actors involved (including the historically dominant ones) consider and engage with potentially problematic elements of their (collective) identity and history. This could, for example, mean the rewriting of dominant historical narratives about the national past as presented in schoolbooks (for example, regarding colonial harm, labour migration, etc.). While, for example, the EU framework on transitional justice suggests that European countries find this a reasonable and logical demand to make of post-conflict countries (EEAS 2015), the idea of critically engaging with one's own troubled past meets with significant resistance when asked of various societal groups within domestic borders.[16]

In sum, while the objective of educational and curricular interventions in Belgium aligns with those of educational reforms taking place within a transitional justice context (i.e. defusing conflict over collective identities), they do not seem to share the intentionality of contributing to greater accountability or recognition of past harm. Indeed, the ambitions of the existing initiatives seem to be much more modest and miss any reference to accountability for or recognition of past (and ongoing) harm, root causes, broader societal dynamics, or historical injustices that might feed or characterise this polarisation. Instead, existing initiatives take a rather ahistorical approach to depolarisation that assumes the appropriateness and effectiveness of managerial approaches to dealing with polarisation, for example, in a classroom context. In the project I proposed, on the contrary, I explicitly sought to introduce transitional justice into this conversation, precisely to foreground these structural and historical dynamics and the need for accountability and recognition.

Response

Of the 21 interlocutors consulted on this topic during the conceptualisation phase of the project, only one actor already actively mainstreamed insights and

16 This is illustrative of some of the inherent flaws of transitional justice mechanisms as an export product (also see Aboueldahab and Saeed in this volume).

South-based expertise (its own and that of its South-based partners) regarding conflict transformation and conflict prevention in the educational and pedagogical work it did in Belgium: *RCN Justice et Démocratie*, a small niche player active in development and peace-building in the Global South as well as in the educational domain in the Global North. This NGO was the only to explicitly conceptualise its own educational and pedagogical programme for Belgium based on insights from its work in post-conflict contexts. While its educational materials use several concepts related to transitional justice, the term transitional justice was not used. This absence of explicit references to transitional justice may be read as a form of contextualisation whereby it avoids a paradigm that could be perceived by institutional actors as disruptive of the legitimacy of the current dominant narrative. Instead, the NGO offered correctives that were acceptable to institutional actors. Yet the opening created by this NGO offers room to think about how insights from transitional justice contexts could be used in educational initiatives in consolidated democracies, in ways that pay more attention to the recognition of past harm. Their work also offers ways to reverse the dynamics of lesson learning and best-practice sharing. As such, even if it is happening on the fringes of the dominant discourse, this work could be read as a non-standardised form of transitional justice in that it proposes innovative practices (both in post-conflict countries and in Belgium) for how expertise and know-how could flow from a (post-)conflict context to consolidated democracies. Despite the innovative and promising nature of their work, their position in the margin of the debate and the field of practice meant that they had little room to shape the public debate.

Institutional stakeholders in the domain of education (within cabinets, administrations, or education providers) were on average much more reluctant to embrace the idea of engaging with transitional justice's intentionality or rhetoric. These actors do not currently engage transitional justice expertise in their work, and reactions to the proposal to do so ranged from reluctant interest (e.g. on the side of certain departments of the administrations), to pushback (e.g. on the part of some education providers) to outright resistance (including among academic reviewers of the project). This range of reactions can be linked to the intentionality of transitional justice versus the intentionality of what these actors are doing on the ground. While there is a shared interest in restoring civic trust in state institutions and among citizens, depolarising potentially conflictual collective identities, and contributing to more inclusive and just societies, Belgian education initiatives do not seem to share transitional justice's intentionality of centring this process around accountability or recognition of past harm. Thus, while some interlocutors rejected the notion of transitional justice because it was understood as something potentially destabilising, others rejected it precisely because they understood transitional justice as a standardised field with a narrow focus on criminal justice and gross human rights violations.[17] Here as well, a concern over transitional justice's disruptive potential seems to be central to explaining the positions of concerned stakeholders.

Lastly, it is interesting to highlight the reaction of several academic reviewers to the notion of 'reverse' lesson learning. Most reviewers praised the project's rigour, societal relevance, impact potential, and reversal of 'the usual tendency to transpose North-based models to the Global South', but their comments reflected problematic biases which challenged the notion that the Global North could learn from the Global South in this regard.[18] This is also in line with the argument that transitional justice is only considered by many North-based actors as part of their foreign policy agenda, but not as a potential internal policy element (see, e.g. Greenland in this volume).

In sum, whereas the first section described an instance of institutionalised actors adopting a specific standardised form of transitional justice that allowed them to formally inscribe themselves within transitional justice's normative logic of ensuring accountability and recognition, what we see here is a rejection by institutional actors of other – non-standardised – forms of transitional justice that could be more disruptive, and that would require a genuine rethinking of power imbalances. So far, trying to inscribe transitional justice into this conversation has failed, illustrating the limited ambition to engage with transitional justice core objectives. Comparing these two cases, we can observe that the context within which they are studied is similar, namely that of a state which is not seeking to rethink its foundational justice conceptions or institutions. This explains why in both cases, there has been limited engagement with those innovative or non-standardised ways of thinking about transitional justice that could lead to disruption. Still, in the first case, disruption might happen through a logic of rhetorical entrapment, but it is strongly hampered by processual factors. In the second case, the non-engagement with transitional justice means that disruption is unlikely to happen, even if niche players seek to open up the discourse. Neither case is thus highly likely to challenge the status quo, which can explain the critique of civil society actors.

17 We should distinguish between resistance and rejection on the one hand, and reluctance on the other. On the side of several practitioners and administrations, for example, there was a budding awareness of the potential of transitional justice interventions. Unfamiliarity with the field and the lack of good empirical studies on the effects of educational reform as a tool to prevent and transform conflict hampered informed and evidence-based policy making in this domain.

18 Comments included 'Why would we assume that experiences from a post-conflict setting are relevant to the challenges of established democracies?', or the advice to rewrite the project so as to drop 'the link between post-transitional and established democracies'.

Implications for the Field of Transitional Justice

The initiatives described in the previous section make clear that it is not possible to speak of a comprehensive transitional justice agenda in the Belgian case. Both the initiative which was formally adopted (i.e. the truth commission) as well as the one which was rejected (i.e. the educational proposal) are only nibbling at the margins of what a comprehensive transitional justice approach aimed at accountability and recognition would look like. Yet, both examples can be used to reflect on the evolution of the field of transitional justice, particularly its innovation and consolidation.

Juxtaposing these examples illustrates the constant interaction between innovation and consolidation of the field, but also its limits. Transitional justice has often been criticised for being too undefined, too catch-all, and too encompassing to have much analytical value (Israël and Mouralis 2013). Yet, the example from the domain of education shows that precisely the existence of a relatively stable core function of transitional justice can explain a lot of the resistance to transitional justice in cases where there is hardly political support for these core functions of accountability and recognition. There needs to be a certain critical mass believing in, and rallying behind, the core intentionality of transitional justice mechanisms (defined transformatively or conservatively), for the paradigm to be considered relevant and to 'stick'. In the case of the Belgian commission, the formal support of both a governing and two opposition parties, as well as the report by the UN Expert Group, provided this critical mass, in a context where there was also societal momentum. In the case of educational reform, this critical mass was not there, and both the proposed project and the work of *RCN Démocratie et Justice* gained little or limited traction. Neither prompted other stakeholders active in the same domain to rally around the notion of transitional justice, which they did not consider the most relevant paradigm to achieve their intentions, nor were these intentions conceptualised in terms of accountability or recognition. This demonstrates that for consolidation-through-innovation to occur, a critical mass is needed of actors who wish to normatively engage with the core intentionality of transitional justice – at least at face value.

The establishment of the Belgian commission can be described as an instance of consolidation-through-innovation in the domain of transitional justice, in that it is the first of its kind to be established by a former colonial state to address the historical truth about the colonial past in overseas colonies. This is precisely the kind of innovation within the field that can be read as a form of consolidation, in the sense that, by adapting the modalities and mandate of the commission to the institutional make-up, political agenda and societal context of consolidated democracies, standardised transitional justice increases its reach and relevance in aparadigmatic cases, making it more broadly applicable. This kind of adaption of model transitional justice can hardly be called innovation per se, but should rather be seen as some 'light' form of contextualisation that consolidates the field and allows it to expand further. At the same time, there is some degree of actual innovation happening in this case in the sense that non-standardised proposals for transitional justice are being introduced in the margin of the model approach. The survey sent out by the expert group to non-affiliated experts, for example, reflected both the four existing pillars of transitional justice (truth, justice, reparation and guarantees of non-recurrence), as well as a focus on more innovative elements (such as education or memorialisation). This constant interaction between standardised and less-standardised transitional justice is not only interesting from a practice-oriented point of view that examines how experts navigate that tension, but also from an analytical point of view in the sense that it says something about the field's malleability and its concern with self-preservation.

Concluding Remarks

The travelling of paradigms requires a more rigorous theorisation of the core concepts underlying transitional justice (e.g. conflict, justice), its objectives (e.g. from the core objectives of accountability and recognition to more ambitious ones of conflict prevention, disruption, or transformation) and its approaches (e.g. bottom-up or top-down). It is precisely the travelling of the model to other contexts that makes this exercise possible. In the Belgian case, for example, actors engaging with forms of transitional justice, moved outside the formal UN definition and took the broadness and ambiguity of mainstream transitional justice norms as elements that they moulded to their own context. In doing so, they implicitly responded to critiques of current practice as too narrow and too restrictively linked to human rights obligations and international humanitarian law.

The fact that policy actors agreed to install one transitional justice element, i.e. a commission on overseas colonial legacies, while resisting educational programmes in line with transitional justice insights, shows that adoption, rejection, and resistance can co-exist within one context. More importantly, it raises the question of what sort of potential disruptions consolidated democracies are willing to allow. Engaging with transitional justice's core intentions of accountability and recognition of past harm, requires the state to engage in, or at least allow for, a rethinking of, and potential challenge to, the legitimacy of the existing state institutions and of the existing narratives about those institutions. In the Belgian case, the way in which the truth commission has been organised raises questions about institutional actors' broad support for these intentions and justifies the commission's critical reception by civil society.

References

Balace, F. and others (2020) 'Eerst het onderzoek, dan het debat'. De Standaard, 17 August. Retrieved from https://www.standaard.be/cnt/dmf20200816_97578124.

Belga (2020) 'La commission spéciale de la Chambre sur la mémoire du colonialisme officiellement installée'. La Libre Belgique, 16 July. Retrieved from: https://www.lalibre.be/belgique/politique-belge/la-commission-speciale-de-la-chambre-sur-la-memoire-du-colonialisme-officiellement-installee-5f106e107b50a677fbf20538.

Belgische Kamer van Volksvertegenwoordigers (2020) *Bijzondere commissie belast met het onderzoek over Congo-Vrijstaat (1885–1908) en het Belgisch koloniaal verleden in Congo (1908–1960), Rwanda en Burundi (1919–1962), de impact hiervan en de gevolgen die hieraan dienen gegeven te worden.* Brussels: Belgische Kamer van Volksvertegenwoordigers.

Brandsma, B. (2018) *Polarisation: Understanding the Dynamics of Us vs. Them.* Schoonrewoerd: BB in Media.

Cessou, S. (2020) 'Passé colonial de la Belgique: la 'Commission vérité et réconciliation' est-elle mal partie?' RFI, 12 July. Retrieved from: https://www.rfi.fr/fr/afrique/20200712-belgique-colonisation-commission-v%C3%A9rit%C3%A9-r%C3%A9conciliation-cvr-mal-partie?ref=tw.

Dubois, J.L. and M. Trabelsi (2007) 'Education in Pre- and Post-conflict Contexts: Relating Capability and Life-skills Approaches'. *International Journal of Social Economics* 34(1/2), 53–65.

Frisancho, S. and F. Réategui (2009) 'Moral Education and Post-War Societies: The Peruvian Case'. *Journal of Moral Education* 38(4), 421–443.

Gready, P. and S. Robins (2014) 'From Transitional to transformative justice'. *International Journal of Transitional Justice, 8*(3), 339–361.

Grymonprez, S. (2020) 'Diaspora zet Congocommissie meteen onder hoogspanning'. De Standaard, 13 July. Retrieved from https://www.standaard.be/cnt/dmf20200712_97565989.

Human Rights Council (2019) 'Report of the Working Group of Experts on People of African Descent. Visit to Belgium'. A/HRC/42/59/Add.1, 14 August. Retrieved from: https://www.ohchr.org/en/documents/country-reports/ahrc4259add1-visit-belgium-report-working-group-experts-people-african.

Israël, L. and G. Mouralis (2014) *Dealing with Wars and Dictatorships: Legal Concepts and Categories in Action.* The Hague: T.M.C. Asser Press.

Lepianka, D. (2018) 'Justice in European Political Discourse: Comparative Report of Six Country Cases'. Utrecht: ETHOS Justice. Retrieved from: https://ethos-europe.eu/sites/default/files//docs/d4.2_loaded_website_version.pdf.

Nsayi, N. (2020) 'Betrek kritische zwarte experts en organisaties bij de commissie over het koloniaal verleden'. De Morgen, 2 July. Retrieved from: https://www.demorgen.be/meningen/betrek-kritische-zwarte-experts-en-organisaties-bij-de-commissie-over-het-koloniaal-verleden~bce61132/.

Ramírez-Barat, C. and R. Duthie (2017) 'Introduction'. In C. Ramírez-Barat and R. Duthie, eds. *Transitional Justice and Education: Learning Peace* (pp. 1–25). New York: International Center for Transitional Justice and UNICEF.

Risse, T., S. Ropp, and K. Sikkink, eds. (1999) *The Power of Human Rights: International Norms and Domestic Change.* Cambridge: Cambridge University Press.

RTBF (2020) 'Commission spéciale 'décolonisation': déjà de grosses tensions sur la désignation des experts'. rtbf.be, 16 July. Retrieved from: https://www.rtbf.be/info/belgique/detail_commission-speciale-decolonisation-deja-de-grosses-tensions-sur-la-designation-des-experts?id=10543825.

Rutazibwa, O. (2020) 'Invitation to join the group of experts for the Special Commission responsible for investigating the Congo-Free State (1885–1908) and the Belgian colonial past in the Congo (1908–1960), Rwanda and Burundi (1919–1962), and the impacts and implications.' Blog entry, 21 July. Retrieved from: https://oliviarutazibwa.wordpress.com/2020/07/21/congo-commissie-why-i-will-not-participate-in-the-expert-group/.

Schimmelfennig, F. (2001) 'The Community Trap: Liberal Norms, Rhetorical Action, and the Eastern Enlargement of the European Union'. *International Organization* 50(1), 47–80.

Tarusarira, J. (2019) 'The Anatomy of Apology and Forgiveness: Towards Transformative Apology and Forgiveness'. *International Journal of Transitional Justice* 13(1), 206–224.

Van Alstein, M. (2018) *Omgaan met controverse en polarisatie in de klas*. Antwerp: Pelckmans Pro.

Vatthauer, J.-P. and I. Weipert-Fenner (2017) *The Quest for Social Justice in Tunisia: Socioeconomic Protest and Political Democratization Post 2011*. PRIF Report 143. Frankfurt am Main: Peace Research Institute Frankurt.

Verberckmoes, Y. (2020) 'Politiek mijnenveld, maar historische kans. Interview with Wouter De Vriendt'. *De morgen*, 17 July, p. 6.

Verdoolaege, A. and P. Kerstens (2004) 'The South African Truth and Reconciliation Commission and the Belgian Lumumba Commission: A Comparison'. *Africa Today* 50(3), 75–91.

Vergauwen, E. (2020) 'Brief koning Filip krijg internationale weerklank: 'Spijt maar geen excuses''. De Standaard, 30 June. Retrieved from: https://www.standaard.be/cnt/dmf20200630_95125247

Willems, E. and others (2020) 'De verlammende angst van de historicus'. Der Standaard, 24 August. Retrieved from: https://www.standaard.be/cnt/dmf20200823_97714965.

Winston, C. (2020) 'Truth Commissions as Tactical Concessions: The Curious Case of Idi Amin'. *International Journal of Human Rights* 25(2), 251–273.

Chapter 9

Transitional Justice for European Terror Actors

Disrupting Europe's Security/Rights Terror Law Impasse

Kerstin Bree Carlson

Introduction

The terror attacks by Islamic extremists in New York City (2001) and Madrid (2004) have shaped a modern understanding of terror. In previous epochs, terrorism was associated with national self-determination, anti-colonialism, or political constructs (Crenshaw 1981; Schmid 1983). Where terror in the 20th century was recognised as political, the rise of the Islamic State (IS) and its attraction to foreigners who joined it, including Europeans, has reified the idea of Islamic extremism (Sheikh 2021). Over the past decade, more than 5,000 European 'foreign fighters' have travelled to Syria to fight for IS, while IS affiliates have conducted several successful terror attacks in Europe. In response to the IS-generated threat, European states have enacted a series of expansive criminal laws ('terror law'), guided by UN and EU directives. These laws, deemed necessary to combat the threat of terror and ensure security, have been widely criticised for violating established rights and norms (Lacey 2019; Ashworth and Zedner 2015) and disproportionately impacting European Muslims and racial minorities (Bigo and Tsoukala 2008; Fadil et al. 2019).

Because the threat of radical Islamic terrorism is usually represented as springing from ideological constructs of Islamic practices (Fadil et al. 2019; Sheikh 2021), it is becoming increasingly difficult to draw the line between impermissible and permissible Islamic practice and belief across Europe. States increasingly regard European Muslims as 'suspect communities' (Breen-Smyth 2014; Coolsaet 2019; Ragazzi 2016; Silke and Brown 2016). At the same time, the inability of European states to manage growing state-sanctioned and institutionalised Islamophobia threatens the rights recognitions that legitimise liberal states (Macmanus 2020; Müller 2021). This situation has led to an impasse which impacts European politics and policy. In the name of security, states are imposing rights-violating policies and practices justified as 'exceptions' to the regular rule-of-law norms in consolidated democracies (Agamben 2005; Schmitt, Strong, and Strauss 2007). Those who critique terror law as illiberal and impermissible in the name of rights are opposed by those who argue for

DOI: 10.4324/9781003289104-10

the necessity of terror law in the name of security. So far, there are no bridges between them.

This chapter considers how a field designed to build bridges – transitional justice – might address the security/rights impasse evidenced by European terror law practices. The chapter lays out a prescriptive argument for the possibility of addressing the security/rights impasse that transitional justice could provide. To do this, the chapter proceeds in two parts. The first examines how terror law practices challenge established rights norms. Here, the chapter explores empirical examples of rights challenges in two paradigmatic European states, Denmark and France. These two countries are selected as representative of European practice more broadly, given that they represent a large and a small state, a strong and a reticent EU ally, and a demographically more diverse versus more homogenous citizenry. Danish and French terror law practices are distinct from each other, but they share the consequence that Danish and French Muslims no longer enjoy the same legal protection as other citizens. This challenges the liberal ideals that legitimise governance structures in consolidated democracies and exacerbates security concerns as marginalised populations are further marginalised. Both security and rights are central liberal principles and are equally endangered by current European policies and/or legal practices. The first part of the chapter describes this security/rights impasse.

The second part of the chapter theorises how applying transitional justice concepts might disrupt the security/rights impasse that has captured European states. Here the chapter examines what the terror law practices of European states, and specifically Denmark's citizenship revocation and France's criminalisation of 'pre-crime', show regarding the axes of *intention* and *response* theorised in the Introduction in this volume. Transitional justice could play a meaningful role in the present impasse precisely because of its deliberate capacity towards accountability and recognition. The chapter concludes by considering how lessons learned from paradigmatic transitional justice cases managing the cessation of armed conflict, such as those obtained in Colombia, might be meaningfully applied to the security/rights impasse presently challenging European states. Such an application would amount to both a consolidation and an innovation for transitional justice, because it would simultaneously reaffirm the accountability and recognition elements that transitional justice shares with liberal governance (Sharp 2018), while disrupting a righteous rights narrative that holds that consolidated democracies have little to learn from other states' experiences of social violence.

Terror Laws in Europe: The Rise of the Illiberal European State

Many European countries categorise themselves as 'at war' with radical Islam and its associated violence. The language of 'war' has important rights implications. First, it suggests that a war-constraining humanitarian law regime rather than a liberal domestic human rights regime should apply to state actions against terror actors. International humanitarian law (IHL), the laws of war, are constructed on the 1949 Geneva Conventions and offer different – mostly lesser – protections than regional human rights treaties and the domestic criminal law they oversee. Murder, for example, can be legal under IHL whereas this is not the case in criminal law or international human rights law. Second, applying the rhetoric of war, with its concomitant IHL legal regime, obfuscates the fact that terror is criminalised within domestic jurisdictions. For example, large-scale criminal trials in Paris are aimed at dozens of actors involved in the 2015 and 2016 terror attacks carried out there. Where ideological converts and sympathisers have also succeeded in smaller-scale violence, like the 2020 beheading of French civics teacher Samuel Paty and the 2015 Copenhagen attacks that killed a film-maker and a volunteer security guard, this violence has been investigated by police and prosecutors and charges have been brought against accomplices, even where the main actors are dead. Terrorism is thus included in the social policy and social control aims that drive and justify criminal law (Duff 2010; Wacquant 2008).

In European welfare states, criminal law has traditionally prioritised the rehabilitation of the offender as social policy (Smith and Ugelvik 2017). Beyond individual and societal benefits, rehabilitation allegedly also transforms the criminal from deviant to norm-following and thus enables a distinction between *doing* wrong and *being* wrong. Modern terror law, however, is challenging this distinction. Over the past two decades European states have transformed their approach to homegrown terrorism from a rehabilitative criminal justice model to a militarised 'security' model (Lister 2015). Modern anti-terrorism practices demonstrate a semiotic shift from defence to prevention, or put another way, from managing danger to managing risk (Drumbl 2006; Edwards 2018; Van Munster 2004). In the criminal law systems of France and Denmark today, the same criminal act can have drastically different penal consequences depending on whether it is characterised as 'terror' or not (Lacey 2019). In France, categorising a crime as 'terror' can double its sentence length. In Denmark, such categorisation opens the possibility that citizenship revocation can accompany punishment. The question of how and to whom the labels 'terror' and 'terrorist' are applied thus becomes very significant.

Criminal law, in particular, is subjected to the most rigorous constitutional/human rights protections, as it is the area where the state, with its nearly unlimited surveillance power and economic resources, directly challenges the liberty of the accused (Duff 2001; Lacey 2016; Teubner 2012). Critics argue that illiberal hard law prevention and deradicalisation measures risk marginalising whole populations and making them amenable to radicalisation; hence, they are ineffective social policy (Bigo 2019; Wacquant 2009). This critical perspective is in the minority in an increasingly populist political landscape where the 'clash of civilizations' argument is often successfully wielded (Sheikh 2021;

Silverstein 2018). This vicious cycle of marginalisation, which leads to security threat, which in turn leads to further marginalisation has become a dominant refrain in political discourse and has yet to field workable solutions.

The Jihadification of Terrorism Policy

Martha Crenshaw (1981) produced a capstone text founding the field of terrorism studies, wherein she posed a seminal question regarding who commits terrorism and why. Four decades later, this question remains unanswered and, for some, abandoned as too difficult (Coolsaet 2019). Put another way, different factions have developed varying theories for who commits terror and why. These factions constitute an internal divide so stark that key figures in terrorism studies have challenged its right to be identified as a 'field' at all (Stampnitzky 2011). States' roles as sponsors and consumers of expertise in terror studies complicate the construction of a bounded area of agreed definitions and approaches (Silke 2004). Critics of terror studies from the left challenge the absence of recognition of state-sponsored violence in discussions of terrorism (Kundnani 2014). Critics of terror studies from the right can accuse researchers of 'sympathy' with terrorists as they seek to eradicate terror violence.

Attacks in the 1990s brought scrutiny to 'Islamic' movements, while security discourse shifted from a focus on political causes to belief systems and ideology (Stampnitzky 2013). This built on social tensions that began in the 1960s with increased migration from Muslim countries and growing minority populations in European countries. The 2001 and 2005 attacks in New York and Madrid cemented a modern understanding of 'radical Islamic terror', that is, a 'religious wave' (Chiangi 2019; Rapoport 2004) motivating terror. While European policy proposals in the 2000s sought to remain neutral towards actors to avoid ostracising or villainising social groups, within a decade policy was focused on Islamic extremism in ways that implicated all European Muslims (Silke and Brown 2016). 'Radicalisation' transformed from a socio-psychological concept to a political construct (Schmid 2013). Within this framework, European Muslims have generally become 'suspect communities' (Ragazzi 2016). Attempts to distinguish extremism from Islam through the use of 'Islamist' instead of 'Islamic', as French President Macron's government does, do not resolve the demonstrated direction of the trend, which is the conflation of Islamic belief and practice with extremism and violence (Fassin 2021).

The construction of terrorism as synonymous with Islamic extremism encourages two problematic directional tendencies for European terror law practices. First, a heightened focus on Muslims as suspect communities has encouraged a narrowing of terror law practice to focus nearly exclusively on activities related to Muslim extremism, where violent acts constitute 'jihad'. This is problematic, because it can lead terror law policy to overlook other violent social behaviour with a collective impact, such as femicide or hate crimes; Norway has suffered several right wing attacks, including a 2011 attack that killed 77 people. It also criminalises non-violent acts, such as wearing face coverings in public. The most obvious example of this practice may be the regulation of female Islamic attire. In the past decade, nearly every European country has debated or passed laws regulating female Islamic dress largely due to resistance to the 'extremism' that Islamic face-and-hair-covering dress connotes for many Europeans (Brems et al. 2017; Carlson and Slosser 2021).

Beyond overlooking other social harms, narrowing terror law practices to focus on Islamic extremism can lead to ineffective social policy. For example, a focus on terror as jihad has resulted in what is arguably an unnecessarily high focus in many European jurisdictions on 'foreign fighters', citizens who travelled, or attempted to travel, to the Levant to assist jihadi groups like IS. There is disagreement among experts regarding both the level of threat that these individuals pose as well as how best to mitigate that threat (Moors 2019). Some social scientists studying terror actors argue that criminal background is a much more relevant criteria for terrorist violence than for example ideology and belief (Dawson 2021; Hemmingsen 2015). This would suggest that knowing what activities foreign fighters engage in while abroad would be a crucial element of assessing the risk they pose upon return. Terror law and practice is not following this evaluation, however. In France and Denmark, foreign fighters are charged as terrorists with an aggravated penalty to match. This is minimum ten year prison sentence in France (although many first instance terror trial judges have refused to impose it, see discussion below). In Denmark, prison sentences are shorter, but dual citizens can, and increasingly do, see their citizenship revoked.

Likewise, the broad lens with which state operatives view Islamic activities has accompanied and supported a state-backed criminalisation of risk. This includes 'prevention', i.e. acts not yet committed or even conceptualised but which would be criminal if carried out. Where terror is synonymous with radical Islam, radical Islamic practices that are not in themselves violent become associated with risk and are made illegal. Terror is criminalised and is represented in domestic criminal codes, but the imprecision of legal definitions, together with the transformation of terrorism's framing from a criminal law problem to a security and war paradigm, has transformed European criminal law policies of reduction and rehabilitation to policies of eradication. Cole (2005) calls this 'enemy aliens'; Lacey (2016, 2) calls it 'character responsibility'. In this construction, the particular circumstances of particular kinds of people justify particular treatment. This is a direct challenge to liberal values and criminal law procedural fairness guarantees.

Illiberal State Terror Law: Examples from Denmark and France

Tolstoy's *Anna Karenina* famously begins, 'All happy families are alike, but every unhappy family is unhappy in its own way'. So it is with modern state responses to Islamic terror. Each state has a unique justification for which central tenets of liberal governance must be suspended in the face of Islamic terror. In Denmark, which has a strong narrative of cultural homogeneity (Schmidt 2019), Muslims can be perceived as aliens (Hervik 2019; Rytter 2010; Sniderman 2016). This has enabled a growing terror law practice of citizenship revocation. In France, on the contrary, which is officially race and religion blind, state-of-emergency measures have gutted established criminal protections, such as standards of proof and specificity of criminal acts, in ways that threaten to make law arbitrary and unpredictable (Garapon and Rosenfeld 2016; Hamilton 2019; Weill 2018). This practice thereby challenges rule-of-law norms.

While the manifestations of countries' 'unhappiness' are unique, they are united by a common security discourse. Security is a central component of state legitimacy; even before the social contract legitimising the exercise of state power, the state must secure a monopoly on the legitimate use of violence to be recognisable as a state (see Winter in this volume). Security is therefore a necessary element of the rights guarantees that underpin liberalism and the legitimacy of governance in consolidated liberal democracies. Although security is often a force that operates in contravention of rights or to override established rights, it is also a necessary foundation for the rights states seek to guarantee. This tension is represented in Figure 9.1 which shows the interconnected balance between security and rights.

This section considers two illiberal practices culled from the terror law of France and Denmark. Both countries were deeply affected by the rise of the Islamic State and its agenda of violence. Proportionate to their populations, Denmark and France saw some of Europe's highest numbers of 'foreign fighters', citizens who left to join IS in Syria or Iraq. The organisation's success in recruiting and training French and Danish citizens had immediate, and tragic, consequences at home. In February 2015, a 22-year-old Danish-Jordanian man killed two people in two attacks before being killed by the police. A month

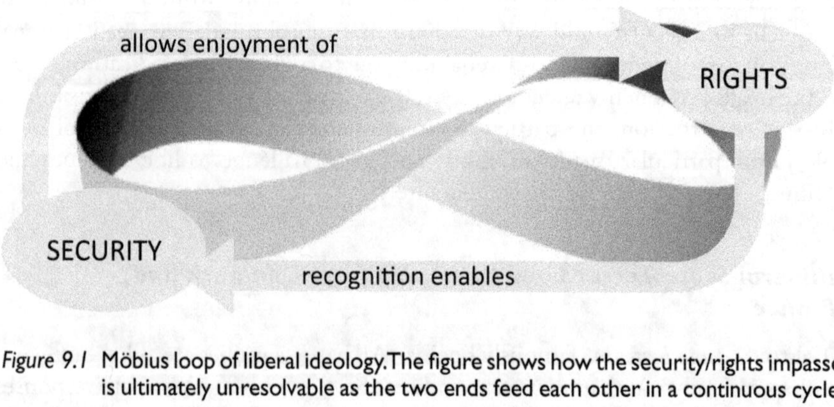

Figure 9.1 Möbius loop of liberal ideology. The figure shows how the security/rights impasse is ultimately unresolvable as the two ends feed each other in a continuous cycle.

earlier, IS-trained militants staged successful terror attacks in France, successfully attacking the offices of the magazine Charlie Hebdo and a kosher supermarket. In November 2015, a series of related terror attacks killed 130 people in Paris. The following year, an IS adherent murdered people by driving a truck down a crowded street in Nice on Bastille Day.

Years before these attacks took place, Denmark and France had been putting laws in place that permitted novel, severe, and arguably rights-violating responses to actions classified as 'terror'. In 2002 and 2006, Denmark passed what is known as 'the terror package' (*terrorpakken*), alterations to its criminal code recognising terror as a specific kind of crime and proscribing particular punishments for it. In conjunction with *terrorpakken*, in 2004 Denmark changed its law to permit citizenship revocation for terror offenders. Due to international legal prohibitions against statelessness, this modern application of 'banishment' is only possible for citizens who enjoy a second citizenship. Although the legal formalities arise around specific questions of dual citizenship, in practice the law treats 'ethnic' and 'non-ethnic' Danes differently. Such discriminatory treatment challenges fundamental norms governing European state practices and is in violation of Denmark's international obligations.

France had begun a legal reordering even earlier. Following the July 1995 St. Michel attack perpetrated by the radical Islamic group Armed Islamic Group, France added to its terror laws by passing in 1996 a law criminalising illegal associations, called *association de malfaiteurs* (AMT). This law has been widely criticised as nothing less than a repudiation of criminal procedure and defendants' rights because it criminalises premeditation, what its detractors call 'pre-crime' (Blisson 2017; Cahn and Alix 2017; Weill 2018).

Presently, several European countries criminalise joining IS, regardless of what role one takes or in which activities one engages. In Denmark, foreign fighters who have returned and faced prosecution have often received low prison sentences (3–4 years). This might suggest low social threat (de Graaf 2019). In France, while sentences have been higher than in Denmark (up to ten years), judges in France's specialised terror court division have generally refused to enact the double penalties the law proscribes, enforcing a more typical 'infraction' and not 'felony' standard that would follow from the nature of the crime committed (were it not labelled as terrorism) (Besnier and Weill 2019).

Citizenship Revocation in Denmark

The first test of *terrorpakken*'s citizenship revocation provisions came in 2007, when a district court found Saïd Mansour guilty of 'inciting terrorism' based on Facebook posts and sentenced him to 3.5 years in jail. Mansour, a naturalised Danish citizen with dual nationality who was born and raised in Morocco, was eligible for citizenship revocation under the terms of Denmark's terror law.

Nonetheless, the district court, in a close 7–5 vote, declined to remove his citizenship.[1]

In 2014, Mansour was arrested again and again put on trial for inciting terrorism via posts on Facebook and other media. This time, after finding him guilty, the court elected to remove his citizenship.[2] The case was appealed and in 2016, the Danish Supreme Court affirmed the decision; it was also affirmed in 2019 by the European Court of Human Rights (ECtHR).[3] Mansour has since been repatriated to Morocco, where he potentially faces a death sentence in connection to his alleged role in a 2003 terror attack in Casablanca.

The 2016 *Mansour* judgement opened the door to citizenship revocation in Danish terror law practice and several more cases followed. Where Mansour was a naturalised Danish citizen with strong connections to his original homeland, the latter cases have involved Danish-born citizens of dual nationality. In November[4] and December 2017,[5] Danish courts stripped two Danish-born citizens with only minimal ties to their second-nationality countries of their Danish passports in conjunction with short criminal sentences for terror-related activity.

Then, in 2018 the Danish Supreme Court weighed in on the debate regarding denationalisation with a startling judgement that deserves close attention. The case involved Adam Johansen, whom the Supreme Court sentenced to four years in prison for his departure from Denmark to Syria as a foreign fighter.[6] Both the trial and appeals court had considered citizenship revocation but rejected it due to Johansen's strong ties to Denmark. The Danish Supreme Court reversed the decisions of the lower courts, determining that Johansen's Danish citizenship could be revoked. The Court engaged in a balancing exercise, weighing which of the defendant's two citizenships exercised greater claim: Denmark, where he was born (Faroe Islands) and raised, and where his wife and child live, or Tunisia, his father's country, which he visited as a teenager, and where he does not speak the local variant of Arabic. The Court found that Johansen's *Islamic practice* tied him more meaningfully to Tunisia than to Denmark, stating:

> [The Defendant] has explained that Islam means everything to him and he practices Islam in everyday life. Even though [the defendant] grew up here in Denmark, the Supreme Court finds, on the basis of the facts before it,

1 Københavns Byret (Court of First Instance), Case No. SS 23-28409/2006 (April 1, 2007).
2 Eastern High Court (Court of Second Instance), Case No. S-3475-14 (June 22, 2015).
3 Supreme Court of Denmark, Case No. 211/2015 (June 8, 2016); ECHR Second Session, February 14, 2019 available at: https://fln.dk/-/media/FLN/Publikationer-og-notater/EMRK/SAID-ABDUL-SALAM-MUBARAK-v-DENMARK.pdf?la=da.
4 Supreme Court of Denmark, Case No. 119/2017 (November 14, 2017).
5 Glostrup Byret (Court of First Instance), Case No. 4506/2017 (December 13, 2017).
6 Supreme Court of Denmark, Case 124/2018 (November 20, 2018).

> that the defendant must be recognized as having an unusual connectedness to Tunisia and Tunisian culture and ways.[7]

In other words, the Court explicitly tied its determination to revoke Johansen's citizenship to his Islamic faith. The court did not see citizenship revocation as a violation of Johansen's right to family life, holding:

> It should also be noted that his cohabiting partner, who, as an 18-year-old, converted to Islam and their now 8-year-old son, who has been attending an Islamic school for a shorter period of time and is now being taught at home by his mother, must not be presumed to be without the necessary background to accompany him to Tunisia.[8]

In this way, the Court extended its rationale to find that Islam could sufficiently connect both the defendant's wife and son to Tunisia, though they have no other connection to that country and are, instead, wholly connected to Denmark. Moreover, the Court's rationale diverges from the ECtHR's argumentation in the earlier revocation of *Mansour*, where the court considered Mansour's background, language skills, and attachment to Denmark in weighing the question of citizenship revocation.

Johansen's case was recently rejected by the ECtHR.[9] In its decision, the ECtHR unanimously recognised and concurred with the Danish Supreme Court's analysis. The ECtHR further noted that Johansen's terror offences themselves 'to a large extent showed his lack of attachment to Denmark and its values'.[10] This decoupling of basic rights (citizenship) in connection to criminal conviction challenges liberal ideals regarding punishment (Lacey 2019; Duff 2001).

The period following the *Johansen* case demonstrates that citizenship revocation has become *de rigueur* in Danish terror law practice. For example, an appeals court in 2019 upheld a 2018 decision to remove Danish citizenship for teenagers who had *unsuccessfully attempted* to travel to Syria (three made it to Turkey, the fourth never left Denmark). The court reported that based on the 'seriousness of their crimes' those defendants eligible for citizenship revocation had their Danish citizenship stripped, in addition to receiving a three-year jail sentence.[11] The court did this 'regardless of their connection to Denmark'.[12] Of

7 Supreme Court of Denmark, Case 124/2018 (November 19, 2018), p 9 (author's translation).
8 Supreme Court of Denmark, Case 124/2018 (November 19, 2018), p 9 (author's translation).
9 *Johansen v. Denmark*, Application no. 27801/19, European Court of Human Rights, March 3, 2022.
10 Ibid., para 70.
11 Eastern High Court (Court of Second Instance), Case No. S-1896-18 (March 7, 2019), case summary available here: https://domstol.dk/oestrelandsret/aktuelt/2019/3/forsoeg-paa-at-tilslutte-sig-is-i-syrien/ (accessed March 22, 2022).
12 Eastern High Court (Court of Second Instance), Case No. S-1896-18 (March 7, 2019), case summary available here: https://domstol.dk/oestrelandsret/aktuelt/2019/3/forsoeg-paa-at-tilslutte-sig-is-i-syrien/ (accessed March 22, 2022).

the four defendants, two were dual citizens born and raised in Denmark and one was an Afghan citizen born and raised in Denmark: these three had their Danish citizenship/residency removed. The final defendant had only Danish citizenship and thus was not implicated beyond the three-year jail sentence.

In cases where citizenship revocation is permissible due to dual citizenship, therefore, the practice now seems more the norm than the exception. In an example of what criminologists call 'normalisation' (Galli 2015) or 'contagion' (Hamilton 2019), this practice has now slipped the bounds of criminal law and is applied in other legal areas as well. In 2019, Denmark passed a 'hasty law' enabling it to remove citizenship without trial or court oversight for dual-citizen Danes trapped in Syria. This law followed the October 2019 Turkish incursion into north-eastern Syria and the subsequent US withdrawal. Thousands of European citizens, including children, were imprisoned in Kurdish and Iraqi camps after the fall of IS in March 2019, generating fear that IS adherents would escape and make their way back to Europe. Most European countries steadfastly refused to repatriate them, a practice that largely continues, with a few exceptions, to this day.

In January 2020, Norway repatriated a Palestinian-born IS adherent due to her child's serious illness. In March 2021 the woman was tried in Norway and sentenced to four years in prison. This pressured the Danish government, which had been refusing to repatriate adult Danish citizens held in Kurdish-run camps, to insist that children alone, without their parents, would be welcome. This was the position of the centre-left Danish prime minister as late as March 2021. Ultimately, the Danish government reversed its position, following the publication of a leaked security briefing that argued that Danish citizens in Kurdish camps posed a security risk if they remained in the camps. In September 2021, 19 Danish women and children were repatriated from the Al Hol camp (Carlson 2021). This number did not include three dual citizens whose Danish citizenship was removed via the 2019 'Hasty Law', nor their children. In this case, both the European Parliament[13] and the UN's High Commissioner for Human Rights[14] urged Denmark to repatriate all Danes.

Denmark's citizenship revocation practice is not singular; several European countries link citizenship revocation to terror prosecution for dual citizens. In the UK, citizenship revocation is possible for dual citizens convicted even of non-terror crime (Gentleman 2020). For many countries, however, citizenship revocation for dual-citizen terror actors is seen as an unacceptable action for a liberal state. France, for example, has contemplated and rejected citizenship

13 EU Parliament, 'European Parliament resolution of 11 March 2021 on the Syrian conflict – 10 years after the uprising (2021/2576(RSP))', available here: https://www.europarl.europa.eu/doceo/document/TA-9-2021-0088_EN.html (accessed March 22, 2022).

14 United Nations Office of the High Commissioner statement February 2021, available here: https://www.ohchr.org/EN/NewsEvents/Pages/DisplayNews.aspx?NewsID=26730&LangID=E (accessed March 22, 2022)

revocation for dual citizens in conjunction with terror, concerned about the weakening of citizenship ties that such a practice would premise.

Most European states now permit dual citizenship, though for some, like Denmark, this is a relatively recent phenomenon. Indeed, it seems possible and even plausible that countries that have recently changed their dual citizenship laws such as Denmark (2015) and Norway (2018) have done so in order to permit convicted terror actors to be excommunicated (Midtbøen 2019). Denmark's example shows the broadening trajectory of illiberal practice, from the introduction of the possibility of citizenship revocation in 2004 to the standardisation of its application today.

Criminalising 'Pre-Crime' in France

Another example of illiberal terror law is demonstrated by the French retraction of criminal law's procedural protections in its terror law doctrine. The *association de malfaiteurs* doctrine does not require specificity regarding plans or actions and instead permits conviction based on shared ideology. This makes it a doctrine capable of prosecuting suspicion (Weill 2020), also known as 'pre-crime' (Garapon and Rosenberg 2016).

The long reach of this doctrine has become evident in trials that were much publicised in France, such as the 2017 Cannes-Torcey network trial (Hecker 2016; Besnier and Weill 2019) and the trial against Mohammed Merah who murdered seven people in 2012, including gunning down three children and a rabbi in front of a Jewish school in Toulouse, before being killed by police. In 2016, a criminal case for complicity in terrorism was brought against his brother, Abdulakar, who was eventually convicted and sentenced to 30 years' prison. The *Merah* trial saw the *mens rea* elements of AMT refined, where Abdulakar Merah's ideas and ideology made him part of a 'criminal association' with the brother who committed the violence. AMT changes the contours of criminal conviction from 'direct proof' to 'proof through an intellectual construct' (Sayare 2018, 12). AMT is now the basis for the mass trials France is conducting, including the 'Charlie Hebdo' trial (2020), the Bataclan trial (2021–2022) and the Nice trial (2022).

The January 2015 *Charlie Hebdo* attacks and subsequent manhunt for the attackers paralysed France. This terror attack marked a turning point in French counter terrorism. In the following months, a series of restrictive legal and administrative measures were instituted under a state of emergency. Police and judges were granted extensive flexibility in terms of prevention and surveillance, including extending pre-trial detention to nearly five years. After these attacks, anyone who left or attempted to go to Syria to join a terrorist armed group was presumed to be willing to participate in their criminal activities. As noted above, these 'foreign fighters' can now be prosecuted for terror and receive sentences of 20 years to life imprisonment. These measures are still in effect in France.

After the three terrorists were killed by the police, a wide net was cast to catch supporters and collaborators of the Charlie Hebdo attacks. Several of the men caught up in this net appeared at the 2020 trial. The perpetrators themselves are dead, while three closest associates who stood accused in absentia are missing in Syria. The 11 defendants present at trial appeared to be a somewhat arbitrary and coincidentally linked assembly of marginalised, largely unemployed, small-time drug and gun dealers and some of their friends. Many had only a passing acquaintance (or none at all) with any of the perpetrators.

The prosecution's case was built on the controversial AMT doctrine, which as discussed above makes it possible to convict individuals for participation in terrorism even where they have not contributed to the terrorist act itself and regardless of whether the act has occurred. The prosecution used AMT to argue that small acts that indirectly assisted the perpetrators in their attacks were terrorism. Some of the acts were indeed criminal: small-time guns and drug trafficking and fraudulent car sales. These would normally be misdemeanours, however, and hardly punishable by decades in prison (and not susceptible to pre-trial detention measures). Other actions were not in themselves criminal, such as accompanying one of the perpetrators when he bought flak jackets and knives in an army store. Because one of the perpetrators wore these items in the attack, AMT allows the prosecution to reach back and make those actions criminal based on a presumption of what the defendants knew about the perpetrator's plans.

On December 15, 2020, the court found all defendants guilty, though several were not found guilty of terrorism. This meant several sentences were significantly shortened, in some cases to little more than time served. The defendants not found guilty of terrorism were a showcase of marginalised despair: unemployed, without prospects, directionless. For example, Christophe Raumel accompanied some of the other defendants on a car trip to Belgium to traffic in illegal guns because the other defendants promised to stop at McDonalds along the way.[15] Raumel was ultimately found guilty of an infraction and sentenced to four years' prison.

Several of the defendants, similarly marginal to the crimes, seemed to be before the court largely due to their connection with Islam. Islam, in the prosecutor's telling, became the 'shared ideology' connecting the defendants to the murderous, dead attackers. For example, the prosecutor drew attention to one defendant's halal diet to argue that he shared the radical extremism of Amedy Coulibaly, the attacker who ended his life murdering shoppers and taking hostages in a Jewish supermarket. The prosecutor did not have other proof that demonstrated that the defendant either knew of Coulibaly's plans or shared his

15 His defense attorney informed the court that he had been present on a car trip to Belgium to review illegal guns in order to get a McDonalds meal. Notes from trial ethnography, December 8, 2020, on file with author.

views. For the *Charlie Hebdo* prosecutors, avoiding pork was a demonstration of that shared ideology. As many of the defence attorneys argued, this use of 'ideology' allows AMT to effectively require defendants to prove their innocence, rather than the other way around

After five years of investigating the Charlie Hebdo attacks, central questions remain unanswered. The network that enabled the Kouachi brothers to murder journalists in Charlie Hebdo's offices with military precision, including supplying their guns, is still undiscovered. Claude Hermant, who brought Coulibaly's guns into France, was convicted by a different (non-terror) court in Lille and has already served his sentence. The connection that moved Hermann's guns to Coulibaly remains unknown. In short, the central elements that enabled the attacks are either still missing or were only tangentially addressed by the trial.

Reframing Terror Law Practices via Transitional Justice: Building a New Paradigm

The first section has demonstrated the problem of an increasingly illiberal European terror law jurisprudence, illustrated by citizenship revocation in Denmark and diminished procedural protections in France. These rights revocations have been made in the name of security, necessary incursions into foundational liberal principles justified by the 'exceptional' circumstances in which the terror threat places European governments. This section considers how transitional justice might address the security/rights impasse challenging European states. It argues that the accountability and recognition elements of transitional justice offer tools that could disrupt static discourses, largely by highlighting problematic intentionality and responses by state actors. The section proceeds in two parts. The first examines how transitional justice could augment the accountability, recognition, and disruption tools that are foundational in the governance ideologies of liberal democracies. The second briefly examines how rule-of-law discourse challenging state intentionality and response is already in use against illiberal terror law in France and Denmark. Although these activists are not reaching for the label of transitional justice, the chapter argues that it applies, and that taking a transitional justice approach to states' treatment of Islamic extremism could address the security/rights impasse.

Transitional Justice for Consolidated Democracies

Traditionally, transitional justice has been applied during or after violent conflict, as a means to end war or to sustain the peace (Gallen 2017; Quinn 2009; Sharp 2018; Teitel 2000; Turner 2008). Emerging scholarship, however, considers what work transitional justice could afford aparadigmatic cases, including consolidated democracies (see Destrooper, Gissel, Hansen, and McGonighle Leyh, respectively, in this volume) and cases of social contestation, such as affirmative action policies in the United States (Joshi 2020).

With Northern Ireland the notable example, European states have not applied transitional justice methods to their own terrorism challenges (Mallinder et al. 2016). This is not because European states are unfamiliar with transitional justice approaches or tools; they are by now a mainstream, global policy and European states support their wide application elsewhere. Moreover, as explored in this volume, European states increasingly apply transitional justice within their own jurisdictions when it comes to violence committed elsewhere or in past times (see Destrooper and Pallí-Asperó in this volume). Contemporary domestic situations still fall outside its ambit, however, including terror law practice in Europe.[16]

The security/rights impasse has constructed an – ever-widening – area of security concern in European states that tracks Islamic practice, as discussed above. We can call these terror law applications illiberal, as many have, but this does not exit the security/rights impasse. That is because the content of Islamic motivation and belief has now become juridically possible to equate with terror (see discussion of AMT, above), and thus triggers security concerns.

The security/rights impasse tracks a divided chasm in political belief regarding how to categorise the risk of Islamic extremism. For the political right, Islamic extremism is fundamentally understood as deriving from Islam itself. This makes all Islamic practices potentially suspect. This point of view echoes 'civilizational arguments' which position Islam in conflict with 'the West' (Fukuyama 1992; Lewis 2002). From this positionality, Islamic ideas contain the possibility of radicalisation, often discussed as a form of 'infection' (Lippens 2004; Picard 2017) and as a cause of violent behaviour (Roex and Vermeulen 2019). This can drive social discussions such as whether to repatriate toddlers trapped after the fall of IS based on the danger they pose to their society of citizenship, what is sometimes called the 'cubs of the caliphate' argument (Vranx 2018). For the political left, on the other hand, jihadi violence is better explained by factors that drive violence more generally, chiefly poverty and social marginalisation, rather than anything particular to Islam. In this view, jihadism is less a radicalisation of Islam than an Islamification of radicalism (Roy 2017). Thus for the political left, rights-violating security discourses that further marginalise already marginalised groups are themselves a causal factor in the proliferation of jihadi violence (Sheikh 2021).

A central chasm between these two views describes motivation and cause. The security/rights impasse affecting European states does not have a method to bridge this divide; either Islam is 'suspect' and Muslims require state surveillance

16 For example, reviews of a proposed research project for a Danish grant rejected the premise that transitional justice could be applied to terror challenges in Europe, arguing that 'transitional justice is not the right approach to be taken [... towards] religious extremists/fanatics whose aim is to destroy the society – because they are not willing to reconcile'. The reviewers further explained that the type of conflict and motivation of actors must be understood to define when and how transitional justice can and should be applied. See also Destrooper in this volume.

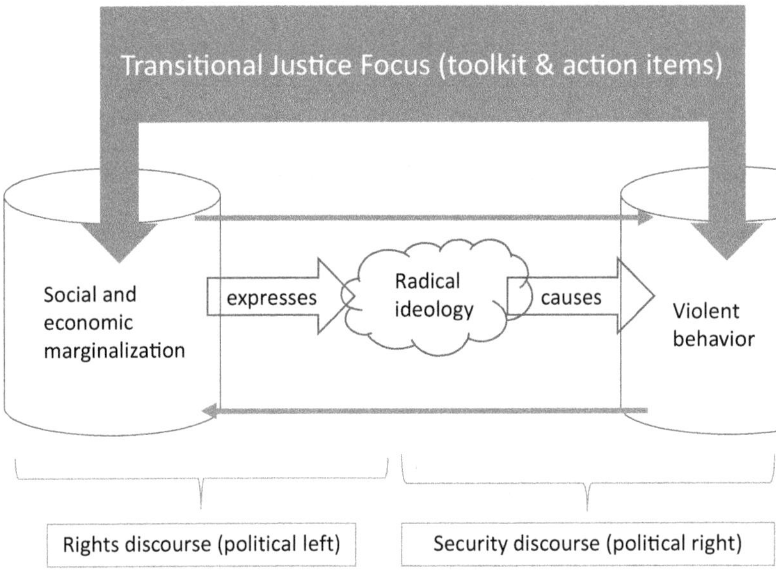

Figure 9.2 How a transitional justice focus bypasses ideological questions.

and control to keep general populations secure, or the rights violations of finding an entire group 'suspect' based on an identity they are free to hold (race and/or religion, depending on how the identity is constructed (Aziz 2021)) are marginalising and encourage radicalisation of the targeted population. It is here that transitional justice offers resolution. This is because transitional justice neutralises deeply held disagreements regarding political positionality, what we can refer to summarily as actors' motivations, via its toolkit of accountability and recognition.

Transitional justice requires all sides, but particularly state actors, to accept compromise in place of absolute victory, i.e. to see compromise as victory. It does so by neutralising, i.e. not interrogating or engaging, actors' political beliefs or historical narratives. We see this most clearly in paradigmatic transitional justice cases. For example, the 2016 peace accord signed in Colombia ending more than 50 years of brutal conflict established a novel transitional justice mechanism, the *Jurisdicción Especial para la Paz* (Special Jurisdiction for Peace; JEP).[17] Its innovative procedure begins by collecting victims' testimonies, followed by engaging criminologists and prosecutors to construct patterns of harm. By grounding its work in the suffering of the civilian

17 Material on the JEP is available here: https://www.jep.gov.co/Paginas/Inicio.aspx (accessed March 22, 2022).

population, a central transitional justice trope, the JEP sidesteps questions of perpetrator ideology. The rationale or comparative justifications behind rebel kidnappings or government 'false positive' murder schemes is not under consideration; the measurable suffering of victims' experiences drives the process. Finally, through a framework that focuses on actions that harmed victims, the JEP recognises perpetrators equally. This has interesting implications for legitimation; for example, the JEP applies IHL – which usually favours state actors – to all actors in the conflict, including criminals and terrorists, to determine who is eligible for amnesties. The laws of war, as discussed in the first section, are designed to limit and humanise the actions of two sovereign states in conflict, and do not imagine that one side has greater rights or legitimacy.

This means that even as transitional justice transpires in Colombia, the leftist *Fuerzas Armadas Revolucionarias de Colombia* (FARC) guerrillas may continue to call for resource redistribution and may represent their struggle as just and necessary. Likewise, the Colombian military may continue to exercise its police powers and insist on the righteous necessity of its cause. Transitional justice does not require narrative movement in how the groups represent their righteous struggles, it requires cooperation with its terms and tools.

It is regarding questions of 'motivation' that transitional justice has potentially the most to offer to European states in the security/rights terror law impasse. Because transitional justice is uninterested in actors' ideological motivations, it has the potential to bridge, or transcend, questions of ideology, motivation, and belief. Transitional justice practice proposes a series of actions – the toolkit – in pursuit of recognition of and justice for victims. This toolkit addresses violence and marginalisation directly, jumping over questions of where ideology fits into actors' rationalisations or motivations. The question transitional justice asks is to what degree progress is made with regard to proposed toolkit actions, not what participating actors think about those tools. The only necessary ideological element for transitional justice to be applied to any given conflict is the recognition of the legitimacy of the other side. This has so far been an impossibly high bar regarding jihadi extremism and its terror actors. The construction of recognition and legitimacy as actors is also exactly where activists and those who are contesting illiberal terror law are focusing their efforts, as discussed briefly in the chapter's next and final section.

Legitimacy Discourses: Recognising Jihadi Terror as Political, Foregrounding the Rule of Law

As the example of Colombia's JEP showed, one can discuss transitional justice in terms of compromise, where compromise becomes a kind of victory. Avishai Margalit (2013) theorises that the first essential element of compromise is recognising the legitimacy of your bargaining partner: Is this someone with whom you can do business, and bargain? Recognition of the legitimacy of the other side is a tall order for many in Europe when it comes to Islamic extremism and jihadi terror. As Didier Bigo (2019, 277) has noted, '[r]adicalisation is not a notion or an academic concept, but an accusation – a way to purify the so-called reactive violence by assigning the blame to one side only'. European states and their populations have little inclination to try to understand, sympathise, or recognise jihadi extremists, and IS adherents and murderous terrorists are often unsympathetic actors. Attempts to reframe discussions of Islamic extremism with a recognition of the contexts in which it occurs, specifically what Habermas called, 'a structural violence [… of] unconscionable social inequality, degrading discrimination, pauperization, and marginalization' (Borradori 2003), is increasingly resisted. In France, speech that 'defends terrorism' is a crime. In both France and Denmark, government policy to constrain scholarly debate that supports what the French call 'Islamo-leftist' ideas has been proposed. So we see in European political and social discourse an ossification of resistance not simply to jihadi terrorism (which violence we should always expect to be resisted) but further to discussions seeking to contextualise, and thereby legitimise, the positionality of those actors who engage in, or are sympathetic to, jihadi extremist ideology.

Here again, however, paradigmatic cases remind us that author legitimacy is always hotly contested prior to transitional justice processes, whether we are speaking of the terrorist FARC or the terrorist Irish nationalists. Both of those groups now enjoy seats in government, following transitional justice processes. Neither the FARC nor the Irish Republican Army joined the government as warring factions; they joined as partners in peace, whereby both they *and the states they were in combat against* undertook to commit and refrain from a series of actions. Their respective ideologies were not embraced by the states against whom they agitated, but rather, those states foundationally accepted the legitimacy of those groups as partners in compromise and worked with them towards solutions.

Contestations over the recognition of legitimacy – as distinct from sympathy or agreement – are driving several contemporary academic and activist movements. Terror researchers are increasingly approaching terror as a political act (Alix and Cahn 2021; Combs 2017) and contesting arguments of terrorist 'irrationality' (Sheikh 2021). This moves academic discussions of terror back to its roots (Crenshaw 1981) and away from the civilisational approaches that inspired several decades of focus on religion as a terror driver (Rapoport 2004).

The drive to categorise terror as political rather than irrational or insane moves responses to terror back towards the criminal law. When terrorism is apolitical, it exists outside of the political spectrum of compromise/negotiation. The 'war on terrorism' discourse turns terror into an enemy act of war, which permits a victory discourse of eradication and/or banishment, rather than a criminal act of violence, which in European welfare states requires a rights-balanced, rationalised punishment which includes rehabilitation and eventual social re-entry. Terror researchers' focus on terror as political violence thus contributes to activist discourses on rule-of-law resolution.

In Denmark, a steady activism surrounding Denmark's refusal to repatriate women and children from camps in Syria has been gaining ground. This movement enjoyed a (partial) victory in April 2021 when Denmark's Prime Minister Mette Frederiksen reversed her position and agreed to repatriate the 'Danish' women and children (Carlson 2021). In September 2021, 17 women and children were returned from Al Hol camp in Syria to Denmark; five children and their mothers were left behind, when three women with dual citizenship were not recognised as Danish after having their citizenship revoked under the 2019 law. In October 2022, Denmark's Supreme Court rejected one woman's request to have her Danish citizenship reinstated.

The shift in Denmark's official position regarding IS adherents in the Levant (women and children, at least) was impacted by aggressive reporting by a Ekstra-Bladet, Denmark's largest circulation tabloid newspaper. Four journalists were awarded Denmark's top prize in journalism, the Cavling Prize, in 2021 for their reporting on the issue. In addition to bringing attention to the unhappy fate of those individuals trapped in camps where both violence and unsanitary living conditions constitute the norm, this reporting broke the story that the governing Social Democrats party had suppressed a report by the Danish security services which found that leaving Danish citizens in the camps constituted a security risk arguably greater than repatriating them.

Reporting by the tabloid press now joined other contestations of state policy, including protests and activism by several international groups. In 2019, the author Jonas Eika won the Nordic Prize for literature. In his speech in Stockholm, with the Danish prime minister in the audience, he called her and her government out for policies that amounted to 'state-sponsored racism' ('*statsracisme*'). The charge of racism is a kind of third rail in Danish political discourse, and this speech brought a great deal of attention and critique, much of it directed at Eika but nonetheless some of it directed at the government's policies.[18]

These moments of protest and activism have for several years been challenges to what was a unified front crossing nearly the entire political spectrum. With the support of left-leaning parties, the Social Democratics took power in 2019 on a slate that echoed right wing and nationalist parties' positions on immigration and security. In the years following their victory, the Social Democrats have made good on these promises. In addition to citizenship revocation policies, they have reduced basic benefits for refugees to half the standard social benefits package available to citizens and residents, parlayed with

18 See debate on DR1: available at: https://www.facebook.com/watch/?v=826424267773780 (accessed March 22, 2022).

Rwanda regarding housing refugees there, signed an agreement with Kosovo to jail deported persons there, and determined that Syria is safe for refugee return, a position shared only by Hungary and critiqued by the EU parliament. Yet the differential treatment of Ukrainian refugees is beginning a new conversation regarding refugee treatment in Denmark. This is an example of the narrative-changing activism that can drive transitional justice processes and proponents.

Conclusion

The difficulties European nations face confronting returnees and domestic terror actors are similar to those of other countries reconciling once warring parties after conflict. They raise questions such as whether and how severely violators should be punished, and how or if they should be permitted to re-join the nation as civilians.

The question of how Europe treats its Muslims and what relation that treatment has to the success of radical Islamic terror movements is ossifying in the political debate. The rise of populism across Europe and its concomitant rejection of human rights has strengthened a politics of ethnic nationalism that often rejects Muslims and other recent immigrants as non-European. There is a mainstream policy tool applied to move forward from intractable conflict, where both sides feel they are right and resist compromise or cooperation: it is called 'transitional justice'.

References

Agamben, G. (2005) *State of Exception*. Chicago: University of Chicago Press.

Alix, J. and O. Cahn, eds. (2021) *Terrorisme et infraction politique*. Paris: Mare Martin.

Ashworth, A. and L. Zedner (2015) *Preventive Justice*. Oxford: Oxford University Press.

Aziz, S.F. (2021) *The Racial Muslim: When Racism Quashes Religious Freedom*. Oakland: University of California Press.

Besnier, C. and S. Weill (2019) 'Les Filieres Djihadistes en Proces: Approche Ethnographique des Audiences Criminelles er Correctionnelles (2017–2019)'. *Mission de Recherche Droit and Justice* Rapport 17.29.

Bigo, D. (2019) 'The Maze of Radicalization: Justification and Professional Interests'. In: N. Fadil, F. Ragazzi and M. de Koning, eds. *Radicalization in Belgium and the Netherlands: Critical Perspectives on Violence and Security*. London: I.B. Taurus.

—— and A. Tsoukala, eds. (2008) *Terror, Insecurity and Liberty: Illiberal Practices of Liberal Regimes after 9/11*. Abingdon: Routledge.

Blisson, L. (2017) 'Risques et périls de l'association de malfaiteurs terroriste'. *Deliberee* 2(2), 16–20.

Borradori, G. (2003) *Philosophy in a Time of Terror: Dialogues with Jürgen Habermas and Jacques Derrida*. Chicago: University of Chicago Press.

Breen-Smyth, M. (2014) 'Theorising the 'Suspect Community': Counterterrorism, Security Practices and the Public Imagination'. *Critical Studies on Terrorism* 7(2), 223–40.

Brems, E., C. Heri, S.O. Chaib and L. Verdonck (2017) 'Head-Covering Bans in Belgian Courtrooms and Beyond: Headscarf Persecution and the Complicity of Supranational Courts'. *Human Rights Quarterly* 39(4), 882–909.

Cahn, O. and J. Alix, eds. (2017) *L'hypothèse de la guerre contre le terrorisme - Implications juridiques*. Paris: Dalloz.

Carlson, K.B. (2021) 'What to Do about Islamic State Supporters Still in Syria? Denmark's Decision Sets a Worrying Trend'. The Conversation, 3 June. Retrieved from: https://theconversation.com/what-to-do-about-islamic-state-supporters-still-in-syria-denmarks-decision-sets-a-worrying-trend-161971.

—— and J. Slosser (2021) 'When Religion Speaks: Denmark's Face Covering Ban and European Human Rights Law'. *Nordic Journal of Human Rights* 39(4), 420–439.

Chiangi, M.A. (2019) 'Theoretical Conception of Modern Terrorism: An Appraisal of David Rapoport's Four Waves Theory'. SSRN scholarly paper, ID 3498569. Rochester: Social Science Research Network.

Cole, D. (2005) *Enemy Aliens: Double Standards and Cosntitutional Freedoms in the War on Terrorism*. New York: The New Press.

Combs, C. (2017) *Terrorism in the Twenty-First Century*, 8th ed. Abingdon: Routledge.

Coolsaet, R. (2019) 'Radicalization: The Origins and Limits of a Contested Concept'. In: N. Fadil, F. Ragazzi and M. de Koning, eds. *Radicalization in Belgium and the Netherlands: Critical Perspectives on Violence and Security*. London: I.B. Taurus.

Crenshaw, M. (1981) 'The Causes of Terrorism'. *Comparative Politics* 13(4), 379–99.

Dawson, L.A. (2021) 'A Comparative Analysis of the Data on Western Foreign Fighters in Syria and Iraq: Who Went and Why?' 10 February. The Hague: International Centre for Counter Terrorism. Retrieved from: https://icct.nl/app/uploads/2021/02/Dawson-Comparative-Analysis-FINAL-1.pdf.

Drumbl, M. (2006) 'The Expressive Value of Prosecuting and Punishing Terrorists: Handman, the Geneva Conventions, and International Criminal Law'. *George Washington Law Review* 75, 1165–1199.

Duff, R.A. (2001) *Punishment, Communication and Community*. Oxford: Oxford University Press.

—— (2010) 'Towards a Theory of Criminal Law?' *Proceedings of the Aristotelian Society* Supplementary 84, 1–28.

Edwards, P. (2018) 'Counter-Terrorism and Counter-Law: An Archetypal Critique'. *Legal Studies* 38(2), 279–97.

Fadil, N., F. Ragazzi and M. de Koning, eds. (2019) *Radicalization in Belgium and the Netherlands: Critical Perspectives on Violence and Security*. London: I.B. Taurus.

Fassin, D. (2021) 'Are 'woke' Academics a Threat to the French Republic? Ask Macron's Ministers" The Guardian, 12 March. Retrieved from: https://www.theguardian.com/commentisfree/2021/mar/12/academics-french-republic-macron-islamo-leftism.

Fukuyama, F. (1992) *The End of History and the Last Man*. New York: Free Press.

Gallen, J. (2017) 'Catherine Turner: Violence, Law and the Impossibility of Transitional Justice'. *Feminist Legal Studies* 25(1), 131–35.

Galli, F. (2015) *The Law on Terrorism: The UK, France and Italy Compared*. Brussels: Bruyant.

Garapon, A. and M. Rosenfeld (2016) *Démocraties Sous Stress: Les Défis Du Terrorisme Global*. Paris: PUF.

Gentleman, A. (2020) 'London-Born Twins Face Deportation to Different Countries'. The Guardian, July 7. Retrieved from: https://www.theguardian.com/uk-news/2020/jul/07/london-born-twins-face-deportation-to-different-countries.

de Graaf, B. (2019) 'Foreign Fighters on Trial: Sentencing Risk, 2013–2017'. In: N. Fadil, F. Ragazzi and M. de Koning, eds. *Radicalization in Belgium and the Netherlands: Critical Perspectives on Violence and Security*. London: I.B. Taurus.

Hamilton, C. (2019) *Contagion, Counter-Terrorism and Criminology: Justice in the Shadow of Terror*. Basingstoke: Palgrave Macmillan.

Hecker, M. (2016) 'Le Djihadisme en Procès'. *Revue des Deux Mondes*, 139–147.

Hemmingsen, A.-S. (2015) *An Introduction to the Danish Approach to Countering and Preventing Extremism and Radicalization*. DIIS Report 2015/15. Copenhagen: Danish Institute for International Studies.

Hervik, P. ed. (2019) *Racialization, Racism, and Anti-Racism in the Nordic Countries*. Cham: Palgrave Macmillan.

Joshi, Y. (2020) 'Affirmative Action as Transitional Justice'. *Wisconsin Law Review* 2020(1), 1–48.

Kundnani, A. (2014) *The Muslims are Coming!: Islamophobia, Extremism, and the Domestic War on Terror*. London: Verso.

Lacey, N. (2016) *In Search of Criminal Responsibility: Ideas, Interests, and Institutions*. Oxford, New York: Oxford University Press.

—— (2019) 'Populism and the Rule of Law'. *Annual Review of Law and Social Science* 15(1), 79–96.

Lewis, B. (2002) *What Went Wrong? The Clash Between Islam and Modernity in the Middle East*. London: Weidenfeld & Nicolson.

Lippens, R. (2004) 'Viral Contagion and Anti-Terrorism: Notes on Medical Emergency, Legality and Diplomacy'. *International Journal for the Semiotics of Law* 17, 125–39.

Lister, C. (2015) 'Returning Foreign Fighters: Criminalization or Reintegration?'. *Brookings Doha Center Policy Briefing*, August. Doha: Brookings.

Macmanus, T. (2020) 'State Crime'. In: *Oxford Research Encyclopedias: Criminology and Criminal Justice (online)*, 17 December. Retrieved from: https://doi.org/10.1093/acrefore/9780190264079.013.362.

Mallinder, L., K. McEvoy, L. Moffett and G. Anthony (2016) 'The Historical Use of Amnesties, Immunities, and Sentence Reductions in Northern Ireland.' Transitional Justice Institute Research Paper 16-12. Retrieved from: https://papers.ssrn.com/sol3/papers.cfm?abstract_id=2801555.

Margalit, A. (2013) *On Compromise and Rotten Compromises*. Princeton: Princeton University Press.

Midtbøen, A. (2019) 'Dual Citizenship in an Era of Securitisation: The Case of Denmark'. *Nordic Journal of Migration Research* 9(3), 293–309.

Moors, A. (2019) 'No Escape: The Force of the Security Frame in Academia and Beyond'. In: N. Fadil, F. Ragazzi and M. de Koning, eds. *Radicalization in Belgium and the Netherlands: Critical Perspectives on Violence and Security*. London: I.B. Taurus.

Müller, J.W. (2021) *Democracy Rules*. New York: Farrar, Straus & Giroux.

Picard, M.H. (2017) "Iraqnophobia': A Biomedical History of State-Rearing and Shock Doctrine in Iraq'. *International Journal for the Semiotics of Law* 30(1), 81–114.

Quinn, J.R., ed. (2009) *Reconciliation(s): Transitional Justice in Postconflict Societies*. Montreal: McGill-Queen's University Press.

Ragazzi, F. (2016) 'Suspect Community or Suspect Category: The Impact of Counter-Terrorism as 'Policed Multiculturalism''. *Journal of Ethnic and Migration Studies* 42(5), 724–41.

Rapoport, D. (2004) 'The Four Waves of Modern Terrorism'. In: A. Cronin and J. Ludes, eds. *Attacking Terrorism: Elements of a Grand Strategy* (pp. 46–73). Washington, DC: Georgetown University Press.

Roex, I. and F. Vermeulen (2019) 'Pre-Emptive Measures Against Radicalization and Local Partnerships in Antwerp'. In: N. Fadil, F. Ragazzi and M. de Koning, eds. *Radicalization in Belgium and the Netherlands: Critical Perspectives on Violence and Security*. London: I.B. Taurus.
Roy, O. (2017) *Jihad and Death: The Global Appeal of the Islamic State*. London: Hurst.
Rytter, M. (2010) '"The Family of Denmark" and "the Aliens": Kinship Images in Danish Integration Politics'. Ethnos 75(3), 301–322.
Sayare, S. (2018) 'Terrorist by Association'. The New Republic. October, 1–20.
Schmid, A. (1983) *Political Terrorism: A Research Guide to Concepts, Theories, Data Bases and Literature*. New Brunswick: Transaction Books.
—— (2013) 'Radicalisation, De-Radicalisation, Counter-Radicalisation: A Conceptual Discussion and Literature Review'. *International Centre for Counter-Terrorism* Research Paper, March. The Hague: International Centre for Counter-Terrorism.
Schmidt, G. (2019) 'Myths of Ethnic Homogeneity: The Danish Case'. In S. Keskinen, U.D. Skaptadóttir and M. Toivanen, eds. *Undoing Homogeneity in the Nordic Region: Studies in Migration and Diaspora*. London: Routledge.
Schmitt, C., T.B. Strong and L. Strauss (2007) *The Concept of the Political: Expanded Edition*. Chicago: The University of Chicago Press.
Sharp, D.N. (2018) *Rethinking Transitional Justice for the Twenty-First Century: Beyond the End of History*. Cambridge and New York: Cambridge University Press.
Sheikh, J. (2021) *Vi Tabte: Hvordan jihadismen besjrede Vesten, og hvordan vi kommer videre som tabere*. Copenhagen: Gyldendal.
Silke, A. (2004) 'Courage in Dark Places: Reflections on Terrorist Psychology'. *Social Research* 71(1), 177–98.
—— and K. Brown (2016) '"Radicalisation": The Transformation of Modern Understanding of Terrorist Origins, Psychology and Motivation'. In: S. Jayakumar, ed. *State, Society and National Security* (pp. 129–150). Singapore: World Scientific.
Silverstein, P. (2018) *Postcolonial France: Race, Islam, and the Future of the Republic*. London: Pluto Press.
Smith, P.S. and T. Ugelvik, eds. (2017) *Scandinavian Penal History, Culture and Prison Practice*. Cham: Palgrave Macmillan.
Sniderman, P. (2016) *Paradoxes of Liberal Democracy*. Princeton: Princeton University Press.
Stampnitzky, L. (2011) 'Disciplining an Unruly Field: Terrorism Experts and Theories of Scientific/Intellectual Production'. *Qualitative Sociology* 34, 1–19.
—— (2013) *Disciplining Terror: How Experts Invented 'Terrorism'*. Cambridge: Cambridge University Press.
Teitel, R.G. (2000) *Transitional Justice*. Oxford: Oxford University Press.
Teubner, G. (2012) *Constitutional Fragments: Societal Constitutionalism and Globalization*. Oxford: Oxford University Press.
Turner, C. (2008) 'Delivering Lasting Peace, Democracy and Human Rights in Times of Transition: The Role of International Law'. *International Journal of Transitional Justice* 2(2), 126–51.
Van Munster, R. (2004) 'The War on Terrorism: When the Exception Becomes the Rule'. *International Journal for the Semiotics of Law* 17(2), 141–53.
Vrankx, R. (2018) 'For the Sins of their Fathers' (documentary series November 2018, available at: https://www.vrt.be/vrtnws/en/2018/11/14/for-the-sins-of-their-fathers-episode-one/)

Wacquant, L. (2008) 'Ordering Insecurity: Social Polarization and the Punitive Upsurge'. *Radical Philosophy Review* 11(1), 1–19.

—— (2009) *Punishing the Poor: The Neoliberal Government of Social Insecurity*. Durham, NC: Duke University Press.

Weill, S. (2018) *Terror in Courts: French Counter-Terrorism, Administrative and Penal Avenues. Report for the Official Visit of the UN Special Rapporteur on Counter-Terrorism and Human Rights*. May. Paris: PSIA, Sciences Po.

Weill, S. (2020) 'Transnational Jihadism and the Role of Criminal Judges: An Ethnography of French Courts'. *Journal of Law and Society* 47(S1), S30–S53.

Chapter 10

Addressing the Legacies of the Past

Historical Commissions in Consolidated Democracies

Cira Pallí-Asperó

Introduction

Consolidated democracies are increasingly facing pressures to come to terms with their violent pasts. An important component is dealing with historical accounts that deny or justify past wrongs and that can lead to, or perpetuate already existing, social divisions. Against this background, stakeholders are increasingly looking for ways to move from dominant and sometimes oppressive narratives towards spaces for contestation and competing narratives. Several governments have established commissions that seek to examine the past to uncover or clarify specific events relating to past abuses; and to contribute to processes of recognition, acknowledgement, and redress on the basis thereof. One such type has been historical commissions.[1]

In this chapter, I introduce state-sponsored historical commissions as an alternative approach to truth-seeking in consolidated democracies, under the transitional justice model's truth pillar. The chapter builds on previous research investigating how 27 historical commissions operated in various political contexts to address the legacies of a contested past. The chapter examines the extent to which historical commissions align with the core objectives of transitional justice, i.e. accountability, recognition, and social change. It explores how historical commissions in consolidated democracies represent an innovation in the field of transitional justice by helping to alleviate some of the tensions emerging from the application of the transitional justice strategy to an aparadigmatic context.

The concept of the state, used in relation to state-sponsored or state-sanctioned historical commissions, is understood as a 'set of entities and practices

1 Commissioned history has several different names in relation to their objectives or the context in which they have operated, such as historical expert commissions (Pettai 2018); historical truth commissions (Hayner 2001); sociohistorical commissions of inquiry (Freeman 2006); historical commissions (Karn 2006, 2015, 2017). Elsewhere, I term them historical clarification commissions (Palli-Aspero 2020). This chapter uses the term historical commissions to generalise the broader phenomenon.

DOI: 10.4324/9781003289104-11

which can function in profoundly different ways depending on the historical, sociocultural or institutional context' (Bevernage and Wouters 2018, 5). The state is a conglomerate of actors, institutions, and other mechanisms that enable particular interventions and practices. These actors are perceived as active players in the construction of historical narratives through a range of practices and institutions. The focus on intentionality presented in the conceptual framework of this volume helps to frame this approach. The state establishes historical commissions to enable a process of inquiry into the past with the intention to address issues of accountability and recognition of harm. Through the endorsement of the emerging historical accounts, the state 'actively grant[s] a specific moral status to particular pasts' (Bevernage and Wouters 2018, 4) in an effort to (re)frame state legitimacy in the present (Winter 2014). Presenting state-sponsored historical commissions as instances of transitional justice in consolidated democracies can be seen, therefore, as a tool for state legitimation under the parameters of accountability and recognition for past wrongdoing.

Historical Commissions

The rise and popularity of historical commissions took place throughout the 1990s in the context of the end of the Cold War. The reopening of archives and the change in the political landscape in many countries generated a new interest by historians in engaging with the politics of the past (Karn 2006). Since then, historical commissions have operated in various contexts, from situations of ongoing conflict and post-authoritarian/totalitarian or (post)conflict contexts, to consolidated democracies (see also the Introduction in this volume). They have had a variety of objectives and functions, such as debunking ill-informed historical narratives; contributing to history textbooks; fostering diplomatic relations; addressing responsibility for crimes and violations of human rights; acknowledgement of past wrongdoing; and/or the redress of historical injustices. This chapter analyses state-sponsored or state-sanctioned historical commissions which are established to help resolve social and political disputes or antagonisms rooted in historical events.

Historical Commissions' Working Paradigm

Historical commissions are defined as state-sponsored bodies of clarification of the past that work towards recognition and moral and political accountability for past wrongs through the creation of new historical frames of interpretation. Historical commissions seek to understand the structural conditions and underlying processes that contributed to the development of the facts investigated, while concentrating on the complexity of historical developments. They do this by enabling a process of critical reflection that considers different interpretations of the past and creates new historical frameworks that shift away from accusatory accounts to more explanatory ones based on accurate and contextualised historical facts. Ultimately, they aim to transform perceptions about the past to correct the historical record, challenge historical myths, and achieve social change.

They are composed primarily of professional historians who engage in an investigative process informed by methodological and ethical standards of historical scholarship to (re)evaluate existing historical knowledge and conduct analysis of new sources (Karn 2006; Pettai 2018). Although their investigation is conducted mainly through the analysis of archival resources, historical commissions sometimes have access to testimonies, either as oral reports about the past or through written submissions from the present or stored in archives. However, in these cases, the use to the testimonies takes a different approach than in other transitional justice mechanisms taking a secondary role within the investigation. This is further explored in the next section.

Historical Commissions as Unique Mechanisms Within Transitional Justice

Scholars debate whether historical commissions can be seen as instances of transitional justice. Hayner (2001) sees historical commissions as official bodies of inquiry operating outside the paradigmatic transitional justice framework. To her, historical commissions are established to inquire into events that took place (and ended) many years ago and are not concerned with 'widespread political repression', but with 'targeted practices that may have affected specific ethnic, racial or other groups' (2001, 17). Freeman (2006, 57) defines historical commissions as human rights investigative inquiries into events that have taken place a generation or more prior to the establishment of the commission. He understands historical commissions to be separate from truth commissions.

Others have framed historical commissions within transitional justice as a historical sub-type of truth commission, arguing that they operate in similar ways and pursue similar outcomes (Grodsky 2009; Stan 2009). For example, they create national narratives about the past that seek to uncover, clarify, and formally acknowledge past abuses. I agree with Pettai (2015b, 241) that approaching historical commissions from the lens of a truth commission risks 'overlooking a number of fundamental differences in the aims, operative work and outcome of both kinds of official investigations'. Historical commissions and truth commissions are functionally and conceptually different in many significant ways. Accordingly, historical commissions as a truth-seeking/clarification mechanism within transitional justice should be understood as a unique mechanism, rather than a sub-category. I do not suggest that one is better than the other, or that truth commissions are inappropriate truth-seeking mechanisms in consolidated democracies. Instead, my intention is to enrich current truth commission practice in transitional justice.

In the following section I explore the differentiation between historical commissions and truth commissions through three overarching themes: the commissions' mandate, their approach to the inquiry, and the commissions' outputs.

Mandate

The mandate of both historical and truth commissions offers the guidelines for the investigation as well as the overarching aim and function that the commissions work towards. Truth commissions are generally established relatively soon after the commencement of a governmental transition in order to support the transitional process. They interrogate recent events related to 'politically motivated or politically targeted repression' and/or investigate 'widespread abuses and violations of human rights' (Hayner 2001, 17). They report on the principal causes and consequences of 'severe violence or repression that occurred on the state during determinate periods of abusive rule or conflict, and mak[e] recommendations for their redress and future prevention' (Freeman 2006, xiii).

Historical commissions have mainly operated in consolidated democracies undertaking inquiries related to inter-group violence or injustices committed in a distant past. Historical commissions are often established as a response to prevalent or resurfacing historically rooted tensions and claims of recognition based on past injustices (Barkan 2009; Pettai 2015b). These involve conflicting, opposite, or accusatory truth claims about past wrongs that challenge long-lasting perceptions, political authority, and social cohesion (Pettai 2015b). Historical commissions are set up to revisit historical records and facts about past wrongs to produce a new critical historical frame that challenges established historical accounts or clarifies some of its contested elements.

Approach to the Inquiry: Forensic Truth vs. Historical Truth

The methodological approach that both commissions take to the investigation is also significantly different. The main objective of truth commissions is to quantify the human rights violations through the recovery of forensic truth – '*who did what to whom*'. To do so, they access the testimonies of victims and witnesses to document political violence committed by state or non-state actors (Grandin and Kullboch 2007). Truth commissions use a legal approach in their methodologies and forms of interrogation and compilation of information by, for example, relying on statements submitted by eyewitnesses and victims of human rights violations (Brahm 2009; Hayner 2001). Within the working parameters of truth commissions, 'truth' is built on the 'subjectivity and authenticity of the victim and eyewitness of abuse' (Pettai 2015a, 5). The emerging accounts are seen to contribute to the idea of closure from a past that should never be repeated, which is reinforced by the notion that truth telling can contribute to reconciliation and nation-building (Bevernage 2014; Grandin and Kullboch 2007; Hayner 2001).

Historical commissions, on the other hand, are located away from the legal paradigm that usually frames transitional justice mechanisms. Historical commissions' main source of evidence are archival resources and do not usually deal with the collection of testimonies because they investigate acts of wrongdoing that took place in a distant time – the victims or witnesses who experienced the wrongful actions are not capable of giving testimony. However, a few historical commissions have had the opportunity to access the testimonies of witnesses and victims. In these cases, the collection of testimonies does not follow the quasi-legal framework characteristic of truth commissions but takes a secondary role. Within the historical commissions' working paradigm, testimonies are treated as another piece of evidence that contributes to the construction of a nuanced contextualisation of the events that sheds light on the broad historical, political, and social-structural factors.

The emerging historical frames pursue historical truth, which is considered 'open' and always subject to 'continuous re-evaluation against new evidence and interpretive frameworks' (Maier 2003, 264). Within this understanding, the work of historical commissions provides a critical scrutiny of the evidence allowing for different perspectives and contestation to coexist. This approach responds to the increasing tendency to highlight the importance of the acknowledgement of the existence of multi-perspectives or interpretations of the same past to establish new historical frames to mend social and political antagonisms in a present context projecting the idea of a common future (Bevernage 2018).

Creation of a New Historical Narratives

Making the past accessible through public knowledge about past crimes is seen as imperative to challenging those representations of the past that serve to legitimise unlawful, criminal and immoral actions. An accurate rendering of the past can help undermine 'the self-serving justificatory narratives of perpetrators – and in the process holding them publicly accountable, even if only symbolically', and offer 'extended recognition to victims and survivors' (Verdeja 2009, 33). Both historical and truth commissions produce (new) historical frames about the past that have a focus on the future with the aim of 'demystifying, delegitimizing the past and strengthening future and current political or social structures or regimes' (Mihr 2017, 2). Therefore, they act as active agents in the process of regime legitimation through the production of historical accounts that allow the state to acknowledge and address past wrongs. However, they differ in terms of the purpose of the emerging account.

First, while historical commissions have the explicit mandate of creating a historical account emerging from a rigorous and extensive historical analysis of the period or event under inquiry, truth commissions do so in order to be able to present their findings to the public in an intelligible manner that contextualise them within their historical context (Scheuzger 2018). The mandate of a truth commissions it is not to produce a historical investigation, but to document human rights abuses and other crimes.

Second, the purpose of historical commissions is to create new interpretative frames that, while presenting accurate historical facts scrutinised through a rigorous process of analysis, 'move the historical discourse away from an accusatory framework' towards an explanatory one that 'offers a new context for historical facts that have been miss-constructed or marshalled differently by rival groups' (Karn 2006, 33). Thus, the process of framing the past through historical narratives is 'not simply a re-write of history, but rather a form of history-making' (McGrattan 2016, 108), in which the intentionality of the sponsoring state is imprinted. This point is explored further below.

As this section has shown, historical commissions have a unique approach to addressing the legacies of the past. The introduction of such commissions within the transitional justice framework in aparadigmatic context – in this case, consolidated democracies, fosters the consolidation of the field through an innovation of the methodological approaches available.

The Links Between Historical Commissions and Transitional Justice

The role of historical commissions within transitional justice ought to be understood as radically different than historiography (i.e. the discipline of history), as historical commissions become active agents in political mythmaking[2] (Pettai 2015b). The inquiry into the past is a response to a particular purpose in the present (Lewis 1975) – in our case, within the intentionality orbit within which the state seeks accountability and recognition for the past wrongs. This approach to history has a strong political function as it responds to external objectives to legitimise, convince, influence, rationalise, or mobilise certain groups within a given society.

Creating history with a purpose is generally related with an 'attempt to arrange historical elements into the relevant context of meaning, made mainly by groups of intellectuals and politicians in control of public representations' (Karlsson 2013, 39). This point is key to the argument of this chapter for the following reason. If one understands the work of historical commissions under the parameters of history for a purpose, it means that the emerging historical narratives are always constructed to make 'sense of the past in light of the needs of the present for the sake of aspirations for the future' (Bevernage 2018, 77). Therefore, social and political junctures surrounding the sponsoring state

2 Mythmaking is defined as a form of 'collective memory that is constructed and institutionalised through top-down mechanisms of state policy' (Pettai 2015b, 243) concerning historical events that are 'politically and institutionally elevated to provide higher meaning to the political or national community' (Pettai 2015b, 244).

are crucial in determining the intentional and functional aspects of the work of historical commissions. The historical accounts emerging from the process of historical clarification are constructed to respond to a particular orbit of intention – which within the transitional justice paradigm seeks to achieve accountability and recognition. These lines of influence are imprinted in the mandate of the commissions by the sponsoring state, which dictates who will take part on the investigation (commissioners); what events will be examined; what resources will be made available to the commissioners; which research methods will be employed in the analysis; and how the findings will be communicated to the public.

Even though establishing the research limits of a historical investigation is necessary to conduct a feasible inquiry, we must be cautious and consider the challenges and limitations of commissioned history and the elaboration of a historical narrative 'on request'. When considering the historian as a political agent working in a state institution, some of these concerns are related to the divergences on what would be considered free academic research and historical research done through commissioned history under a political mandate. In the framework of historical commissions, there is a fine line 'between ideological or power-political instrumentalization, and the necessary impartiality of credible historical research' (Pettai 2015a, 5). As states can indeed be 'deeply involved in politics of historical denial and can severely violate academic freedom' (Bevernage and Wouters 2018, 3), the sponsoring-party ideology may try to, directly or indirectly, influence the commission's approach to the investigation.

The promotion of 'critical historical inquiries from officially established institutions, [can act] as a vehicle to destabilize those unreflective historical narratives that are constructed to serve a particular agenda' (Verdeja 2009, 152). However, there might also be social or political constraints about what is (morally and ethically) acceptable to reveal, or even limitations on the sources that are available. While the state may use the work of historical commissions to facilitate access to new evidence to shed light on previously unknown events, it may also limit access to specific archives or other resources to maintain the *status quo*. Finally, governments, political parties, or other groups may use specific rhetorical discourses as a means of legitimation and use the work of historical commissions as a mechanism to reinforce (new) accusatory accounts or strategically privilege specific approaches to investigating particular events for a political purpose. Its work can be instrumentalised to justify past wrongs, avoid responsibilities, or highlight particular events, for a strategic political end.

Historical Commissions as Instances of Transitional Justice in Consolidated Democracies

To explore the role of historical commissions within transitional justice in consolidated democracies, I will use three of the transitional justice working hypothesis (namely, the temporal dimension, its core objectives of accountability and recognition, and victim's participation) as reference points for discussion. By examining these three dimensions, I explore the expansion of the core elements of transitional justice when transported into an aparadigmatic context, as well as how the work of historical commissions offers an alternative approach to truth-seeking while still aligning with the core pillars of transitional justice.

In the section, the three dimensions, while being heavily intertwined with one another, are discussed separately. In consolidated democracies, the inquiries into the past are often set to investigate events that took place in a distant past (temporal dimension), but that still have an impact in the social and political relations in the present (continuity in time rather than a moment of rupture). This means that the engagement with those who experience the events first-hand is limited or impossible (this includes victims, testimonies, and perpetrators), resulting in the need to apply different methodological approaches to the investigation. I explore the potential role of historical commissions in relation to the three dimensions by introducing illustrative examples of historical commissions that had operated in other contexts. Although all the examples can be seen to contribute to accountability, recognition, and social change, I have decided to highlight certain elements of their work to complement the discussion of each dimension.

The temporal logic of transitional justice assumes a clear break with the past, in which the process of transition is seen 'as a process of closure' (Ní Aolain and Campbell 2005, 182). Transitional justice politics and mechanisms are set to legitimate 'the new order by declaring that, despite necessary continuities, political institutions will henceforth bear a very different character' (Winter 2014, 17). The idea of a clear rupture between the past and the present is, in itself, widely contested within the domain of transitional justice; but it becomes even more problematic in aparadigmatic settings, as it is in consolidated democracies, where continuity, not rupture, is the state of affairs (Álvarez-Berastegi 2017). In these contexts, what we find, instead, is a change in regimes of legitimacy that does not lead 'an inauguration of a new state' (Winter 2014, 34), but rather represents a process of (re)legitimation of the political orders in the present. Furthermore, the work of historical commissions challenges the idea of 'rupture' with the past by exploring those historical events that despite having taken place in a distant past continue to have an impact in the present. Thus, these commissions play a key role in understanding the social and political junctures in the present. In these lines, historical commissions carry on an inquiry into the past that becomes both 'retrospective' (in coming to terms with the past), and 'prospective' (Schaap 2005, 91) in fostering accountability, recognition and social change.

Challenging 'Historical Myths' About the Past

To illustrate this, I will refer to the Study Mission on the Spoliation of Jews (1997) in France which is often included as part of a bigger group of Western

European commissions known as Holocaust commissions[3] (Karn 2015). The late 1990s and early 2000s saw a growing interest in investigating the international system of looting and policy of extermination that characterised the national-socialist regime during the Second World War. Despite its focus on spoliated property,[4] the commissions worked beyond the mandate to establish evidence of collaborations from governments, national banks and other institutions with the Third Reich. The emerging accounts challenged previous national discourses used to avoid taking responsibility for the crimes committed during the Nazi occupation.[5]

In France, the historical narrative that had prevailed after the end of the Nazi occupation was built on the 'parenthesis theory' (Rousso 1994), by which the resistance against Nazi Germany was glorified, while distancing the discourse from the dark years of the Vichy regime operating after the Nazi occupation of France. It is referred to as parenthesis theory because it considers the Vichy regime as a parenthesis in the history of the nation, and for which the post-Vichy French government was not to be held accountable. However, that changed during the mid-1990s, with a shift in how the political and academic spheres related to the years of Nazi occupation and policies of the Vichy regime. In 1996, President Jacques Chirac apologised for the anti-Semitic policies of the Vichy government (Simons 1995), acknowledging, for the first time, the involvement of France in the Holocaust. President Chirac's apology 'opened the nation's history for critical revision and amendment' (Karn 2015, 34). As a response, the French government established the Study Mission on the Spoliation of Jews, known also as the Mattéoli Commission.

The Mattéoli Commission was tasked with studying the conditions in which the Jews of France were spoliated of their properties by the Nazi occupier and the Vichy authorities (Mattéoli 2000). The commission was seen as a mechanism to address moral, political, and historical responsibilities towards the past. The final report sought to achieve more than an inventory of stolen goods and to present a new historical frame that would highlight the 'moral rehabilitation'

3 These are Switzerland's Independent Commission of Experts (ICE) in 1996; Belgium's Study Commission on Jewish Assets in 1997; France's Study Mission on the Spoliation of Jews in France in 1997; Italy's Commission for the Study of the Acquisition of Goods of Jewish Citizens by Private and Public Bodies in 1998; and Austria's Historical Commission in 1998.

4 The term spoliation refers to the deprivation of property rights of the European Jews during the years of Nazi occupation.

5 This political and historiographic attitude towards the past was built on the claim that the states, as known in the present, did not exist under the Nazi occupation and, therefore, the governments of the time had no control over the actions. These attitudes towards the past have been explored by many in relation to different countries. For instance, the parenthesis theory in France (Karn 2015; Mattéoli 2000; Rousso 1994); the resistance myth in Italy (Anselmi 2001; Karn 2015); the theory of occupation (Jabloner 2007) and the victim thesis in Austria (Art 2006; Karn 2015; Pelinka 1989); and the myth of neutrality in Switzerland (Bergier 2002; Karn 2006).

(Karn 2015, 37) of the nation through the acknowledgement and recognition of the crimes committed during the Vichy regime.

In consolidated democracies where the state usually operates within a political space characterised by a certain degree of acceptance and consent among its citizens, the core objectives characteristic of paradigmatic transitions – i.e. issues of accountability and recognition – are likely to take a radically different meaning from those of post-authoritarian or post-conflict settings (Hansen 2011; McAuliffe 2011; Ní Aolain and Cambell 2005; Teitel 2010, 2017). For example, in a context in which accountability through criminal justice may not be possible due to the distance in time in relation to the crimes, the objective of achieving accountability may consist, in the first place, of 'labelling certain practices as unjust in the public domain' (Hansen 2011, 42), rather than actual prosecutions through criminal justice (as would be the case in most 'classic' transitional justice contexts). In these cases, political accountability through recognition of the past wrongs becomes a key element (Haldemann 2008; Schaap 2005).

Historical commissions can contribute to addressing issues of political accountability through a process of clarification of the past that leads to the acknowledgement and recognition of the past wrongs and the articulation of political and moral responsibilities (regime legitimation in the present). In this framework, political accountability, or political responsibility (Schaap 2005), for the past wrongdoing ought to be seen as grounded on the acknowledgement that those societies that live in the present, are entangled with those in the past, 'irrespective of [any] particular motives and intentions' (2005, 123). It is this historical aspect that sustains the argument that state-sponsored historical commissions contribute to political accountability and recognition. There are various forms in which the work of historical commissions may lead to expressions of political accountability. For example, state redress through institutional reform, public acknowledgement for historical injustices, official apologies, public and official statements recognising the responsibility for past wrongs, or forms of symbolic reparation such as commemorations and memorials are all characteristic of transitional justice practice (Winter 2014).

State Redress as Form of Political Accountability

An example of state redress of historical injustices can be found in historical commissions established by settler nations to redress the historical injustices of the colonial past in Australia, Canada and Chile.[6] These commissions were

6 These are the Australia's National Inquiry into the Separation of Aboriginal and Torres Strait Islander Children from Their Families in 1995; the Royal Commission on Aboriginal Peoples and the Truth and Reconciliation Commission of Canada – Indigenous Residential Schools set up in Canada in 1991 and 2007, respectively; and Chile's Historical Truth Commission and New Treaty with Indigenous Peoples in 2001.

established by the settler states to deal with issues of social justice and structural inequalities through institutional and policy reforms that would ensure more social and political egalitarian treatment and the acknowledgement and recognition of the suffering of the native communities at the hands of the settler government (Winter 2014).

In 2006, the Canadian government and the Assembly of the First Nations signed the Indian Residential Schools Settlement Agreement with the main objective 'of bringing a fair and lasting resolution to the legacy of the Indian Residential Schools' (Indigenous and Northern Affairs, Government of Canada 2019). In the framework of the agreement, the Aboriginal communities pressured the government to obtain both material and symbolic reparations for the harm done through the Residential Schools. In this framework, the Truth and Reconciliation Commission of Canada – Indigenous Residential Schools was established in 2007 as part of the Indian Residential Schools Settlement Agreement to look into the Residential Schools for Aboriginal People.[7] The Indigenous Residential Schools (IRS) commission had as a main objective to foster acknowledgement, recognition, and healing, as well as the compilation of recommendations to the Canadian government to redress the harm done by the Residential Schools, in particular; and redress nation-to-nation relations through institutional reform, in general.

Although the IRS commission was called a truth and reconciliation commission, its mandate was stripped of some of the most common characteristics of such bodies of inquiry. It stated that the IRS commission would not mimic a legal proceeding nor use quasi-legal methodologies in its approach to the inquiry[8] – i.e. it would not hold public inquiries and the testimonies would be collected in community events or by written submission (Government of Canada 2007). Furthermore, the process of truth-seeking was not linked to compensation and reparations, as these were addressed by other independent bodies (i.e. the Common Experience Payment and the Independent Assessment Process) (Stanton 2011). The purpose of the IRS commission was to produce a historical investigation that would 'reveal the structural and institutional nature of the human rights violations that occurred in order to recommend ways in which to prevent future recurrences' (Stanton 2011, 9).

7 The Residential schools for Aboriginal people operated from the 1870s and were funded by the government and run by the church with the objective of eliminating parental involvement in the intellectual, cultural, and spiritual development of Aboriginal children (see also the National Centre for Truth and Reconciliation n.d.).

8 This was the result of an extreme discontentment and dissolution by survivors and their families and other members of the community with previous criminal and civil litigation procedures, particularly the lack of political response that those had had (Stanton 2011).

The final report compiled 94 calls for action[9] in the areas of justice, treaty rights, education, child welfare, health, and language and culture; of which very few have been implemented (Nagy 2020). However, from the publication of the report in 2015 to the moment in which this chapter is being written (2021), the government of Canada has completed only 8 of the 94 recommendations. In addition, any progress addressing systemic and structural elements that continue to produce social inequalities have been, at best, 'minimal and cosmetic' (Jewell and Mosby 2019 cited in Nagy 2020, 227).

The last point of discussion is the transitional justice's strong emphasis on victim participation. There is consensus that transitional justice processes should be victim-centred, as it directly contributes to the consolidation of victims' rights to truth, and to processes of rehabilitation and individual and/or societal reconciliation (Méndez 2016; McEvoy and McConnachie 2013). However, victim-centred approaches can become challenging in consolidated democracies where, due to the long-distance of the inquired events, access to direct survivors becomes a difficult and sometimes impossible task bringing to the fore complex debates of transgenerational victimhood (Wayman 2019). Against this background, historical commissions provide an alternative approach to the inquiry. Through the application of the critical historical method, historical commissions offer a different approach to truth-seeking when testimonies of those who experienced the wrongdoing are not available, alleviating some of the tensions of transgenerational victimhood, and in those cases in which a victim-centred approach is not seen as a pivotal part of the inquiry. It is worth noting that, deciding to design a mandate that moves away from a victim-centred approach should not be understood as dismissing the victims of the wrongdoing or neglecting their rights; rather, I would like to point out that in some cases where the intended outcome of the inquiry into the past is to conduct a historical clarification investigation, a victim-centred approach may not be pivotal to the inquiry.

Condemning Past Wrongdoing Through a Historical Investigation

To reflect on the above, I bring forward a case of a historical commission which operated in Romania in 2006, the Presidential Commission for the Analysis of the Communist Regime (PCACDR). Although this commission operated within a post-totalitarian context (and not in a consolidated democracy), it is useful to illustrate how historical commissions may offer an alternative truth-seeking mechanism within transitional justice in consolidated democracies.

9 For further information, see the government of Canada's website for the Truth and Reconciliation Commission of Canada: www.rcaanc-cirnac.gc.ca/eng/1450124405592/1529106060525.

Nearly two decades after the Romanian revolution that ended Nicolae Ceaușescu's regime, the PCACDR was established in 2006 by then President Traian Băsescu to investigate the Communist regime and compile a comprehensive report that would provide the basis for its moral and political condemnation of the Soviet regime. It had the mandate to analyse the 'nature, aims and effects of the totalitarian communist regime' with focus on its 'ideology, power and political practices in Romania [from] 1945–1989' (PCACDR 2006, 9). The PCACDR commission, has been defined by Stan and Tismăneanu (2015) as a truth-commission-like mechanism because it was an *ad hoc* body of inquiry established to conduct an inquiry into a recent past to investigate patterns of violence and abuse over a period of time, and which compiled the findings of its work on a final report. However, they then continue to signal one of the main methodological characteristics that differentiate the PCACDR from a truth commission, is that its work did not relay on the collection of testimonies from 'victims and victimizers of the communist regime' (Stan and Tismăneanu 2015, 27). This methodological approach did not mean that the testimonies of those who suffered would not be taken into consideration, but rather 'they would be integrated into a comprehensive historical narrative [...]' (Stan and Tismăneanu 2015, 27).

Its final report was released in December 2006, less than one month before Romania became a member of the European Union. PCACDR's work was seen as contributing to the building of a 'new beginning' marked by a political shift that would be reinforced by the new historical frame provided by the commission. It represented a process of legitimation of the state during which the communist totalitarian experience was exposed acting as a 'moral judgment on the defunct dictatorship and invite a reckoning with the past [...]' representing a 'symbolic step toward national reconciliation by means of clarifying and dealing with the past' (Tismăneanu 2011, 178). For some, however, the commission was seen as a political instrument part of the political strategy to become a member of the European Union. That political orientation was seen to be imprinted in the commission through the selection of its commissioners, which included former dissidents to the Communist regime, who would work towards the (re)construction of the past according to the present interests (Hogea 2010).

This section has shown how historical commissions seek to meet the core objectives of transitional justice – accountability, recognition, and social change – through a different conceptual and methodological approach to the inquiry into the past.

Conclusions

Historical commissions have been presented in this chapter as an alternative methodology within the truth-seeking dimension. Such commissions are located away from the legal paradigm that usually frames transitional justice mechanisms. Their approach to the investigation pursues a historical truth, through the analysis of archival sources with the application of the ethical and methodological standards of historical scholarship, rather than by quasi-legal approach to the inquiry. It explores how (1) historical commissions can act as accountability mechanisms for crimes and other violations of human rights committed in a distant past in those contexts where criminal justice is not possible, (2) the use of historical commissions as truth-seeking mechanisms in consolidated democracies can alleviate tensions emerging from transgenerational victimhood or limited access to testimonies, (3) a historical commissions' prospective approach fosters transformation of the political and public perception of the past to promote social change. The introduction of historical commissions as unique mechanisms within the transitional justice frame in consolidated democracies would contribute to the consolidation of the field through innovation within the truth pillar.

References

Álvarez-Berastegi, A. (2017) 'Justicia Transicional en Estados Democráticos: Uso y Abuso de los Límites Conceptuales. In: R.J. Aranguren, ed. *Justicia Transicional: Historia y Actualidad* (pp. 69–86). Cizur Menor: Thompson Reuters Aranzadi.

Anselmi, T. (2001) 'Introduzione (english_version)'. In: Presidenza del Consiglio dei Ministri, ed. Commissione per la ricostruzione delle vicende che hanno caratterizzato in Italia le attività di acquisizione dei beni dei cittadini ebrei da parte di organismi pubblici e private: Rapporto Generale. Retrieved from: https://web.archive.org/web/20190322081503/http://presidenza.governo.it/DICA/7_ARCHIVIO_STORICO/beni_ebraici/english_version/5_9_ms.pdf.

Barkan, E. (2009) 'Historians and Historical Reconciliation'. *American Historical Review* 114(4), 899–913.

Bergier, J.F. (2002) 'Commissioned History in Switzerland'. In: O. Rathkolb, ed. *Revisiting the National Socialist Legacy: Coming to Terms with Forced Labor, Expropriation, Compensation, and Restitution* (pp. 43–50) Abingdon: Routledge.

Bevernage, B. (2014) 'Transitional Justice and Historiography: Challenges, Dilemmas and Possibilites'. *Macquarie Law Journal*, 13, 7–24.

—— (2018) 'Narrating the Pasts for Peace: A Critical Analysis of Some Recent Initiatives of Reconciliation through 'Historical Dialogue' and 'Shared History''. In: S. Hegelson and J. Svenungsson, *The Ethos of History: Time and Responsibility* (pp. 70–93). New York and Oxford: Berghahm Books.

—— and N. Wouters, eds. (2018) *The Palgrave Handbook of State-Sponsored History After 1945*. London: Palgrave Macmillan.

Brahm, E. (2009) 'What is a Truth Commission and What Does it Matter?' *Peace and Conflict Review* 3(2), 1–14.

Freeman, M. (2006) *Truth Commissions and Procedural Fairness*. New York: Cambridge University Press.

Government of Canada (2007) 'Indian Residential Schools Settlement Agreement. Schedule N, Mandate for the Truth and Reconciliation Commission'. Ottawa. Retrieved from: https://www.residentialschoolsettlement.ca/SCHEDULE_N.pdf

Grandin, D. and M.T. Kullboch, eds. (2007) 'Truth Commissions: State Terror, History and Memory'. Special journal issue. *Radical History Review* 7(97).

Grodsky, B. (2009) 'Beyond Lustration. Truth-Seeking Efforts in the Post-Communist Space'. *Taiwan Journal of Democracy* 5(2), 21–43.

Haldemann, F. (2008) 'Another King of Justice: Transitional Justice as Recognition'. *Cornell International Law Journal* 41(3), article 3. Available at: https://scholarship.law.cornell.edu/cilj/vol41/iss3/3.

Hansen, T.O. (2011) 'Transitional Justice: Toward a Differentiated Theory'. *Open Review of International Law* 13(1), 1–46.

Hayner, P. (2001) *Unspeakable Truths: Confronting State Terror and Atrocity*. New York and London: Routledge.

Hogea, A. (2010) 'Coming to Terms with the Communist Past in Romania: An Analysis of the Political and Media Discourse Concerning the Tismăneanu Report'. *Studies of Transition States and Societies* 2(2), 16–30.

—— (2019) 'Indian Residential Schools Settlement Agreement'. Website. Ottawa: Indigenous and Northern Affairs. Available at: https://www.rcaanc-cirnac.gc.ca/eng/1100100015576/1571581687074 (Accessed 6 December 2019).

Jabloner, C. (2007) 'Scholarly Investigation and Material Compensation: the Austrian Historical Commission at Work'. In: D. Diner and G. Wunberg, eds. *Restitution and Memory: Material Restoration in Europe* (pp. 105–116). New York: Berghahn.

Karn, A. (2006) 'Depolarising the Past: The Role of Historical Commissions in Conflict Mediation and Reconciliation'. *Journal of International Affairs* 60(1), 31–50.

—— (2015) *Amending the Past: Europe's Holocaust Commissions and the Right to History*. Madison: University of Wisconsin Press.

Karlsson, K. (2013) 'Public uses of History in Contemporary Europe'. In: H. Jones, K. Östberg, and N. Randeraad, eds. *Contemporary History on Trial: Europe since 1989 and the Role of the Expert Historian*. Manchester: Manchester University Press.

Lewis, B. (1975) *History: Remembered, Recovered, Invented*. Princeton: Princeton University Press.

Maier, C.S. (2003) 'Overcoming the Past? Narrative and Negotiation, Remembering, and Reparation: Issues at the Interface of History and the Law'. In: J. Torpey, ed. *Politics and the Past: On Repairing Historical Injustices* (pp. 295–304). Lanham: Rowman & Littlefield.

Mattéoli, J. (2000) 'Rapport Général. Mission d'étude sur la spoliation des Juifs de France'. Retrieved from: http://www.civs.gouv.fr/images/pdf/matteoli/Mission_Matteoli-rapport_final.pdf.

McAuliffe, P. (2011) 'Transitional Justice's Expanding Empire: Reasserting the Value of the Paradigmatic Transition'. *Journal of Conflictology* 2(2), 32–44.

McEvoy, K. and K. McConnachie (2013) 'Victims and Transitional Justice: Voice, Agency and Blame'. *Social & Legal studies* 22(4), 489–513.

McGrattan, C. (2016) *The Politics of Trauma and Peace-Building: Lessons from Northern Ireland*. Abingdon: Routledge Press.

Méndez, J.E. (2016) 'Victims as Protagonists in Transitional Justice'. *International Journal of Transitional Justice* 10(1), 1–5.

Mihr, A. (2017) 'An Introduction to Transitional Justice'. In: O. Simic, ed. *An Introduction to Transitional Justice* (pp. 113–131). Abingdon: Routledge.

Nagy, R. (2020) 'Settler Witnessing at the Truth and Reconciliation Commission of Canada'. *Human Rights Review* 21, 219–241.

National Centre for Truth and Reconciliation (n.d.) *Truth and Reconciliation Commission Reports*. Website. University of Manitoba.

Ní Aolain, F. and C. Cambpell (2005) 'The Paradox of Transition in Conflicted Democracies'. *Human Rights Quarterly* 27(1), 172–213.

Palli-Aspero, C. (2020) 'The Uses of the Historical Method in Conflicted Societies: Understanding Historical Clarification Commissions'. Doctoral Thesis, Ulster University. On file with the author.

Pelinka, A. (1989) *Austria: Out of the Shadow of the Past*. Boulder: Westview.

Pettai, E.C. (2015a) 'Negotiating History for Reconciliation: A Comparative Evaluation of the Baltic Presidential Commissions'. *Europe-Asia studies* 67(7), 1079–1101.

—— (2015b) 'Interactions between History and Memory: Historical Truth Commissions and Historical Reconciliation'. In: S. Kattogo, ed. *The Ashgate Research Companion to Memory Studies*. Abingdon: Routledge.

—— (2018) 'Historical Expert Commissions and Their Politics'. In: B. Bevernage and N. Wouters, eds. *The Palgrave Handbook of State-Sponsored History After 1945* (pp. 687–712). London: Palgrave Macmillan.

Presidential Commission for the Analysis of the Communist Regime (2006) 'Raport Final'. Bucuresti. Retrieved from: https://www.wilsoncenter.org/sites/default/files/media/documents/article/RAPORT%20FINAL_%20CADCR.pdf.

Russo, H. (1944) *The Vichy Syndrome: History and Memory and France since 1944*. Cambridge MA: Harvard University Press.

Schaap, A. (2005) *Political Reconciliation*. London: Routledge.

Scheuzger, S. (2018) 'Truth Commissions and the Politics of History: a Critical Appraisal'. In: B. Bevernage and N. Wouters, eds. *The Palgrave Handbook of State-Sponsored History After 1945* (pp. 621–636). London: Palgrave Macmillan.

Simons, M. (1995) 'Chirac Affirms France's Guilt in Fate of Jews'. New York Times, 17 July. https://www.nytimes.com/1995/07/17/world/chirac-affirms-france-s-guilt-in-fate-of-jews.html.

Stan, L. (2009) 'Truth Commissions in Post-Communism: The Overlooked Solution?' *The Open Political Science Journal* 2, 1–13.

Stan, M. and V. Tismăneanu (2015) 'Coming to Terms with the Communist Past: Democracy and Memory in Romania'. In: L. Stand and D. Vancea, eds. *Post-Communist Romania at Twenty-Five: Linking Past, Present, and Future* (pp. 23–39). Lanham: Lexington Books.

Stanton, K. (2011) 'Canada's Truth and Reconciliation Commission: Settling the Past?' *The International Indigenous Policy Journal* 2(3). Retrieved from: https://ir.lib.uwo.ca/iipj/vol2/iss3/2.

Teitel, R.G. (2010) 'Global Transitional Justice'. Center for Global Studies Working Paper 8, George Mason University, Washington DC. Retrieved from: https://centers.gmu.edu/globalstudies/publications/hjd/hjd_wp_8.pdf.

—— (2017) 'Genealogía de la justicia transicional'. In: R.J. Aranguren, ed. *Justicia Transicional: Historia y Actualidad* (pp. 31–67). Cizur Menor: Thompson Reuters Aranzadi.

Verdeja, E. (2009) *Unchopping a Tree: Reconciliation in the Aftermath of Political Violence*. Philadelphia: Temple University Press.

Winter, S. (2014) *Transitional Justice in Established Democracies: A Political Theory*. London: Palgrave MacMillan.

Chapter 11

Theorising Transitional Justice in Ongoing Conflict[1]

Stephen Winter

Introduction

Canonically, the practice of transitional justice emerged in the 1980s in response to atrocities committed by repressive South American regimes (Arthur 2009). Then, as the Introduction in this volume relates, analysts and practitioners extended the concept to new geographical areas and to polities transitioning (it was hoped) from violent conflict to peace. In the now paradigmatic understanding:

> Transitional justice refers to the ways countries emerging from periods of conflict and repression address large-scale or systematic human rights violations [...]
>
> (International Center for Transitional Justice n.d.)

As the field expands, scholars have begun to address practices in the (apparently) aparadigmatic contexts of consolidated democracies and ongoing violent conflicts (Engstrom 2013; Hansen 2011; Winter 2014). But critics of the possibility of, and prospects for, transitional justice in aparadigmatic cases are vocal and influential (De Greiff 2020, 254; Hayner 2002, 17; Murphy 2017, 77–80). These criticisms stem from what people think transitional justice is. A descriptive theory of transitional justice must identify how practices of *justice* – giving people what they are due – respond to systemic[2] wrongdoings in ways relevant to a *transition*, which one influential author understands as 'a normative shift in the principles underlying and legitimating the exercise of state power' (Teitel 2000, 213). If we reflect on that definition, the aparadigmatic circumstances of consolidated democracies and ongoing conflict may appear inept. In the

1 I would like to thank Tine Destrooper, Geoffrey Kemp, Stephen Galoob, Line Engbo Gissel, Katherine Smits, and Roxane Winter for their helpful comments on previous versions.

2 I use 'systemic' in place of the International Centre for Transitional Justice's 'systematic' because the latter can mean 'regular' or 'frequent' when I think the key point is that such injuries are structural (See Lu 2017, 33–34).

DOI: 10.4324/9781003289104-12

case of consolidated democracies, the principles underlying the legitimacy of state power remain apparently stable (Hansen 2013, 119). In cases of ongoing conflict or fragile states, there has been no transition from conflict (McAuliffe 2011, 37; see also the Introduction in this volume). It might seem that neither context presents us with a transition.

I think a unified theory can embrace both aparadigmatic circumstances. By re-reading Karl Jaspers' 'The Question of German Guilt' (Jaspers 2001 [1947]), this chapter carries what I call the 'legitimating account' of transitional justice into conditions of ongoing violent conflict. The chapter is structured as follows. The next section outlines the legitimating account of transitional justice. The following section exhibits two challenges that confront the legitimating account in circumstances of ongoing conflict. To respond to those challenges, the next section reviews Jaspers' political-constitutive reading of the Nuremberg trials. I then use that reading of Jaspers to work through the challenges already identified. By the end of the chapter, I hope to have dispelled some concerns that might otherwise encumber a theory of transitional justice in circumstances of ongoing conflict.

The Legitimating Account

My argument that transitional justice can occur in aparadigmatic contexts depends upon what transitional justice is. I previously set out what I call the 'legitimating account' to theorise transitional justice in consolidated democracies (Winter 2013, 2014). This section sketches that theory, which derives from the rationalist tradition in political theory. That tradition understands a reasonable political order as necessary to a decent human life. In turn, a reasonable political order requires the rule of law. To have the rule of law, a polity needs institutions with authority to create binding rules (laws).[3] The law provides reasons for citizens to do or to not do certain things – a citizenry is a body of people bound by a common set of laws. If law is to bind the citizenry, it must be legitimate, which requires that people can rationally endorse what the law demands and how it is made (Kant 1970, §46; Raz 1985, 18–22; Williams 2005, 5–6).[4] A law-making authority's legitimacy, therefore, consists in the reason(s) a citizen has to endorse it (Copp 1999). Jaspers is part of that tradition. For him, the rule of law depends upon an accord between positive

3 Political authorities exercise powers other than rule-making, but that core power is enough for my purposes.

4 It may help to disambiguate the rationalist conception of legitimacy from the sociological understanding common in the transitional justice literature. For the sociologist, legitimacy is the citizenry's predilection to conform to the law and a legitimate authority is an office that issues directives that are likely to be obeyed. For the rationalist, the phenomenon of obedience is secondary because the primary conditions of legitimate authority exist in the reasons that a citizenry has to conform.

law and the 'Right',[5] where the 'Right' is an ideal of reasonable legitimating values that enable political authority.[6]

Right is the sublime idea of men who derive their existence from an origin which is secured by force alone, but not determined by force. Wherever men become aware of their humanity and recognise man as man, they grasp human rights and base themselves on a natural law to which both victor and vanquished may appeal (Jaspers 2001 [1947], 31).

Determinate rules must be 'secured by force' if humans are to engage with one another as reasonable beings. Legitimate political authority rests upon people's need for a reasonable political order – reasonable because it is Right and Right because it is necessary for freedom.[7] When both the procedures for making law and its substantive content enables the recognition of each person as equal and free, the law's use of coercive force supplies a necessary ingredient of a reasonable political order.

If the citizenry must be able to endorse the law that governs them, law-making institutions will become authoritative by accomplishing purposes that are reasonable for the citizenry. In other words, legitimacy requires enactment (Simmons 1999). That is why real history is important to a state's authority. States that act in ways that citizens could not reasonably endorse become less legitimate. Political wrongdoing can burden or vitiate legitimacy. An authority is *burdened* when it inflicts systemic injuries that undermine the reasons the citizenry has to endorse the laws (Galoob and Winter 2019; Muldoon 2003; Shelby 2007; Spinner-Halev 2007). For example, an authority might be burdened when injurious laws discriminate against certain groups. The worst crimes against humanity are cases where offending states simply fail to exercise authority vis-à-vis their intended victims (see, for example, Aboueldahab in this volume). Diane Orentlicher (1994, 2542) argues that persistent failures to protect the citizenry from injustice can negate political authority. Legitimacy is *vitiated* when purported authorities either fail to enact legitimating reasons or violate the citizenry in ways that negate authority's fundamental purpose of creating and maintaining a reasonable political order. Legitimacy is, therefore, a practical, historical phenomenon that depends upon what political authorities actually do (Habermas and Rehg 2001, 768; Zurn 2010, 224–225).

This rationalist-historical approach to authority and legitimacy underpins my account of transitional justice. I think that transitional justice responds to widespread and fundamental problems of political illegitimacy. Transitions both expose problems of illegitimacy and permit their remedy. As Ruti Teitel

5 Note that the German *Recht* encompasses law, order, and rectitude.

6 Jaspers (1959 [1951], 86–102) anticipates this account of the relationships between *Recht*, law, politics and force in his 1931 *Die Geistige Situation der Zeit*.

7 Jaspers understands freedom as constitutive of humanity. As an aside, I think that many reasons besides freedom can legitimate authority, just as there are many different procedural, substantive, and hybrid accounts (Klosko 2004).

(2000, 213) argues, transitions involve 'either a reinterpretation of the salient justifications underlying the prevailing normative order or a turn to an independent source of alternative legal norms'. Regime transitions entail changes in discursive practice. Where authorised practices were, or are, injurious, the transition is often accompanied by demands for accountability, recognition, and redress – in other words, for justice.

Responding to those demands, transitional justice enacts legitimating reasons. The standard transitional justice toolkit of criminal trials mitigated by amnesties; material and symbolic reparations; constitutional reform and lustration of implicated officials; and truth telling exercises are all justice practices that enable states to exercise political authority: states enact legitimating reasons by doing justice. Transitional justice, as such, is both performative and political. Where systemic human rights violations burden or vitiate political authority, states discharge duties of justice to create a more reasonable political order. In this way, transitional justice is a driver of transition, bringing state practice into accord with developing legitimating discourses (Skaar 2013, 60). This is the essence of the legitimating account of transitional justice: transitional justice enacts legitimating reasons as a remedy in cases where systemic wrongdoing has burdened or vitiated authority.

A short illustration will help animate the account. In the paradigmatic case of Argentina's 'Dirty War', an authoritarian government used the military to annihilate their leftist opponents (Inter-American Commission on Human Rights 1980, §G1). Only extermination would suffice. Rear Admiral César Guzzetti's oft-cited 1976 newspaper proclamation (quoted in Pereira 2005, 133) reads:

> the social body of the country is contaminated by an illness that in corroding its entrails produces antibodies. These antibodies must not be considered in the same way as microbes. As the government controls and destroys the guerrilla, the action of the antibody will disappear [...] This is just the natural reaction of a sick body.

Some 'microbes' were incarcerated indefinitely, without being charged, but there would be no legal process for those who were disappeared (Pereira 2005, 129). A justificatory regime that mixed Catholic conservatism, neoliberal economics, and national security concerns supported the military's actions. Atrocities, such as disappearance, were systemic (structural) because the military acted with the acceptance and/or complicity of political authorities.

After the 1983 election of the former human rights lawyer, Raúl Alfonsín, Argentina slowly began to subject the military to the rule of law. The Argentine transition displaced the previous legitimating discourses with liberal-democratic values and norms disseminated by highly mobilised human rights organisations (Sikkink 2008). But those changes in the ways politics was conducted left Argentina with political institutions whose legitimacy was burdened by systemic wrongdoing. In response, Argentina employed what would become standard transitional justice techniques. Argentina's truth commission, criminal trials and amnesty, monetary reparations, memorial day, and public apology are well-established paradigmatic exemplars. The legitimating account understands those remedial practices as enacting legitimating reasons; they are remedies for the state's failures (among other things). Those responses make the state more legitimate by enacting reasons that citizens can endorse.

Two Challenges That Arise

I think we can use the legitimating account to understand the role of transitional justice in circumstances of ongoing conflict. But this section first exhibits two credible challenges to that aparadigmatic extension. I do not pretend that these are the only problems with the account, but they are significant and engaging with them will help develop the theory.

I understand circumstances of systemically violent conflict to involve radical insecurity resulting from pervasive credible threats to one's life and person. A persistent feature of such conditions is the absence of political authority with the capacity to enforce a reasonable rule of law. Without effective authority, arbitrary coercion and violence structures human existence and, as a result, it is impossible to secure the preconditions of a decent human life (Hobbes 1998, Chapter 1). That characterisation exposes the apparent challenges to the legitimating account of transitional justice in ongoing conflict. The first challenge argues that *systemic wrongdoing is not the problem* and the second that there is *no transition* in these cases. So as to be comprehensive, I develop two different ways that each challenge might be stated.

I start with the challenge that *systemic wrongdoing is not the problem.* The legitimating account describes transitional justice as responding to a specific type of problem – illegitimacy created by authorised wrongdoing. Consider the Argentinian case. A key feature of authorised atrocities like disappearance was that wrongdoing was part of the political system, involving the military, police, courts, and the political executive. But that kind of authorised wrongdoing is not a necessary condition of conflict. In the standard conception of war, opposing sovereigns can reasonably engage in conflict. If all parties have appropriate justifications for engaging in war, conduct the war adhering to relevant laws and conventions, and then conclude an equitable peace treaty, they need not engage in authorised wrongdoing and, therefore, are not plausible candidates for the legitimating account of transitional justice. In another scenario, conflict might emerge when outlaws employ illegal violence, committing atrocities without pretending to exercise political authority. Outlaw violence might be met with justified repression, not authorised wrongdoing. When violence committed by outlaws is aberrant, not systemic, *systemic wrongdoing is not the problem*, for it does not occur. Lastly, if only politically authorised wrongdoing can be systemic, then transitional justice could not address violence committed by non-state actors, such as non-governmental organisations (NGOs) and multi-national corporations. If political authorities do not commit systemic wrongdoing, it seems that transitional justice could not happen, at least not in the terms prescribed by the legitimating account. If that is right, then the account could not support the attribution of transitional justice in all circumstances of ongoing conflict.

A similar conclusion might be seen from a different perspective. As a theory of what transitional justice is, the legitimating account is state-centric. By focusing on political authority and legitimacy, the account may appear elite and institutionalist. Perhaps, therefore, it fails to represent the needs and understandings of many people in, and recovering from, conflict. Alexander Hinton (2018) argues that a participant-focused theory should prioritise the understanding of stakeholders. Hinton observes that transitional justice often undergoes processes of 'thick translation', wherein internationally-recognised transitional justice concepts and values are transmuted into ideas that make sense to those involved. Participants understand transitional justice practices in ways that are shaped by their particular histories and conceptual frameworks. Therefore, good theoretical description must 'focus on phenomenology – lived experience, the interstitial spaces in which "justice" is "translated," and the on-the-ground understandings and practices in which it is enacted' (Hinton 2018, 248).

Just as transitional justice needs to be understood in local terms, one might think that it needs to respond to local concerns. Recall that paradigmatic transitional justice responds to 'systematic human rights violations' (International Center for Transitional Justice n.d.). Critics express concerns with the centrality of human rights in that paradigmatic definition. The human rights industry's legal framework prescinds from the lived experience of survivors and appropriates their voices (Madlingozi 2010). As the Introduction in this volume notes, a narrow legalistic approach can be inadequate. Too often, transitional justice backgrounds the 'root causes' of conflict (Miller 2008, 288). For people engaged in conflict, the remedy of human rights violations may not be urgent. Locals might be more focused on the 'everyday' injuries of conflict, including poverty, homelessness, malnutrition, and disease. Helena Cobban (2007, 60) observes, 'study after study of the needs and preferences of people living in post-conflict, post-atrocity societies shows that economic and social stabilization has been absolutely their main priority'. Insofar as my argument centres upon political legitimacy, it may fail to respond to the immediate concerns of real people in terms that they recognise, meaning that *systemic wrongdoing is not the problem* that best represents the understandings and needs of stakeholders.

I now bring forward a second challenge concerning the absence of transition in circumstances of ongoing conflict. Contemporary conflict is often characterised by chronic violence. Circumstances of 'no war, no peace' are socially, economically, and politically embedded in ways that enmesh people in ongoing conflict (Collier 2003; Mac Ginty 2016, 77–78; Muggah 2005, 240–241). This poses another problem for the legitimating theory: circumstances of ongoing conflict are not circumstances of transition. The problem of *no transition* holds that transitional justice cannot happen in conflicts that simply continue.

Another way of developing the *no transition* challenge has Marxist inflections and is pessimistic regarding the very possibility of a reasonable political order. In this argument, the law institutionalises ongoing conflicts between classes, genders, and ethnicities. Therefore, if transitional justice aims at creating a reasonable rule of law, it aims only at a dangerous fantasy: law necessarily leaves some people exposed to systemic violence. Shana Tabak (2011) argues that the conflict/post-conflict is a false dichotomy in which violence is relegated to the past. When transitional justice talks about post-conflict states, it obscures violence that continues, hidden in the private sphere or normalised by oppressive legal structures. This problem of *no transition* suggests that the paradigmatic ideal of the rule of law re-inscribes injurious insecurity. This challenge is not merely critical of the application of transitional justice to circumstances of ongoing conflict; radical versions would condemn state-building more generally.

To summarise the problems identified with carrying the legitimating account into circumstances of ongoing conflict, *systemic wrongdoing is not the problem* if no authority acted wrongfully or if those involved in conflict do not understand transitional justice as a means for resolving authorised wrongdoing. Equally, they might not think it should. Second, circumstances of conflict may present cases of *no transition* because violent conflict continues either in the absence of the rule of law or under its aegis.

Jaspers' Constitutive Account

To argue that the legitimating account can explain how transitional justice happens in circumstances of ongoing conflict, I need to show how the challenges exhibited in the previous section can be overcome. For help I turn to Karl Jaspers' 1947 lectures on international criminal justice, known to English readers as 'The Question of German Guilt' (Jaspers 2001 [1947]). Those lectures are known for distinguishing four different types of guilt – criminal, political, moral, and metaphysical; however, Jaspers' larger purpose is to explain how Germans (and everyone else) should understand the International Military Tribunal (IMT) at Nuremberg. The IMT is a recognised antecedent of present-day transitional justice (McGonigle Leyh 2016). And post-war Germany was a quintessential weak post-conflict state. However, Jaspers is not focused on German politics; his argument concerns the IMT's role in developing a global rule of law. Jaspers' reflections develop the constitutive practice of justice in the systemically violent, anarchic, and pervasively insecure domain of international relations. What Jaspers says about the IMT's constitutive international potential can help develop the legitimating account of transitional justice in ongoing conflict.

International relations is often thought to be an anarchic realm where the strong act and the weak suffer. In that light, Jaspers confronts the charge that Nuremberg represents 'victor's justice', that it is merely the exercise of brute force dressed up in legal clothing – a form of authorised wrongdoing. If the coercion enacted by the IMT was not part of a reasonable political order, then it would be antithetical to freedom and, for that reason, illegitimate. The accusation has some merit (Ash 2011; Rabkin 1999). The Allies operated a military occupation in Germany. The IMT's judges represented the victorious Allies, there was no neutral and no German representation. Defendants faced charges concerning acts that were not recognised as crimes at the time of their commission, leading critics to object that the IMT violated the legal principle of *nulla poena sine lege*. History would prove the IMT to be profoundly biased. Despite evidence of Allied war crimes, including the 1939 Soviet wars of aggression against Finland and Poland and the fire-bombing of German cities by American and British airplanes, no Allied leader ever faced analogous charges.

Jaspers' defence of the IMT concerns the relationship between law and politics. Jaspers presents the IMT as a step in the development of a new international political order. As a constitutive act, the decision to hold the Nazi leadership legally accountable was a political, not legal, performance. In 1947, international criminal law was a nascent domain with few institutional authorities. The political decision to construct a legal process began the process of turning force into authority via the rationalist character of law. A trial must operate in ways that participants can understand and endorse, which in turn enables people to freely participate in procedures that limit and shape the exercise of coercive force. The possibility of freedom is the critical move. Unbridled and arbitrary coercive force is antithetical to political order (and to freedom). The law's bridling of force is necessary to secure the conditions of a decent human life. Therefore, when a political institution enables a legal process, it constitutes a necessary ingredient of a decent human life. That is what makes it legitimate.

Responding to critics of the IMT's legal shortcomings, Jaspers argues that it would be unreasonable to expect ideal legal procedures in the extraordinary (transitional) attempt to create political order out of international anarchy. 'The answer to all arguments against the trial is that Nuremberg is really something new' (Jaspers 2001 [1947], 54). The new is an act of politics, not law.[8] Unlike the Goddess Athena birthed fully formed and armoured, political forms do not emerge puissant and capable of self-defence: there is a messy and debilitating process of delivery. The IMT lacked much that a legal process should have had. Held against the standards of a mature legal order, constitutive acts will present 'flaws, mistakes and failings in detail' (Jaspers 2001 [1947], 54). The IMT's flaws increase the risk that the trial will be stillborn, its 'feeble, ambiguous' potential unrealised (Jaspers 2001 [1947], 54). Jaspers asks his

8 Jaspers' friend and colleague, Hannah Arendt (1977), would later make that point famous.

audience not to use those flaws to attack or reject the IMT – instead they are reasons to nurture it.

Jaspers argues that creating the IMT committed the Allies to the aim of constituting a new regime, the transition to which would displace force as the dominant organising principle of international relations. But the constitutive work of politics is not immediate. One trial, one process, one institution cannot create political order. The value of the IMT depends upon it taking its place within an emerging legal order, in which, 'the Nuremberg trial comes to be a link in a chain of meaningful, constructive political acts' (Jaspers 2001 [1947], 53). But in 1947, it was yet too soon to offer a final verdict on the IMT. Humanity needed to await history's verdict to tell us whether Nuremberg's:

> political trial will have become a legal one, with law creatively founded and realized for a new world now waiting to be built. Or disappointment by untruthfulness will create an even worse world atmosphere breeding new wars; instead of a blessing, Nuremberg would become a factor of doom, and in the world's eventual judgment the trial would have been a sham.
>
> (Jaspers 2001 [1947], 53)

Viewed from our 21st century vantage point, we know that the post-war transition to a global political order was partial and flawed. International law remains biased in implementation, limited in reach, and faulty in substance. However, the position of the IMT in the genealogy of transitional justice suggests it was not entirely a sham. Returning to the legitimating account, I think transitional justice works in the same way that Jaspers describes the IMT. Because transitional justice is a form of constitutive politics that enacts legitimating reasons, it can happen in contexts of ongoing violent conflict.

Returning to the Two Challenges

Jaspers' insights as to how transitional justice's constitutive functions develop political authority through practice can help answer the two challenges I exhibited above. Answering those challenges will help develop the legitimating account of transitional justice in circumstances of ongoing conflict.

The first identified challenge was that *systemic wrongdoing is not the problem.* I concede that the scenarios of just war and outlawry are circumstances in which transitional justice does not, and need not, apply. However, those scenarios are highly idealised. In the real world, conflicts relevant to transitional justice usually involve competing authorities (often a recognised state and other aspirants) that commit atrocities. Therefore, in most ongoing conflicts there are authorised wrongdoings to which transitional justice can respond. But I think that answer is both too easy and does not adequately illuminate the strength of the legitimating account. Because it is broadly accepted that transitional justice can/should respond to injuries inflicted by non-state actors, it is important to see how the account accommodates those practices.

If transitional justice responds to systemic/structural injuries, what systemic injuries are characteristic of conflict? Drawing upon a previous observation, one answer might run as follows: in ongoing conflict, injurious insecurity is pervasive and the institutions of international law offer inadequate security. Consider the law of war. The distinction between combatants and civilians 'has been characterised not only as one of the fundamental principles of international law, but as its greatest triumph' (Nurick 1945, 680). But the law prohibiting the killing of civilians is ineffective. As of November 2020, after 17 years of conflict, the NGO Iraq Body Count (2020) estimates that Iraqi civilian deaths outnumber those of combatants around 2:1.[9] Many of those who died were killed by non-state actors (Bengio 2021). The situation in Iraq is representative: despite strict legal protections for noncombatants, personal insecurity is pervasive in violent conflict.

So far, I have tended to describe injuries as systemic when they are authorised wrongdoings: wrongdoing is systemic to a political order when it was carried out or permitted by those seeking to exercise political authority. But that is only one way a structure can engender systemic injuries; equally, profound insecurity might be structurally pervasive in circumstances of ongoing conflict (Balasco 2013). People experience structural insecurity when arbitrary force rules in the absence of the law. I think that, in cases like Iraq, where systemic violence is inflicted by non-stage actors, transitional justice can still occur (by for example, putting violent agents on trial) in ways that, following Jaspers, enact political authority. However, if the experience of pervasive insecurity is a form of systemic injury, incorporating that injury requires amending the legitimating account of transitional justice. In the revised account, systemic injury can take (at least) two forms, either as structurally injurious insecurity or authorised wrongdoing. These two forms of injuries are unified in that they both require the absence of an ingredient necessary to decent human life, effective and legitimate political authority.

That response only addresses one of the supporting arguments for the challenge that *systemic wrongdoing is not the problem*. Recall the second argument that the state-centric and institutionalist character of the account fails to represent the needs and understandings of real people in conflict. If transitional justice is to be participant-focused, their interests and understandings should shape the theory of what it is (Hinton 2018, 248). My response addresses the methodology of descriptive theory. Hinton emphasises what local stakeholders think.

9 Iraqi Body Count records 185,395–208,419 civilian deaths out of 288,000 total fatalities as of November 2020 (Iraqi Body Count 2020). Those are underestimates. For comparison, a 2013 study attributes nearly 500,000 total fatalities to the conflict between 2003–2011 (Hagopian et al. 2013). The difference is due to methodology. The Iraqi Body Count systemically undercounts fatalities because it relies on newspaper reporting, while the 2013 study was a survey of 2,000 Iraqi households.

It is undoubtedly true that what people think must be part of any descriptive political theory. Humans are, to some extent, what we understand ourselves to be. And a failure to respect someone's understanding can be a form of injury – I have in mind cases such as when someone is told that they are not 'really' the gender they identify as. However, imagine if someone identified as Mahatma Gandhi. I would not endorse that descriptive claim merely on the basis of their self-understanding, no matter how sincere they were. I would need other data.

What data is relevant to a descriptive theory of transitional justice? I think popular understandings are not *ir*relevant, but they are certainly not dispositive. It is hard to know if scholars like Hinton propose their phenomenological approach as a means to a general theory, or, if they simply point out the importance of paying attention to people's actual understandings, interests, and needs. The practical claim is salutary. But the theoretical approach is not. The claim that justice is whatever someone thinks it to be is unsupportable. Even if we grant local stakeholders' interpretive precedence, they are unlikely to agree among themselves. Indeed, people hold inconsistent views on what transitional justice is. After all, disagreement about justice is the stuff of politics.

How should a theorist respond to disagreement about what transitional justice is? Following John Rawls (2001, 29–32), the best account of transitional justice should make sense of what occurs in practice while providing a coherent account of the values involved. In the process of engendering a reflective equilibrium, the theorist uses data from both theory and practice.[10] The previous discussion provides an example of how this works. Having developed an account of transitional justice as a response to authorised wrongdoing, I then confronted the possibility of constitutive justice practice in conflicts where there was no authorised wrongdoing. Because those practices and their constitutive function offered both practical comprehension and theoretical coherence, I advanced an adapted understanding of systemic injury that includes the absence of what is necessary to a decent human life. This move deployed a more fundamental description of the political problem that transitional justice aims to redress that embraced both pervasive insecurity and authorised wrongdoing as forms of structural injury. The result is a more stable united account that includes widely accepted practices of transitional justice and their constitutive functions.

Returning to the challenge that the legitimating account fails to represent the needs and understandings of real people in conflict, I doubt most stakeholders would interpret their experience of transitional justice in the terms of the legitimating account. But being participant-focused need not mean endorsing everything that everyone thinks. Hinton describes how Neth Phally, a Cambodian participant in the trial of 'Duch', understood transitional justice as calming his

10 A fuller justification of the legitimating account also requires testing it against alternative theories, such as Colleen Murphy's (2017) societal transformation account, which I discuss below.

deceased brother's spirit (Hinton 2018, 245). I do not denigrate Neth Phally's belief if I exclude it from a descriptive method aiming for a public and stable account of transitional justice across humanity's universe of cases. But that does not mean his beliefs are irrelevant. The legitimating account founds transitional justice on the need for a universal human good – a more reasonable political order. If local stakeholders do not in fact perceive transitional justice as helping to constitute a more reasonable order, or it fails to materialise, that information should shape practice. Sensitivity to local understandings and needs might be crucial to identifying what transitional justice should do – what techniques it should use – without determining its general description. The legitimating theory of transitional justice offers a general account that explains the practice in terms of how it functions. It does not prescribe practice.

Having answered two versions of the *systemic wrongdoing is not the problem* challenge, I now address the *no transition* challenges in cases of ongoing conflict. I first consider the substantive character of transition, which turns out to be relatively straightforward. The existential variant of the *no transition* challenge argues that it would be impossible to conduct transitional justice in cases of ongoing conflict, because transitional justice could only occur after the transition had concluded or where the transition is imminent. To illustrate, although people now say they are conducting transitional justice in places such as Syria and Libya, given that those efforts are not likely to be followed by significant change, they should, therefore, be excluded from the field (McAuliffe 2011, 37).

This challenge is not significant for an account that accepts the success of transitional justice as a contingent possibility. Recall Jaspers' point that the IMT should be understood as a faltering step towards a global political order. Operating in non-ideal circumstances, transitional justice is not the work of a mature political order, rather it offers the 'contingent possibility of politics' (Schaap 2008, 251). On the legitimating account, transitional justice enacts the values of a new regime in circumstances where those values are not realised in effective law. The practice of justice is transitional in the sense that it aids in constituting (potentially) a new regime, and thus has disruptive potential–even if this potential does not always materialise. Failure is possible. Jaspers' worries about the IMT were well-founded – brute coercive force continues to determine much of what happens in international relations. But the possibility of failure does not make transitional justice in the midst of conflict impossible. To return to the birth metaphor, transitional justice can be part of something new, even something that fails to thrive in a hostile world. If that is right, it is easy to distinguish between a failure to succeed and a failure to occur.

The second *no transition* challenge criticises the elitist and institutionalist character of the theory. Some people argue that the relevant form of transition must include significant changes to people's lived experience through broad-ranging psychological or behavioural transformation (Brown 2012; Gready and Robins 2019, 33–34; Madlingozi 2010). Colleen Murphy argues that transitional justice aims to effect 'societal transformations', which she understand as the remedy of structural inequalities that shape interpersonal relationships, attitudes, and ethos (Murphy 2017, 121). In that approach, moving a polity from circumstances of conflict to that of peace requires transitional justice to engage with the sources of conflict in economic and gender injustices, ethnic division, environmental degradation and other fundamental causes. If Murphy is right in thinking that transitional justice works by changing people's attitudes and actions, the transition must be a demotic phenomenon.

A theorist like Murphy might think Jaspers' abstract ideas about the constitutive role of the criminal trial backgrounds the real lives and real concerns of real people. Yet, I think the legitimating account can accommodate the challenge. Transitional justice processes that hope to provide ingredients for a more legitimate political order must speak to ordinary people. Murphy follows the general trend in transitional justice scholarship by employing a sociological understanding of legitimacy.[11] From that perspective, transitional justice processes are supposed to engage with the psychological and behavioural aspects of conflict. But I follow Jaspers in thinking that transitional justice is not a technique for effecting popular attitudinal change, instead, it is a step towards a more reasonable political order.

Recall that a reasonable political order is a fundamental precondition for the possibility of living a decent human life. The legitimating account's foundation in a universal human need means that it is state-centric and institutionalist, but it is not elitist. All those who are subject to the law must have reasons to endorse it. That means the law must accomplish purposes that are reasonable for each citizen. That popular aspect is central to the account. Because transitional justice aims to enact legitimating reasons for all citizens, the legitimating account can endorse critiques of practices that background the 'everyday' injuries of conflict, such as poverty, marginalisation, homelessness, malnutrition, and disease. The account supports the need for transitional justice practices that respond to locally-relevant injuries.

The chapter previously observed that persistent failures to protect the citizenry from injury vitiate political authority. To illustrate, David Roberts (2011, 416) observes that there are few preconditions more important to the right to life than the provision of clean water. If access to clean water is a basic right, then the legitimacy of political authority may depend upon its provision. Further the procedural aspects of the legitimating account emphasise the need to get processes right for local stakeholders (Gready and Robins 2019, 45). In the ideal, transitional justice can create positive feedback-loops as effective authority develops legitimating reasons that engender the popular confidence needed for continued development (Mihr 2018, 57). Confronting the injury of pervasive insecurity, the demand for transitional justice can be an effective

11 See Footnote 3.

technique to prevent any peace agreement from ignoring structural injustices that may have preceded, or helped cause, the conflict. In other words, the conceptual framework of transitional *justice* helps resist side-lining justice in pursuit of an unstable 'negative peace' (Sharp 2015, 167).

But perhaps the *no transition* challenge is better understood as concerned with the very existence of political authority. Underlying some concerns with the centrality of the law in transitional justice theory, one can detect deeper (Marxist/anarchic) concerns with the reality of the state. From that critical perspective, the law cannot be reasonable, at least not universally so: it is necessarily oppressive and will inevitably perpetuate structural injustices (Brown 1995, 109; Turner 2016, 171). Insofar as those critical concerns are ultimately founded upon convictions that political authority is incompatible with human freedom, I doubt anything I can say in response could be convincing.[12] I think, with Jaspers, that no decent human life can exist without political authority. However, if the concern is not with the existence of authority but rather the repressive character of particular laws, I would observe that the legitimating account does not rely on thick value descriptions. The legitimating account requires the transitional enactment of reasons relevant to citizens. But it does not say very much about what the political order should look like, apart from that it requires a reasonable rule of law. The rule of law is a flexible constraint. What is reasonable to people in one context can be unreasonable to others: such human variation is at the core of modern political theory. Therefore, the theory does not specify much in the way of substantive content. It does not require a system of private property or democracy or that the law must recognise the individual as a discrete rights-bearer. But neither do I hold to the contrary. Transitional justice's existence does not depend upon the realisation of an author's preferred state of affairs.

Conclusion

This chapter argues that a unified theory of transitional justice can encompass the aparadigmatic context of ongoing conflict. The legitimating account holds that political institutions necessarily aim to exercise political authority. However, systemic failures undermine or vitiate authority's legitimacy. Transitional justice can legitimate political authorities that have negated their purpose by committing systemic injuries and/or when their weakness or when their absence requires the constitution of new institutions. By enacting reasons that legitimate authority, the work of transitional justice in ongoing conflict offers the contingent possibility of new political forms.

12 Although, with apologies to Joan Robinson, I might observe that the misery of being subject to political authority is nothing compared to the misery of its absence.

References

Arendt, H. (1977) *Between Past and Future: Eight Exercises in Political Thought* (Enlarged ed.). Harmondsworth: Penguin Books.

Arthur, P. (2009) 'How 'Transitions' Reshaped Human Rights: A Conceptual History of Transitional Justice'. *Human Rights Quarterly* 31(2), 321–367.

Ash, T.G. (2011) 'Trials, Purges, and History Lessons'. Atlas of Transformation. Retrieved from http://monumenttotransformation.org/atlas-of-transformation/html/h/history/trials-purges-and-history-lessons-timothy-garton-ash.html.

Balasco, L.M. (2013) 'The Transitions of Transitional Justice: Mapping the Waves From Promise to Practice'. *Journal of Human Rights* 12(2), 198–216.

Bengio, O. (2021) 'The 'Non-State' State in Iraqi Political Discourse and Action'. Tel Aviv Notes, 15(3). Retrieved from: https://dayan.org/content/non-state-state-iraqi-political-discourse-and-action.

Brown, K. (2012) "What It Was Like to Live through a Day': Transitional Justice and the Memory of the Everyday in a Divided Society'. *The International Journal of Transitional Justice*, 6(3), 444–466.

Brown, W. (1995) *States of Injury: Power and Freedom in Late Modernity*. Princeton: Princeton University Press.

Cobban, H. (2007) 'Transitional Justice and Conflict Termination: Mozambique, Rwanda and South Africa Assessed'. In: E. Hughes, W. Schabas and R. Thakur, eds. *Atrocities and International Accountability: Beyond Transitional Justice* (pp. 42–64). Tokyo, New York, and Paris: United Nations University Press.

Collier, P. (2003) *Breaking the Conflict Trap: Civil War and Development Policy*. Washington, DC: World Bank Publications.

Copp, D. (1999) 'The Idea of a Legitimate State'. *Philosophy and Public Affairs* 28(1), 3–45.

De Greiff, P. (2020) 'The Future of the Past: Reflections on the Present State and Prospects of Transitional Justice'. *The International Journal of Transitional Justice* 14(2), 251–259.

Engstrom, P. (2013) 'Transitional Justice and Ongoing Conflict'. In: C. Sriram, G.-G. Jemima, J. Herman, and O. Martin-Ortega, eds. *Transitional Justice and Peacebuilding on the Ground: Victims and Ex-Combatants* (41–61). Abingdon: Routledge.

Galoob, S. and S. Winter (2019) 'Injustice, Reparation and Legitimacy'. In: D. Sobel, P. Vallentyne and S. Wall, eds. *Oxford Studies in Political Philosophy*. Oxford: Oxford University Press.

Gready, P. and S. Robins (2019) 'From Transitional to Transformative Justice: A New Agenda for Practice'. In: P. Gready and S. Robins, eds. *From Transitional to Transformative Justice* (pp. 31–56). Cambridge: Cambridge University Press.

Habermas, J. and W. Rehg (2001) 'Constitutional Democracy: A Paradoxical Union of Contradictory Principles?' *Political Theory* 29(6), 766–781.

Hagopian, A., A.D. Flaxman, T.K. Takaro, S.A.E. Al Shatari, J. Rajaratnam, S. Becker... and W.M. Weiss (2013) 'Mortality in Iraq Associated with the 2003–2011 War and Occupation: Findings from a National Cluster Sample Survey by the University Collaborative Iraq Mortality Study'. *PLoS Med* 10(10), e1001533.

Hansen, T. O. (2011) 'Transitional Justice: Toward a Differentiated Theory'. *Oregon Review of International Law*, 13(1), 1–54

—— (2013) 'The Vertical and Horizontal Expansion of Transitional Justice: Explanations and Implications for a Contested Field'. In: S. Buckley-Zistel, T.K. Beck, C. Braun, and F. Mieth, eds. *Transitional Justice Theories* (pp. 117–136). Abingdon and New York: Routledge.

Hayner, P. (2002) *Unspeakable Truths: Confronting State Terror and Atrocity*. New York: Routledge.

Hinton, A. (2018) *The Justice Façade: Trials of Transition in Cambodia*. Oxford: Oxford University Press.

Hobbes, T. (1998) *On the Citizen (De Cive)* (R. Tuck, Trans.). Cambridge: Cambridge University Press.

Inter-American Commission on Human Rights (1980) 'Report on the Situation of Human Rights in Argentina'. OEA/Ser.L/V/II.49, doc. 19 corr.1, 11 April. Retrieved from: http://www.cidh.oas.org/countryrep/Argentina80eng/toc.htm.

International Center for Transitional Justice (n.d.) 'What is Transitional Justice?' Website. Retrieved 8 July 2020 from: https://www.ictj.org/about/transitional-justice.

Iraqi Body Count (2020) Iraqi Body Count, 31 October 2020. Retrieved 12 November 2020 from: https://www.iraqbodycount.org/.

Jaspers, K. (1959 [1951]) *Man in the Modern Age* (E. Paul and C. Paul, Trans.). London: Routledge.

Jaspers, K. (2001 [1947]) *The Question of German Guilt* (E. B. Ashton, Trans.). New York: Fordham University Press.

Kant, I. (1970) 'The Metaphysics of Morals' (N.B. Nisbet, Trans.). In: H. Reiss, ed. *Kant's Political Writings*. Cambridge: Cambridge University Press.

Klosko, G. (2004) 'Multiple Principles of Political Obligation'. *Political Theory* 32(6), 801–824.

Lu, C. (2017) *Justice and Reconciliation in World Politics*. Cambridge: Cambridge University Press.

Mac Ginty, R. (2016) *No War, No Peace: The Rejuvenation of Stalled Peace Processes and Peace Accords*. New York: Springer.

Madlingozi, T. (2010) 'On Transitional Justice Entrepreneurs and The Production of Victims'. *Journal of Human Rights Practice* 2(2), 208–228.

McAuliffe, P. (2011) 'Transitional Justice's Expanding Empire: Reasserting the Value of the Paradigmatic Transition?' *Journal of Conflictology* 2(2), 32–44.

McGonigle Leyh, B. (2016) 'Nuremberg's Legacy Within Transitional Justice: Prosecutions Are Here to Stay'. *Washington University Global Studies Law Review* 15, 559–574.

Mihr, A. (2018) *Regime Consolidation and Transitional Justice: A Comparative Study of Germany, Spain and Turkey*. Cambridge: Cambridge University Press.

Miller, Z. (2008) 'Effects of Invisibility: In Search of the 'Economic' in Transitional Justice'. *The International Journal of Transitional Justice* 2(3), 266–291.

Muggah, R. (2005) 'No Magic Bullet: A Critical Perspective on Disarmament, Demobilization and Reintegration (DDR) and Weapons Reduction in Post-conflict Contexts'. *The Round Table* 94(379), 239–252.

Muldoon, P. (2003) 'Reconciliation and Political Legitimacy: The Old Australia and the New South Africa'. *Australian Journal of Politics and History* 49(2), 182–196.

Murphy, C. (2017) *The Conceptual Foundations of Transitional Justice*. Cambridge: Cambridge University Press.

Nurick, L. (1945) 'The Distinction between Combatant and Noncombatant in the Law of War'. *The American Journal of International Law* 39(4), 680–697.

Orentlicher, D. (1994) 'Settling Accounts: The Duty to Prosecute Human Rights Violations of a Prior Regime'. *The Yale Law Journal* 1000(8), 2537–2615.

Pereira, A.W. (2005) *Political (in) Justice: Authoritarianism and the Rule of Law in Brazil, Chile, and Argentina*. Pittsburgh, PA: University of Pittsburgh Press.

Rabkin, J.A. (1999) 'Nuremberg Misremembered'. *SAIS Review* 19(2), 81–96.

Rawls, J. (2001) *Justice as Fairness: A Restatement*. Cambridge, MA: Harvard University Press.

Raz, J. (1985) 'Authority and Justification'. *Philosophy & Public Affairs* 14(1), 3–29.

Roberts, D. (2011) 'Post-Conflict Peacebuilding, Liberal Irrelevance and the Locus of Legitimacy'. *International Peacekeeping* 18(4), 410–424.

Schaap, A. (2008) Reconciliation as Ideology and Politics. *Constellations* 15(2), 249–264.

Simmons, A.J. (1999) Justification and Legitimacy. *Ethics* 109(4), 739–771.

Sharp, D.N. (2015) 'Emancipating Transitional Justice from the Bonds of the Paradigmatic Transition'. *International Journal of Transitional Justice* 9(1), 150–169.

Shelby, T. (2007) 'Justice, Deviance, and the Dark Ghetto'. *Philosophy & Public Affairs* 35(2), 126–160.

Sikkink, K. (2008) 'From Pariah State to Global Protagonist: Argentina and the Struggle for International Human Rights'. *Latin American Politics and Society 50*(1), 1–29.

Skaar, E. (2013) 'Reconciliation in a Transitional Justice Perspective'. *Transitional Justice Review* 1(1), article 10, 54–103.

Spinner-Halev, J. (2007) 'From Historical to Enduring Injustice'. *Political Theory* 35(5), 574–597.

Tabak, S. (2011) 'False Dichotomies of Transitional Justice: Gender, Conflict and Combatants in Colombia'. *New York University Journal of International Law & Politics* 44, 103–163.

Teitel, R.G. (2000) *Transitional Justice*. Oxford: Oxford University Press.

Turner, C. (2016) *Violence, Law and the Impossibility of Transitional Justice*. Abingdon: Routledge.

Williams, B. (2005) 'Realism and Moralism in Political Theory'. In G. Hawthorn, ed. *In the Beginning Was the Deed* (pp. 1–18). Princeton and Oxford: Princeton University Press.

Winter, S. (2013) 'Towards a Unified Theory of Transitional Justice'. *The International Journal of Transitional Justice* 7 (2), 205–223.

—— (2014) *Transitional Justice in Established Democracies: A Political Theory*. London: Palgrave Macmillan.

Zurn, C. (2010) 'The Logic of Legitimacy: Bootstrapping Paradoxes of Constitutional Democracy'. *Legal Theory* 16(3), 191–227.

Concluding Remarks[1]

Tine Destrooper and Par Engstrom

Introduction

This book theorises and empirically examines the recent and rapid expansion of transitional justice, both as a field of practice and as a scholarly field. Transitional justice has seen dramatic expansion in contexts of ongoing violence (such as Syria or the DRC), fragile states (such as Kenya or Burundi), or occupied territories (such as Afghanistan or East Timor). Similarly, transitional justice initiatives have been developed in 'old' democracies (such as Belgium or France) and in settler democracies (such as Australia or Canada). These aparadigmatic cases are not emerging from conflict or authoritarian rule and there has been no transition of political authority. So far, however, few studies have sought to examine what we can learn from a comparative analysis across these various types of contexts in which transitional justice is currently commonly invoked. Yet, the invocation of transitional justice in these contexts is affecting what we understand transitional justice to be and what we expect it to do.

In these aparadigmatic cases, transitional justice initiatives are not in the first place implemented to respond to abuses committed by repressive predecessor regimes or to consolidate a recent political transition (McEvoy and McGregor 2008, 6). Instead, various justice actors take recourse to transitional justice because of the visceral appeal of the postulate that accountability for and recognition of past and ongoing wrongs are necessary to break cycles of violence and ensure a peaceful and just future (Quinn 2014). Moreover, they find in transitional justice a standardised and comprehensive, yet versatile, range of tools and practices to work towards its normative ambition of more just societies.

Transitional justice's expansion towards these aparadigmatic cases where no political transition took place raises the question of what is transitional about transitional justice. In Teitel's (2014) view, the 'transition' of transitional justice needs to involve a political transition. Yet, in many cases where transitional justice is used today, reality is far removed from this widely accepted

1 Part of this research was funded through ERC Starting Grant 804154 VictPart. No conflicts of interest to declare.

DOI: 10.4324/9781003289104-13

conceptualisation. Rather than relegating these realities to other fields of study, like peace-building or conflict studies, this book goes beyond the definitional debate of whether what we are observing is transitional justice or not, and instead starts from the empirical reality that an increasingly diverse group of justice actors are engaged in practices and draw on norms they themselves understand to constitute 'transitional justice'.

The book develops a conceptual and analytical framework that seeks to understand the practice of transitional justice in a more context-sensitive, bottom-up, and actor-oriented way. The contributions to the book share a foundational perspective on transitional justice as a time- and place-based practice embedded in existing power relations (see the Introduction in this volume). Such a perspective helps us rethink what change might be possible in the absence of regime transition and acknowledges the complexity and messiness of the practice of transitional justice. This book seizes this complexity and the cognitive dissonance it generates to proposes new ways of thinking about what transitional justice is and can do and ensures that our theorisation of the field follows the expanding reach of the practice of transitional justice.

The framework proposed in the Introduction in this volume revolves around intentions and responses as a lens for capturing the multi-layered and complex dynamics of transitional justice in an actor-oriented way. As such, the book moves beyond a critical deconstruction and proposes not a *model*, but an analytical lens and vocabulary to engage with reality on the ground. The primary aim is not to develop cross-case comparisons, but to analyse what various kinds of 'outlier' cases tell us about the broader domain of transitional justice, and to consider how conceptual unease, whether within or between the cases, can inform our understanding of the practice and the field of transitional justice.

The chapters in this volume use the framework to foreground modalities, intentions, and responses to transitional justice. Equally, they highlight the importance of considering degrees of inbetweenness (Goodale and Merry 2007), and of carefully accounting for the dynamic changes in context, issues, strategies, and positioning that happen over time and across issues, because every position may inherently contain within it its opposite (e.g. attempts at accountability may conceal efforts to avoid accountability in other domains, or resistance to some elements of the discourse may co-exist with the adoption of others). The chapters illustrate how the various intentions and responses interact and co-exist with each other and how actors can move across various positions over time. As such, the framework sheds light on the dynamic normative positionality of actors who (refuse to) engage with the transitional justice paradigm.

In this concluding chapter, we take these empirical insights to engage in a more self-reflective exercise, exploring what sort of disruptions the domain of transitional justice permits and can accommodate. This is a question about transitional justice's future, and about whether the paradigm, practice, and discourse are sufficiently adaptable to these changing circumstances: Are the innovations that are happening in these various contexts leading to a profound dynamic of consolidation by making the field more context-sensitive and broadly applicable, or are we, on the contrary, observing a moment of theoretical and practical overstretch that will eventually lead the field of transitional justice to disintegrate? The chapters show that innovation may both add to the relevance and usefulness of transitional justice in a broader range of cases, thereby contributing to its consolidation, or they may challenge the paradigm and disrupt it to the extent of radically transforming it.

To address these questions, this concluding chapter introduces five themes that surface in the empirical chapters when transitional justice travels to aparadigmatic cases. We also offer some brief reflections on how this pushes the boundaries of what transitional justice is and can be expected to do.

Pluralism and Transitional Justice's Unsettled Character

One recurring theme throughout the chapters is transitional justice pluralism. In contexts where there has been no political transition, and sometimes not even a functioning state, transitional justice is often spearheaded by non-state actors who may operate without or against the state. The chapters in this book describe both the increased – and qualitatively different – involvement of civil society organisations (CSOs) in standardised transitional justice mechanisms, as well as CSOs setting up non-standardised transitional justice mechanisms themselves. Nisan Alıcı's chapter, for example, examines the unofficial Diyarbakır truth commission set up by activist organisations, lawyers, psychologists, and academics in 2007, which had all characteristics of a 'classic' truth commission, even if the state was not involved. In addition, the chapters highlight new types of actors 'doing' transitional justice. Brianne McGonigle Leyh's, for example, explores the role of citizen groups raising funds to set up a local truth commission, while Huma Saeed explores how institutions in host countries of refugees could be seen as transitional justice actors that could, for example, set up truth-seeking initiatives to recognise the suffering of people living on their territory. Pluralism does not only characterise those who 'do' transitional justice, but also those who should be held accountable within the transitional justice framework. Noha Aboueldahab's chapter, for example, opens up the conversation about the accountability of multi-national companies and former colonisers.

This multitude of actors means that the state becomes only one of the elements in a broader transitional justice ecosystem. This decisively shifts the analytical focus from the state-level to that of other stakeholders. Moreover, analysing the intentions and responses of these actors prompts us to examine who is doing what as the starting point for conceptualising what transitional justice means for those using it. What are they imagining it can do, and who is doing the imagining? This may lead to a reconceptualisation of the field as new actors might attach new or different meanings to existing transitional justice processes and mechanisms.

The growing number of actors taking ownership over transitional justice practice foregrounds the political contestation and struggles within the practice of transitional justice. While not exclusive to aparadigmatic cases, these political struggles and contentious politics become even more obvious in cases where the distinctly unsettled, political, and messy character of transitional justice is accentuated by the multitude of stakeholders. As such, the chapters show that, in addition to accountability and recognition, disruption can be seen as a core objective of transitional justice, explaining why both the promotion of transitional justice, as well as resistance to it, can sometimes come from unexpected actors. Noha Aboueldahab's chapter illustrates this nicely when showing how CSOs resist transitional justice as a state practice that consolidates power, while at the same time adopting innovative approaches to transitional justice as a tool in their struggle for social justice.

Acknowledging pluralism thus highlights the extent to which transitional justice is far from consensus-driven and fundamentally unsettled. This also turns our focus to how power relations may shift when the state is no longer the only focal point. As Herremans and Bellintani (in this volume) demonstrate for the Syrian case, access to the ground and knowledge of the context has made CSOs pivotal justice actors with significant power in providing some modicum of justice for Syrians. In this specific case, the traditional focus on criminal justice may still be strong, but the processes surrounding these criminal justice processes are markedly CSO-driven. The pivotal role of, and reliance on, CSOs has led certain international actors, such as the International, Impartial and Independent Mechanism for Syria, to adopt a two-tier approach in dealing with CSOs, in an attempt to mitigate some power imbalances, e.g. with regards to agenda setting. This contrasts with cases in which the involvement of the International Criminal Court for example has been argued to lead to decontestation and a change in local actors' justice agendas. This increasingly important role of CSOs and their innovative take on criminal accountability mechanisms has resulted in an increased sense of ownership and has expanded the gaze of criminal justice as CSOs sought to leverage broader accountability and recognition, as well as bringing considerations about disruption to the centre of the debate. This development may even be argued to take the field of transitional justice to a place closer to its origins, where disruption was also a prominent concern.

The Standardisation of Localised Justice Initiatives

The chapters not only foreground new actors, but also new ways of doing transitional justice, including initiatives proposed by grassroots actors who do not have easy access to the formal transitional justice architecture. Despite significant differences, what these actors have in common is that they use transitional justice rhetoric and tools innovatively and rethink how these can be made relevant to their context, including in ways that fall well outside the formal UN definition of what constitutes 'transitional justice'.

As such, a second topic running through all chapters is the tension between standardisation and contextualisation. While transitional justice has in some ways become a standardised model, neither its origins nor the way in which it is implemented in various settings around the world today, are best described as abstract idealised models. Rather, transitional justice consists of a highly contextualised and historically contingent set of practices that developed in response to lived experiences of violence, repression and exclusion. The chapters thus show that the critique of transitional justice having become too professionalised or too institutionalised to speak to realities on the ground in a meaningful manner, is mitigated by the fact that many forms of contextualisation take place when practices and concepts travel, especially to contexts that are far removed from the ones for which they were initially developed. By applying the label of transitional justice to these various kinds of efforts taking place in different settings, the chapters facilitate a sharing of insights that can help to re-imagine the field and practice.

This is crucial since transitional justice's implementation in this diverse range of contexts has already resulted in a degree of flexibility regarding modalities as well as objectives. Transitional justice norms are so broad that many aims and ways of achieving those aims can be, and have been, attached to them. They are neither inherently disruptive nor inherently contributing to a status quo. While transitional justice aims, normatively, to unsettle and challenge past practices and conditions, whether it will actually disrupt depends on the modalities of its implementation, particularly in contexts of historically exclusionary and oppressive societies. Moreover, as the chapters also show, power relations and exogenous factors specific to a concrete context explain whether – standardised or non-standardised – transitional justice will disrupt or consolidate political power relations, and several chapters highlight the risk of – temporary – elite capture.

As such, the flexibility that is needed to implement transitional justice in aparadigmatic contexts means that the notion of transitional justice as a set of constitutive and prescriptive norms about what a society should look like, should increasingly be complemented with a notion of transitional justice as primarily a procedural or deliberative framework that privileges values and political guiding principles such as participation, representation, accountability, etc., which may serve a number of objectives in various settings. This procedural understanding of transitional justice offers a lens to examine issues related to the standardisation-contextualisation tension in a more practice-based way.

Innovation is often seen as inherently desirable, whereas standardisation is seen as bad for justice actors on the ground. This assumption is questionable. As the Syrian case shows, for some victims, criminal justice processes are important, even if they are not a panacea. Thus, while acknowledging the

– discursive – narrowing that may come with standardisation, and especially standardisation towards more legal approaches, we should refrain from casting these standardised legal approaches as *inherently* problematic. Moreover, here as well, the constant interaction between innovation and contextualisation on one hand, and standardisation on the other, is crucial to acknowledge. Furthermore, innovation can lead to consolidation of the field by making it more broadly relevant, as much as it can disrupt or destabilise it by challenging foundational assumptions. Similarly, consolidation can reaffirm unequal power relations as much as it can be a backstop to protect the most vulnerable or a means to make the practice of transitional justice more coherent and efficient. Approaching transitional justice as a procedural or deliberative framework that privileges principles such as participation, representation, and accountability can help to better understand the consequences of contextualisation and innovation as well as standardisation and consolidation.

This relates to the point about actor-centredness and understanding practices as they are understood and translated by actors on the ground within their context (Hinton 2018; Merry 2006). Several actors studied in this volume, for example, propose practice-driven ways to rethink accountability, beyond a narrow focus on criminal accountability. These interpretations are crucial to highlight, as they offer a way to keep accountability at the centre of transitional justice practice and politics. In an era where transitional justice has often been criticised for being too undefined and too all-encompassing to have any analytical value, it is precisely the centrality of accountability as a core objective that holds the practice of transitional justice together – and makes it either appealing to or threatening for certain actors.

Ongoing Transitions

The chapters in this book, through their focus on actors' intentions and responses, also challenge transitional justice's assumptions about temporality. They conceptualise transitional justice beyond the transitional moment, i.e. the idea that there is a brief window of opportunity that constitutes a clean break with the past and during which legacies of a repressive and violent past regime should be addressed before moving towards a peaceful and democratic future (Hansen 2017; Turner 2017). Also within paradigmatic contexts this idea has been increasingly challenged (De Haan and Destrooper 2021), but it becomes even more problematic in aparadigmatic settings where continuity, not rupture, is the state of affairs (Álvarez-Berastegi 2017, cited in Pallí-Asperó in this volume).

The chapters show that if we leave straightforward temporal assumption behind, new questions emerge about whether and when transitional justice tools can and should be applied, and what it means to designate various justice-seeking efforts as 'transitional justice'. Crucially, the chapters demonstrate that even if transitional justice might not depend on the occurrence of a clear political transition, it still needs to be prompted by some political change or shift, or at least the aspiration thereof, in order for initiatives to be meaningful, or at least not to be entirely superficial. If there are no – aspired to – political shifts, then the risks are high for instrumentalisation or limited impact of transitional justice. At the same time, the chapters underline the importance of acknowledging the unsettled and unsettling nature of transitions. In aparadigmatic cases, the nature of transitional justice as inescapably 'unfinished business' becomes clear: always in the making, never finished, and without clear ends.

The chapters in this book challenge and problematise this understanding of rupture and linear progress, as they cover long, intermittent, juxtaposed, or complex timelines. As one of Nisan Alıcı's interviewees, for example, argued: 'There is a slow transition in place starting from [the] 1930s'. Such an understanding of transition foregrounds both the activism of actors on the ground in pushing for change, as well as elements of structural injustice that contribute to harm. As such, letting go of binary temporal assumptions about the violent past versus the peaceful present, the chapters also shed light on the relevance of transitional justice for present and ongoing violations, as well as for how historical injustices contribute to these. Thomas Obel Hansen's chapter, for example, examines how certain elements from the transitional justice toolkit, could be used – and are *de facto* resisted due to their potentially disruptive nature – to seek accountability for human rights violations committed by the United Kingdom's armed forces in recent military campaigns. Kerstin Bree Carlson discusses how the transitional justice toolbox could be used to deal with Europe's 'home-grown' terrorism because it upholds principles of legality while transcending political disagreement.

Moving beyond a binary and linear temporal logic that is pinned on a teleological understanding of what transitional justice should do, is not a mere conceptual debate. It also has consequences for transitional justice practice. As Noha Aboueldahab's chapter illustrates, many stakeholders have an interest in the transitional justice discourse, but it is precisely the temporal assumptions of transitional justice that make them renounce the paradigm. This is also the case for Syrian justice actors, for whom an overly-strict adherence to the notion of 'transitional' has nurtured opposition among some practitioners and victims regarding the desirability of applying the paradigm in the Syrian context, while others argue that these definitional debates risk hampering the substantive work transitional justice could do for efforts to overcome the justice impasse (Herremans and Bellintani in this volume).

Political Will and Legitimacy

A fourth topic running through all chapters implicitly or explicitly is that of political will and legitimacy. A standard theory of political authority holds that a reasonable political order is necessary to a decent human life, that such an order requires political authority, and that authority depends on legitimacy meaning that citizens can reasonably endorse actions (see Winter in this volume). Transitional justice institutions can enact this legitimacy when the state accomplishes purposes that are reasonable for the citizenry, and notably when it accomplishes these through legal or quasi-legal processes that are widely accepted. From this point of view, transitional justice politics are, in essence, a radical change in the legitimating regime of the state. Yet, the empirical chapters show that ongoingness is the state of affairs in most aparadigmatic cases, and that as such transitional justice is best conceptualised as a form of progress politics that is reform oriented rather than revolutionary in character. This is not to say that transitional justice cannot be a catalyst of change: even if its liberal underpinning and normative ambitions can hardly be argued to be inherently revolutionary, it has disruptive potential.

As Cira Pallí-Asperó's chapter shows, changes often happen through the reform of already existing institutions, by providing public acknowledgement for historical injustices, offering material or symbolic reparations for those who suffered the consequences of the wrongdoing, or by installing historical commissions that act as 'active agents in the construction of the new legitimating regime through the production of new historical frames that allow the state to acknowledge and address the past wrongs'. This hints at the importance of transitional justice interventions being state-sanctioned and the extent to which standardised approaches of transitional justice both depend on and strengthen politico-legal authority. This is also illustrative of the extent to which an ideology that began in opposition to the state was successfully appropriated by the state (see the Introduction in this volume).

As some chapters illustrate, the invocation of transitional justice rhetoric by CSOs to hold the state accountable for its missteps can, however, also challenge the legitimacy of the regime. In Turkey, for example, there has never been an official, overarching transitional justice agenda to deal with the human rights abuses related to the Kurdish conflict. Yet, grassroots organisations, in partnership with international actors, used the transitional justice discourse to put pressure on the government in their pursuit of truth, justice, and accountability, in an attempt to disrupt the official politics of silence (see Alıcı's in this volume).

The discussion of political legitimacy also leads to the question about political will: the willingness of those in power to engage with transitional justice discourse and practice will likely depend on their assessment of whether it will strengthen or weaken their political authority and legitimacy. As Destrooper's chapter shows, the context in which transitional justice is being discussed in Belgium is that of a state that does not (wish or seek to) question its own identity as a liberal rule-of-law state, nor change anything to the basic make-up of its core state institutions or justice discourse. The proposal to borrow insights from the domain of transitional justice met with a lack of political will in one instance, and with political co-optation in another. A fundamental engagement with transitional justice's core objectives of accountability for and recognition of past harm would, in this case, require a rethinking of the legitimacy of existing state institutions and of the associated narratives. Similarly, Line Engbo Gissel's chapter on transitional justice in the North Atlantic analyses the Danish government's rejection of participation in the Greenland Reconciliation Commission. She argues that while the commission aimed for recognition rather than accountability, the fear of disrupting and decolonising the relationship between Denmark and Greenland likely motivated this official refusal to engage with the commission. The Belgium and Denmark cases relate to the point we raised above: even if a formal political transition is not required for transitional justice, some form of transition must be intended for meaningful transitional justice initiatives to take shape.

In cases of ongoing conflict as well as in consolidated democracies the political will to engage in such a transition may be low to non-existing on the side of those state actors. This explains why, in these cases, non-state actors are often the ones pushing for some form of transitional justice in their quest for accountability and recognition. It also relates to the abovementioned innovative methods and the contextualisation-standardisation tension, since these actors (a) do not always have (easy) access to, or influence within, state bodies or (b) because they perceive non-standardised approaches to be more in line with their agenda or modus operandi. In Syria, for example, where there is no political will nor a transition, new modi operandi have been proposed by CSOs (e.g. rooted in universal jurisdiction or artistic practices).

Bridging the Scholar–Practitioner Divide

Lastly, the chapters highlight the importance and possibility of bridging the scholar–practitioner divide. When analysing the empirical cases in this book through the analytical framework proposed in the Introduction in this volume, the question surfaces for whom it matters whether we call something an instance of transitional justice or not, and how we define intentions and responses. On the one hand this is about the question of which lessons scholarship can draw from practice, and on the other it is about how practitioners can use these theoretical lenses in their own practice. The chapters show that discussions about the field of transitional justice are not a mere scholarly debate. The importance of this question for practitioners is clearly illustrated by one of Alıcı's interviewees, who argues that:

> The discussions in transitional justice literature are very valuable for me because they provide a basis to think. The only hardship is that I get stuck because the practicalities of TJ in ongoing conflicts have not been studied enough. I am a lawyer; this is not my specialty. We get stuck because we are trying to find the methodology by ourselves.

Other interviewees cited in this volume also mention the extent to which activists are interested in learning from other contexts and actors about how transitional justice can further their cause, but that they are too deeply invested in the practice of transitional justice to reflect much on the broader picture. Several practitioners cited in this volume were moreover actively looking for a stronger conceptual framework to interpret and shape their own actions. They are seeking to expand the transitional justice paradigm to better serve their struggle. Practitioners and stakeholders therefore are not indifferent to considerations about what their actions in concrete situations mean for transitional justice as a broader field of practice.

This relates to the point we raised above about seeing transitional justice as a deeply contextualised and historically contingent set of practices that is developed in response to lived experiences of violence, repression, and exclusion, and that responds to often intractable political, legal, moral, and social problems. It is in this sense that transitional justice developed as a result of efforts to respond to demands for a practical language and practices of justice. It is also in this sense that transitional justice as a field of practice and a field of scholarship are intractably related. The field is a representation and a retelling of what actors are doing and experimenting with. As such, the examination of the broader field of transitional justice, too, is important for justice actors as it relates to whether and how justice actors can innovate and use the paradigm to further their own struggles. The conversation between the empirical chapters and the theoretical introduction tells us something about where the field could move in the future.

How Aparadigmatic Cases Push the Boundaries of Transitional Justice

The 'outlier' cases examined in this volume allow us to reflect on what they tell us about the broader field of transitional justice. There are five elements to note as a basis in favour of systematically including aparadigmatic cases in efforts to theorise and analyse the field.

First, opening up the practice and theorisation of transitional justice to include aparadigmatic cases makes sense because of the positive effects this can have for actors engaged in struggles for justice. The cases discussed in this volume – and the actors in them – push the boundaries of transitional justice by implementing it in contexts where there have been no formal political transitions. They do this not only because the transitional justice paradigm holds the promise of accountability, recognition, and disruption, but also because of the abovementioned procedural understanding of transitional justice as a deliberative framework that privileges principles such as participation and representation. These normative commitments are tangible and meaningful for actors on the ground. In Syria, for example, several justice actors see – non-standardised forms of – transitional justice as the most apt paradigm to achieve a modicum of justice in a context where redress of millions of victims and the prosecution of thousands of perpetrators is otherwise unimaginable. While others may be more sceptical of how much significant work can be conducted before a transition is in place, innovative and context-specific interpretations of transitional justice demonstrate that certain justice issues can be addressed even in the absence of a political transition. Not doing so, McGonigle Leyh (in this volume) argues, may be a missed opportunity, since transitional justice offers tools to establish new and ad hoc structures to address – historical or ongoing – injustices, that may not be available within the established human rights or criminal justice architecture. She argues that:

> inclusive, participatory structures can be created where the voices of marginalized or oppressed groups can be heard [...] human rights should of course underpin any transitional justice response, even when those responses take shape in so-called stable democracies grappling with a past of serious abuse. And, importantly, the human rights-frame will remain long after the need for transitional justice passes.

The frames of transitional justice, criminal justice, and human rights should thus be seen as complementary and mutually reinforcing, also in aparadigmatic contexts. Especially in cases of mass victimisation and historical injustice the combination of the various frameworks offers the potential to ensure a robust and holistic response to both direct and structural harm.

A second reason for systematically including aparadigmatic cases in the practice and theorisation of transitional justice is its potential to decolonise the field. A Global North–South divide continues to characterise much of mainstream transitional justice scholarship. The classic (post-)conflict/post-authoritarianism versus consolidated democracy binary reflects a postcolonial bias that is typically not explicitly acknowledged. As such, transitional justice scholarship has, so far, not sufficiently addressed (a) the nature and extent of shared challenges of legacies of violence, nor (b) the role of international actors (from foreign states to corporate actors) in creating conflict, nor (c) the role of hegemonic power discourse in overpowering local justice demands. These blind spots underscore the importance of unsettling existing binary thinking and moving beyond alleged divides between various forms of political authority.

The empirical chapters in this book show that political authority can be understood as a spectrum whereby transitional justice can be relevant in many contexts, including to address colonial violence and harm or to hold corporate actors accountable for their role in past or ongoing injustices. The hyperdiversity and contextualisation described in this book moreover shows the decreasing relevance of conceptualising transitional justice as a standardised 'all in' menu, hinting at the extent to which such approaches may lead to processes of othering, and of proposing a set framework that 'applies to others not to us' – the 'us' being consolidated democracies (see, for example, Aboueldahab, Gissel, and Saeed and in this volume). Failing to move beyond this conceptualisation of transitional justice as a standardised toolbox to deal with a certain type of exceptional violence explains the growing scepticism of some South-based actors who increasingly come to see transitional justice as a part of North-based (including EU and the UN) actors' foreign policy toolkit that these North-based actors do not apply domestically to deal with their own legacies of violence; these latter actors may even resist transitional justice as a potential internal policy element to deal with colonial harm, corporate harm, or democratic challenges. By making explicit the logic behind certain instances of rejection or opposition to transitional justice, the chapters shed light on what is being rejected: the intentionality or mechanisms of transitional justice, or the othering discourse it has come to entail.

Moreover, the chapters show that analysing various kinds of aparadigmatic cases alongside one another offers opportunities to reverse the traditional dynamics of lesson learning and best-practice sharing from North to South. Destrooper's chapter, for example shows how a small CSO in the domain of education is taking insights from work in post-conflict settings to develop educational programmes in Belgium. In doing so, the organisation acknowledges and taps into the wealth of knowledge of South-based actors, and challenges who is typically cast as the knowledge producer. This also goes to the point underlined in several chapters about the interwovenness of epistemic injustice and other forms of – direct, structural, historical and ongoing – injustice, and the importance of disrupting these different injustices in a comprehensive manner.

This relates to a third reason for systematically including aparadigmatic cases in the practice and theorisation of transitional justice, namely by offering a new perspective on what can be expected of transitional justice. The chapters show how the practice of transitional justice in aparadigmatic contexts has led to adaptation, in the form of adding new elements to the existing toolkit and discourse in ways that expand transitional justice's repertoire (i.e. accepting new practices as transitional justice), as well as by going back to the roots of transitional justice (i.e. asking how foundational ideas of transitional justice, which were often developed in opposition to the state, can once more be relevant). Both strategies are answers to the question of how transitional justice is done in different contexts, and what 'doing transitional justice' in different contexts tells us about the field. Sometimes both strategies co-exist. For example, when Syrian CSOs are relying on new technologies, such as those proposed by Forensic Architecture Bellingcat, they are tapping into the potential of this innovative technology to further their struggle for accountability.

At the same time, some activists are going back to some of the mechanisms of early transitional justice by proceeding on the basis of universal jurisdiction, a procedure which had long been placed on the backburner. Both strategies problematise the current state of the field at different levels and can be a way to 'futureproof' it. They both have the potential to enrich the debate and to open up the transitional justice imagination by offering a new perspective on what can be expected of transitional justice and how in terms of curbing injustices and stretching the boundaries of what is conceivable in terms of justice, accountability and recognition (Herremans and Destrooper 2021). Various kinds of initiatives taking place in these aparadigmatic cases are doing precisely that. The Diyarbakır Prison truth commission and the Greensboro Commission, for example, show how an unofficial commission, established by independent justice actors and citizens, respectively, could work and what it could achieve (see Alıcı and McGonigle Leyh in this volume). Similarly, an improbable coalition of Syrian justice actors shows how some new – or revived – justice avenues are opened when all formal multilateral mechanisms are blocked, or how documenting housing and property rights violations can happen during conflict with a view to laying the foundation for future restitution and compensation mechanisms. Whereas Alıcı's chapter suggests that in a climate of oppressive rule where human rights activists are being threatened, there may seem to be limited imagination and creativity to reflect on what innovative forms of transitional justice could look like, other chapters demonstrate that it is precisely under these unaccommodating conditions that innovations and disruption take place. They show that even in times when advancing justice for victims of international crimes seems futile, it is possible to push the boundaries of justice. This is crucial because it allows for disruption and the upsetting of binaries that invisibilise the ambiguity and complexity of lived reality.

Concluding Remarks

Due to its normative, political, and geographical expansion, non-transitional or aparadigmatic states today make up the majority of cases where transitional justice is taking place. As such, the cases discussed in this book can hardly be termed 'outliers' and the extent to which these cases shape how we have come to understand transitional justice can hardly be overestimated. The chapters in this book show that the contemporary practice of transitional justice takes many different forms, which are shaped and constrained by context. They problematise certain taken-for-granted assumptions of transitional justice, including its state centricity, the assumption of a formal political transition, and the question of disruption. By exposing the limits of paradigmatic transitional justice and its assumptions, the studies in this book interrogate and shed new light on the field of transitional justice.

This book offers a theoretical framework for a more fine-grained empirical analysis that sheds light on issues that surfaces across cases that find themselves in very different positions with regards to political authority, as well as allowing for a reflection on what these similarities mean for the field of transitional justice. In this concluding chapter, we highlight five such similarities: pluralism, deep contextualisation, ongoingness, struggles over legitimacy, and the need to bridge the scholar–practitioner divide. The fact that these themes emerge in cases as diverse as the ones discussed in this book suggests that there are lessons to be learnt across alleged divides. These lessons can only be learnt if we systematically open up the transitional justice paradigm and include these aparadigmatic cases in our theorisation and further empirical exploration of the field. Doing so allows for transitional justice to become more relevant for various kinds of justice actors, to decolonise the field by overcoming existing biases, and to futureproof it by offering a new perspective on what can be expected of transitional justice.

References

De Haan, M. and T. Destrooper (2021) 'Using Restorative Justice to Rethink the Temporality of Transition in Chile'. *International Journal of Restorative Justice* 4(2), 206–228.

Goodale, M. and S.E. Merry (2007) *The Practice of Human Rights: Tracking Law Between the Global and the Local*. Cambridge: Cambridge University Press.

Hansen, T.O. (2017) 'The Time and Place of Transitional Justice'. In: C. Lawther, L. Moffett and D. Jacobs, eds. *Research Handbook on Transitional Justice* (pp. 34–51). Cheltenham: Edward Elgar.

Herremans, B. and T. Destrooper (2021) 'Stirring the Justice Imagination: Countering the Invisibilization and Erasure of Syrian Victims' Justice Narratives'. *International Journal of Transitional Justice* 15(3), 576–595.

Hinton, A.L. (2018) 'Justice, Temporality and Shame at the Khmer Rouge Tribunal'. In: L. Hinton and H. Willemsen, eds. *Temporality and Shame: Perspectives from Psychoanalysis and Philosophy* (pp. 186–213). New York: Routledge.

McEvoy, K. and L. McGregor (2008) *Transitional Justice From Below: Grassroots activism and the Struggle for Change*. Oxford and Portland: Hart.

Merry, S.E. (2006) 'Transnational Human Rights and Local Activism: Mapping the Middle'. *American Anthropologist* 108(1), 38–51.

Quinn, J. (2014) 'Whither the 'Transition' of Transitional Justice?' *Interdisciplinary Journal of Human Rights Law* 8(1), 63–79.

Teitel, R. (2014) *Globalizing Transitional Justice*. Oxford: Oxford University Press.

Turner, C. (2017) 'Transitional Justice and Critique'. In: C. Lawther, L. Moffett, and D. Jacobs, eds. *Research Handbook on Transitional Justice* (pp. 52–73). Cheltenham: Edward Elgar.

Index

For Product Safety Concerns and Information please contact our EU representative GPSR@taylorandfrancis.com
Taylor & Francis Verlag GmbH, Kaufingerstraße 24, 80331 München, Germany

www.ingramcontent.com/pod-product-compliance
Lightning Source LLC
LaVergne TN
LVHW010549300926
849162LV00002B/277
* 9 7 8 1 0 3 2 2 6 6 1 7 6 *